Meet
Dr. Franklin

Edited by
ROY N. LOKKEN, Ph.D.
Professor of History, East Carolina University

Introduction by
I. BERNARD COHEN, Ph.D.
Professor Emeritus, Harvard University

Preface by
BOWEN C. DEES, Ph.D.
President of The Franklin Institute

ERRATA

Please take note of the following typographical errors that appear in the article, "Benjamin Franklin, Educator," by Thomas Wendel of San Jose State University:

page 69 San Jose University should read San Jose State University.

page 77 *Conservation in Early American History* should read *Conservatism in Early American History.*

page 81 *The Way to Health* should read *The Way to Wealth.*

ISBN Number: 0-89168-035-7
Printed in the United States of America.

Published by The Franklin Institute Press[SM]

Preface

The Franklin Institute's main building bears the legend "In honor of Benjamin Franklin." Dr. Franklin's contributions to mankind were so varied and so significant (as this book amply demonstrates) that it is difficult to find an area of human endeavor in which he did not in some way involve himself. To honor such a man is thus both easy and difficult — easy because one has no trouble showing he was important to the development of any one of many institutions and activities; but difficult because one would like to honor the whole man — the entirety of Franklin — and there is no easy way of doing that: he looms too large on the historical horizon.

Even so, there are special times when we feel we must try to perpetuate and honor his memory. One such time is on the occasion of the 275th anniversary of Franklin's birth: January 17, 1981. Hence the publication at this time of this book, which introduces the reader to a number of facets of Dr. Franklin's many-faceted career.

Some of the essays herein were published under the same title in an earlier edition — but there is much new material in this version of *Meet Dr. Franklin*. We hope and believe that its publication will help us fulfill our charter roles — with us since our founding in 1824 — to perpetuate the memory of Benjamin Franklin and to promote the advancement of science and technology.

BOWEN C. DEES

President
The Franklin Institute

January 1981

iii

Table of Contents

Introduction

The volume *Meet Dr. Franklin* is based primarily on a series of lectures on various aspects of Benjamin Franklin's career, given at the Franklin Institute from 1939–43. The original volume contained an introductory lecture by the dean of Franklin scholars, Carl Van Doren, which has been deleted, plus a final summing-up by Van Doren (also deleted), in which he attempted to take cognizance of the research relating to Franklin which had appeared since the lectures were given and initially published in the *Journal of the Franklin Institute*. The present collection contains most of the contributions to the original volume but some have been omitted as no longer as useful as they had been over 30 years ago. Several new essays have been introduced so as to give the reader a view of the major facets of Franklin's thoughts, actions, and career. These essays from the original collection, that are reprinted here, have been brought up to date by the annotations prepared by Roy N. Lokken. A paragraph has been deleted, here and there, that is no longer an accurate representation of the state of Franklin scholarship.

In many ways, the most significant area of Franklin research since the 1940's, when the original lectures were given, has been in relation to Franklin's science. For instance, the first modern scholarly edition of Franklin's book on electricity was published only in 1941, too late to be used by Robert A. Millikan in his lecture and essay on "Benjamin Franklin as a Scientist," but just in time to be mentioned by Carl Van Doren in his original concluding essay to *Meet Dr. Franklin* in 1943. Since that time, many scholarly articles on Franklin's science have appeared, including a full-length monograph (for which see the following essay on "The Science of Benjamin Franklin") and — just recently — a lengthy presentation of Franklin's electrical researches in the context of the eighteenth century by John L. Heilbron. The latter, in his book on *Electricity in the 17th and 18th Centuries* (Berkeley-Los Angeles-London, 1979) devotes one of the five major sections of the work to "The Age of Franklin."

For most readers the major event in Franklin scholarship since the first publication of *Meet Dr. Franklin* in 1943 has been the new edition of *The Papers of Benjamin Franklin*, a chronological assemblage of all of Franklin's writings and correspondence, sponsored by the American Philosophical Society and the Yale University Library; Leonard W. Labaree was the inaugural editor, William B. Willcox is the present editor. The first volume was published in 1959 by the Yale University Press, the twenty-first (covering the period from 1 January 1774 through 22 March 1775) in 1978. Another memorable event was the parallel text edition of Franklin's autobiographical writings, containing an accurate transcription of the original manuscript, edited by Max Farrand as *Benjamin Franklin's Memoirs* (Berkeley-Los Angeles, 1949). A more recent scholarly edition, based on manuscript sources, is Leonard W. Labaree, Ralph L. Ketcham, Helen C. Boatfield, and Helene H. Fineman (eds.), *The Autobiography of Benjamin Franklin* (New Haven-London, 1964). Among other works, attention may be called to Charles C. Sellers, *Benjamin Franklin in Portraiture* (New Haven, 1962), Claude-Anne Lopez, *Chere Papa: Benjamin Franklin and the Ladies* (New York, 1966) and Claude-Anne Lopez and Eugenia W. Herbert, *The Private Franklin: The Man and his Family* (New York, 1975); and also Alfred Owen Aldridge, *Franklin and his French Contemporaries* (New York, 1957) and Antonio Pace, *Franklin and Italy* (Philadephia, 1958).

The continuing appearance of scholarly monography and popular books and articles on Franklin and his career — far too numerous to be listed here — provide testimony to the continuing attraction that this man has had and continues to have for researchers and writers all over the world. The present collection contains informative essays for the non-specialist on almost every aspect of Franklin's life and thought. But no collection of reasonable size could do justice to each and every facet of this versatile man.

I. Bernard Cohen

Self-Portraiture:
The Autobiography

MAX FARRAND

Max Farrand (1869-1945) was the Director of the Henry E. Huntington Library and Art Gallery from 1927 to 1941. He began his study
of Franklin's autobiography in 1926. Convinced that no acceptable
text of the autobiography had ever been published, he planned an edition of Franklin's original manuscript with the William Temple
Franklin edition of 1818, the French translation by Louis Guillaume le
Veillard, and another French translation (incomplete) published in
1791 by Buisson in Paris. Farrand had solved the major problems involved in editing the four texts before his death, and members of the
Huntington Library staff completed the work, published in 1949 as
The Parallel Text Edition of *Benjamin Franklin's Memoirs*. In 1964 the
Yale University Press published a new edition of Franklin's original
manuscript of the autobiography, preserved at the Huntington
Library. In 1976 P.M. Zall warned that neither edition contains all of
the alterations Franklin had entered on the margin of almost every
page of the original manuscript.[1] It appears that both Farrand's
Parallel Text Edition and the 1964 edition by Leonard W. Labaree and
others are less than perfect. Nevertheless, Farrand's *Benjamin
Franklin's Memoirs* remains as close to a variorum edition as we have,
although it should be compared with the Labaree edition of 1964.

The following essay was delivered in the Hall of The Franklin Institute on January 5, 1940 as one of the papers in the "Meet Dr.
Franklin" Conference.

My immediate interest in Benjamin Franklin centers in his
autobiography and was stimulated through the more or less ac-
cidental circumstance of the Huntington Library being the fortunate possessor of the original and only known manuscript of that
important document. Therein lies a story that cannot be told here.
One need only say that the editing of the manuscript for publica-

---

[1] P.M. Zall, "The Manuscript and Early Texts of Franklin's *Autobiography*,"
The Huntington Library Quarterly, 39 (August 1976), 375-384.

tion presents an intricate problem in textual criticism. While seeking a solution to that problem over several years, these questions persistently intruded: What led Franklin to write his memoirs? And what are the qualities in those memoirs that have made them one of the great autobiographies of all literature and the first great American literary classic?

You may notice that the word "memoirs" is used, for that is what Franklin always called them. The *Oxford English Dictionary* gives the date of the first use of "autobiography" as 1809 by Southey in the *Quarterly Review*.

What is said to you this afternoon carries answers to the questions propounded, having only this much weight and value: they are the most acceptable the speaker has found as yet. He wishes, at this point, to express his gratitude for the suggestions and criticisms of his friend, George Simpson Eddy, Esq., of New York City, the most knowledgeable student of Franklin we have today.

Many biographies of Franklin had, of course, been examined but the autobiography is also a part of our literary heritage. So not long ago, having gathered several ideas for presentation on this occasion, I made the fatal mistake of going to the shelves where in one section were gathered a large number of histories of American literature. To my dismay I found, on looking through twenty or thirty different works, that almost everything I intended to be said here had already been expressed and far better than I could pretend to put it. More than that, everything that ever *could* be said about Franklin seemed already to have been put into print. But much of it was concealed in a flood of verbiage and was scattered through a mass of hopelessly second-and third-rate stuff. Like Gratiano's "two grains of wheat hid in two bushels of chaff: you shall seek all day ere you find them: and when you have them, they are not worth the search."

Sometime I am going to let myself go on the subject of undigested, ill-thought-out productions that are being inflicted upon a long-suffering public. Anybody can write, a goodly number can write well, but there are only a few who not only have ability but are also willing to subject themselves to the discipline, amounting at times almost to torture, that is necessary to produce a work worthy of permanent preservation. I trust I am not adding to the mess.

One is inclined to think we'd be better off, so far as our *understanding* of Franklin is concerned, if nothing had been published except James Parton's *Life and Times of Benjamin Franklin,* which appeared in 1864. Perhaps an exception might be made in favor of Sainte-Beuve's unrivalled essay on Franklin among his "Portraits." Please notice that the word used was "understanding." There is no doubt that our knowledge concerning Franklin has greatly increased, especially in recent years. I like the definition in Webster's "Dictionary" that quotes Thomas Gray: "Knowledge and intelligence . . . alone do not constitute wisdom."

Even the best of the recent lives—Carl Van Doren's readable and informative "Benjamin Franklin"—has not superseded Parton. Van Doren has brought together much from hitherto inaccessible or inconveniently located sources and has added some things that are new, and told the whole story in an attractive, not to say fascinating, manner. But in the preface he wrote, "In effect Franklin's autobiography is here completed on his own scale and in his own words." Perhaps the purpose of this address is to show that he attempted something beyond the power of any person except Franklin himself to achieve.

Apparently the correct thing, these days, to say about Franklin is that he was a child of the Enlightenment. When there is any accepted agreement as to just what is meant by the "enlightenment," we may be able to concur in the opinion that Franklin was its child. Until such time, I, for one, prefer the late William P. Trent's way of putting it—Franklin "is, perhaps, the most complete representative of his century that any nation can point to." Such a statement may be equally vague, but to me at least it sounds more comprehensible.

Trent gives us a further explanation of Franklin's immortality in the United States—that "he is a typical and unapproachable product of what his countrymen are pleased to call 'true Americanism.'"

I shall come back again and again to those estimates of Franklin as a product of the eighteenth century and the personification of what have come to be regarded as American characteristics. There are persons who go so far as to blame him for some of our present traits and qualities.

Thomas Carlyle has been quoted as saying that Benjamin Franklin was the father of all the Yankees. Charles Angoff ("A Literary History of the American People," 1931) claims that this "was a libel against the tribe, for the Yankees have produced Thoreau, Hawthorne, and Emily Dickinson," He then proceeds to castigate Franklin unmercifully and to make him primarily responsible for much that is common and vulgar in American life today.

Angoff has been cited deliberately, for he presents the point of view and even the considered judgment of some persons. But why lay this all up against Franklin? He was essentially a child of his times, as we all are of ours. He was a product of the eighteenth century. Some fifteen years ago a prominent Englishman, so high in station that he should not be identified by name, expressed in conversation his irritation that many people complained of the so-called "Americanization of England." "All that the United States has done," he said, "is to be about twenty years ahead of England. Industrialization is inevitable with all its faults and virtues. We [i.e., the English] are simply experiencing what the people of the United States have already gone through. That isn't Americanization." So Franklin should be regarded as the forerunner rather than the author of some of our less admirable traits and practices.

Benjamin Franklin bears the reputation of having been a shrewd and a wise man. It might be adduced in support of that reputation that he showed those qualities at an early age by the choice of his parents. True, Josiah Franklin, the father, was only a tallow chandler, but he lived to be eighty-nine years old, and the mother to the age of eighty-five. In other words, he came of a long-lived and, it might be added, of an industrious stock.

This child, born [1706] at the beginning of the eighteenth century, in humble circumstances, reared in poverty, largely self-taught, altogether self-made, rose from such conditions to become one the world's great figures and literally to stand before kings. The story has all the elements of success and romance that constitute the ideal of millions of Americans.

Fortunately, it is not necessary to go into the details of Franklin's life; many of this audience are better acquainted with them than is the speaker. And so we may turn directly to the autobiography but, in doing so, one point ought to be emphasized, because it is so frequently overlooked, and that is the conditions under which the writing of the autobiography was begun.

Franklin was, as is well known, on his second mission to England; but it should be remembered also how happy he was in that country. During his previous mission, as you will recall, he

communicated to one of his friends that he had spent in Scotland
"six weeks of the densest happiness I have ever met with in any
part of my life." After returning to America he wrote to Mary
Stevenson in 1763:

> Of all the enviable Things England has, I envy it most its People. Why should that
> petty Island, which compar'd to America, is but like a stepping-Stone in a Brook, scarce
> enough of it above Water to keep one's Shoes dry; why, I say, should that little Island
> enjoy in almost every Neighbourhood, more sensible, virtuous, and elegant Minds, than
> we can collect in ranging 100 Leagues of our vast Forests? ("The Writings of Benjamin
> Franklin," Ed. Smyth, IV, 194).

Benjamin Franklin was a person of importance in his world,
and no one knew it better than Franklin himself. He had succeeded
beyond his greatest expectations. He was not disagreeably con-
ceited—he was pleasantly, even delightfully, vain. Franklin appreciated that, too, for in the very beginning of his autobiography
he admits that his writing will

> a good deal gratify my own *Vanity*. . . . Most People dislike Vanity in others . . .
> but I give it fair Quarter wherever I meet with it, being persuaded that it is often produc-
> tive of Good to the Possessor. . . . And therefore . . . it would not be quite absurd if a
> Man were to thank God for his Vanity among the other Comforts of Life.

So it was in that humor, in 1771, at the age of sixty-five, when
he was on a fortnight's holiday at Twyford with his friends the
Shipleys, of whom he was very fond, that he indulged himself in
something he had long wanted to do—to tell the real story of his
life and to give his own explanation of his success.

Certain facts of his career were common property. Other facts
were known to a few. In his memoirs Franklin is telling his son,
and very probably expecting through his son to tell the world, the
things that other people didn't know, and furthermore what lay
back of those facts. Through the whole story runs an extraordinary
analysis of the motives that inspired his several activities.

Even for such a piece of self-indulgence, Franklin carefully
made out a list of topics to be taken up, which, in the copies now
extant, covers three pages, seven by ten inches. The memoirs
themselves were written on larger-sized sheets, approximately thirteen inches by eight, and were always inscribed in the same
fashion—that is, in a long column on the outer half of the page or
on the right-hand half, leaving the other half as a wide margin for
additions and corrections.

When he had written a little more than eighty-six pages in this way, he stopped. From the outline we know that he was not a third of the way through—in fact, the story had come down only to 1730; he had not reached the point of his great successes; but all that was written was evidently just what it purported to be—a story for his son and immediate family and, perhaps, if they saw fit, to be made public. It is Franklin at his best.

They are, as Van Doren has said, "the homeliest memoirs that had ever been written in the plainest language." But they are something more than that. They tell the story of a printer and shopkeeper who was infinitely bigger than his job but was not above it; of a tradesman who had risen to greatness but was not ashamed of his origin nor of his station. He never shirked any of the menial tasks he had to perform. In fact he quickly saw their advertising value. Even as a youngster—who, again forecasting later American qualities, was to become the great "publicity artist" of his time—Franklin played up these menial tasks. A passage in the autobiography is often quoted but will bear repetition:

> In order to secure my Credit and Character as a Tradesman, I took care not only to be in *Reality* Industrious and frugal, but to avoid all Appearances of the Contrary. I drest plainly; I was seen at no Places of idle Diversion: I never went out a fishing or shooting; a Book, indeed, sometimes debauched me from my Work; but that was seldom, snug, and gave no scandal: and to show that I was not above my Business, I sometimes brought home the Paper I purchased at the Stores, thro' the Streets on a Wheelbarrow.

And now to take up the qualities revealed in the Memoirs, that have made them famous. Franklin's first love was what his contemporaries called "philosophy" but we should call "science." One of the chief reasons he gave for retiring from active participation in the printing shop was to get more time to devote to his experiments. To speak of his scientific qualifications is stepping outside of my field but the ideas used are common property. The line of thought here followed is taken from Lord Jeffrey, as refined by Sainte-Beuve, and adapted to our modern parlance with the help of a scientific friend whom the Franklin Institute has honored with its medal—Dr. Edwin P. Hubble.

Franklin was not a mathematician—that is, he was not a theorist. He was a natural philosopher, a physicist, keenly observant and everlastingly curious as to the whys and wherefores of natural phenomena. He made simple, searching, decisive experiments and then by his clear reasoning was able to offer convincing demonstrations.

The prime qualification of any person who would succeed in science, or in scholarship, is the ability to disassociate himself, his feelings, and his prejudices from the undertaking in hand, so as to make thoroughly impartial and impersonal observations of facts; then, in the same spirit, to record those facts; and, eventually, if possible, to find the explanation.

That is, to me, a leading intellectual quality of Franklin—his ability to take a detached, impersonal, dispassionate point of view.

But Franklin was also interested in human behavior and, in his observations of how human beings acted, he displayed one of the rarest of all qualities. His own doings were, of course, the ones about which he knew the most, and he observes and records them with complete detachment from self. He was not in the least morbidly introspective; if anything, he was whimsically amused. Benjamin Franklin was merely one of the curious human phenomena he was studying and whose acts he was recording. Then he attempted to explain how this person had been able to function so effectively.

He succeeded, as almost no one else has ever done, and that fact is attested by the place accorded to the Memoirs in the world's esteem.

An explanation has been offered to show why the autobiography is such a remarkable human document. There still remains the question of why it is regarded as a literary classic. Franklin could tell a good story, and it is not surprising that he should tell his own story extraordinarily well. That makes a good start. He also possessed a delightful humor, which adds to the enjoyment of the reader.

At this point the interpretation here presented diverges from much of the current opinion. The difference is largely in the use of terms, but the most discriminating—and that means the best—critics apparently do not accept Franklin as one of the great "men of letters." Franklin was the essence of practicality, the embodiment of common sense. He was always constructive, but it is claimed, and with that claim I am inclined to agree, that he was not possessed by the genius that forces men to write whether they will or no, and is necessary to produce great literature.

Sainte-Beuve was apparently making the same point when he wrote:

> Here a reflection begins to dawn upon us. An ideal is lacking in this healthy, upright, able, frugal, laborious nature of Franklin—the fine flower of enthusiasm, tenderness, sacrifice,—all that is the dream, and also the charm and the honour of poetic natures.... He brings everything down to arithmetic and strict reality, assigning no part to human imagination.

His writings generally were in the nature of journalism and most of them were published in newspapers. To disregard them is perhaps to treat "literature" too exclusively as belles-lettres. This is not to deny that Franklin influenced both his contemporaries and his successors in their writing in ways that we think were for their betterment, because in accord with our present-day standards. He may therefore be regarded as a "literary figure" but that hardly makes him a great man of letters, if his sole lasting contribution to literature is the autobiography. This would seem to be the substance of the opinion expressed by such recognized literary historians and critics as Henry A. Beers ("Initial Studies in American Letters," 1891); William P. Trent ("History of American Literature," 1929); and Stuart P. Sherman (in "Cambridge History of American Literature").

All of these critics, however, are agreed upon the directness and simplicity of Franklin's style. It is from the autobiography that we learn how he used the *Spectator* as a model, and taught himself to improve his writing and to express his ideas clearly and concisely. Of course, the first essential is to think clearly, and that was one of Franklin's strongest points. But anyone who imagines that clarity and conciseness in expressing one's thoughts may be achieved and learned once and for all has another guess coming. Undoubtedly many have a gift in that direction. Practice improves one but no person has yet been born who could write continuously and consistently in a clear and concise manner. Like poetry, such writing is the product of infinite pains.

The best way to learn to write is to write and to keep on writing, provided one is critical of one's own work, which was Franklin's habit. It would seem that among the most helpful things he did for his own style was the composition of the maxims for *Poor Richard's Almanac*. In the compilation of these aphorisms Franklin borrowed freely from everywhere. As he himself said,

"They were the wisdom of many ages and nations." But they were transmuted by him, pointed with his wit, and avoiding Latin words and obscure phrases, put into direct and simple English. They stand practically alone in the eighteenth century—the type of humor henceforth to be known as American.

There are people who complain of the broadness of some of the witticisms, and the coarseness of some of the anecdotes. Just to see if there might be any relation between the two productions, I turned to Joe Miller's "Jests," the first edition of which was printed in 1739. There was no resemblance. In comparison with the Jest-Book, "Poor Richard" might well be used as a textbook in a young ladies' finishing school.

Franklin's method of composition and form of written expression, laboriously acquired in his youth, developed in all his newspaper writing, sharpened by the sayings he gathered and prepared for "Poor Richard," undoubtedly had much to do with the wide acceptance of the results of his experiments in electricity. He also found a worthy opportunity for their use to advantage in giving the account of his own life.

These are the final qualities—the simplicity of presentation and the crystal clearness of the style—that, in the flood of memoirs deluging the eighteenth century, raised Benjamin Franklin's story to preeminence.

Some things the autobiography does not reveal. Nothing is said about Franklin's social life. Apparently to him there was little that was new or of interest in the story of a simple, frugal household. But nevertheless there are certain features of consequence in understanding and forming a correct estimate of the man.

Society with a capital S didn't know him. Aristocratic Philadelphia seems to have refused to recognize him socially, although it, especially the menfolk, found him useful and indeed essential in public enterprise. That didn't bother Franklin. He cared less for Society than Society did for him. I doubt, however, if he ever realized one particular thing he had missed: it is a great pity that in his early impressionable years Franklin was not privileged to have had acquaintance and friendship with cultivated and refined womanhood. What the effect might have been is pure speculation, but that it would have been of benefit to so observing and receptive a youth, eager to improve himself, seems beyond question.

The same social inexperience might account for Franklin's failure to develop the art of conversation. The lack is generally recognized, and many references might be quoted to that effect. He was a good listener, but his contribution to social conversation and even to more serious discussions consisted frequently in telling a good story—humorous and apt. And how characteristic that is of Americans today!

We also get no hint of one of Franklin's most lovable traits—his fondness for children and his delight in companionship with young people. Van Doren has brought these out admirably. His affectionate nature, his gentleness and whimsicality, are displayed to the best advantage in letters to his young friends. Theodore Roosevelt said of his own "Letters to His Children," "I would rather have this book published than anything that has ever been written about me." So one wishes that Franklin's letters to young people might be permitted to tell their own story and reveal his attractive and natural self, without a trace of the tradesman's expediency that alienates many people.

The first part of the autobiography is the best, so far as self-revelation is concerned, not only because Franklin enjoyed doing it and let himself go, but also because "the child is father to the man" and the first part covers the character-forming years of his life. The later parts, however, have their own significance.

For over ten years nothing was heard of what Franklin had written. It is doubtful if more than a very few knew of its existence. In the meantime he had returned to America, and after the outbreak of the War for Independence he had been sent as a commissioner to France. His incredible reception by the French and his astounding popularity, when he was the idol of Paris and crowds blocked the streets to see him, are too well known to bear repeating. His fur cap was just another piece of clever publicity, when he had to give up wearing a wig because of an eczema of the scalp.

Just as the peace negotiations were drawing to a close, Abel James wrote from Philadelphia that the memoirs commenced at Twyford had come into his hands. He begged Franklin to go on with them, and enclosed a copy of the outline, as a reminder of what was still to be done. Franklin turned the letter over to his young friend Benjamin Vaughan, with a request for his opinion. Le Veillard, the mayor of Passy, with whom Franklin had developed a warm friendship, was also consulted. They and others urged him to continue the story of his life. But even with the conclusion of peace it was not until 1784 that Franklin again took up the autobiography. When he resumed writing he inserted Vaughan's reply along with James's letter. They make a disconcerting break in the flow of the narrative, but evidently were put in to justify the resumption of the story and to emphasize the change in the character of the memoirs. Franklin prefaced the letters with a note that the first part of the account of his life was written for the family and that the following was "intended for the public." And what a difference there is! Franklin was now over seventy-eight years old. He was not merely a man of consequence; he was one of the great figures of the world. Science may have been his first love, but the passion of his life was the improvement of others as well as of himself, and even in his greatness he never forgot it. Where this motive came from is not clear. It may have been from his New England Calvinistic training but whatever its source it certainly was one of the great forces in his life.

Accordingly, when Franklin again took up the autobiography, he was no longer writing the simple story of his life, for the benefit of his son: he was consciously preaching virtue, as exemplified in his own practices and experience; he was writing to instruct youth.

The value of the second part consists in the revelation of his methodical plan for "arriving at moral perfection," and in the calm way he describes his own deficiencies and limitations. You remember that Franklin listed thirteen virtues and determined to give strict attention to the practice of each of them successively for a week at a time. His reference to this systematic plan of self-improvement as a "a Course compleat in Thirteen weeks, and four Courses a Year" sounds very modern.

Through all of the second part one feels a greater emphasis than was noticeable in the first instalment that others might well profit by his example.

Franklin returned to America in the summer of 1785. On the eve of sailing from Southampton he said in a letter to a friend: "I purpose, on my voyage, to write the remaining notes of my life, which you desire." Instead, he wrote three of his most extensive and useful essays: one on navigation, another on smoky chimneys, and the third a description of his smoke-consuming stove. So for one reason or another he kept putting off the continuation of his memoirs.

He had long been troubled with gout, but for several years he had been suffering from a more serious and painful malady—stone in the bladder. He has been quoted as having said that, during the last two years of his life, he had not had two months, in all, of freedom from pain. In December of 1787 he fell down the steps leading to his garden. He was badly bruised, his right wrist sprained, and the shock was followed by a severe attack of the stone. Not long afterward he began to put his house in order for the end which he saw inevitably approaching. He made his will, which bears the date of July 17, 1788. When the continuation of the autobiography was taken up, Franklin made a note in the margin of the manuscript: "I am now about to write at home, August, 1788."

The third instalment of his memoirs, then, was not commenced until after he had made his last will and testament. He was well on in his eighty-third year and was suffering grievously—to such an extent that he was forced at times to the use of opium. He was apparently engaged for several months in writing this part. He did the best he could, but he was an old man and his story shows the effects of age. One misses, particularly, the spontaneity and the zest with which Franklin had commenced his memoirs. At Twyford he was writing almost gleefully, reliving his youth. In Philadelphia he was making a forced effort; only at times could he forget himself in the interest of the story he was telling.

But there is a quality revealed in the third section that had not appeared so clearly before. Many writers refer to Franklin's frugality. That isn't especially characteristic of him. It was truer of Mrs. Franklin. Franklin's success in his printing shop and other activities—so great that he could retire at the age of forty-two—was due not to economy but to his business efficiency. He was also quick to see and seize an opportunity. When those abilities were combined with an extraordinary insight into human nature, it is little wonder the achievements were remarkable.

The third part of the autobiography describes the emergence of a tradesman into a man of affairs, the growth of a citizen of local importance into a person of consequence throughout the colonies, and into a scientist of reputation not only in England but also on the Continent.

Franklin knew his life was nearly over and that he would never finish his memoirs. Accordingly, in 1789, he had his grandson, Benjamin Franklin Bache, make two "fair copies" of so much as had then been written. One was sent to Vaughan, and the other to Le Veillard. The original manuscript, with its many corrections, was interlined, confused, and in places difficult to read. At some stage in the copying, changes were made. This statement is positive, for, although neither of these copies is now to be found, the evidence in support of it is convincing. To what extent these changes were made or approved by Franklin will probably never be known.

Sometime before his death Franklin added seven and one-half pages to his memoirs. This is the fourth and last part, and for present purposes its chief significance is due to its not being included in the copies sent to Vaughan and Le Veillard.

Franklin died in 1790. His grandson, William Temple Franklin, was made his literary executor. Years passed, and Temple Franklin failed to bring out the promised edition of his grandfather's works. He was probably absorbed in various land speculations from which he expected large profits. It was no small task to select from and to edit his grandfather's papers. He is said to have found particular difficulty in transcribing the manuscript of the most important of all the documents—the autobiography. On one of his visits to Paris, in 1791, or 1792, he saw the fair copy that had been sent to Le Veillard and finally gave the original manuscript in exchange for it.

Temple Franklin's edition of his grandfather's works at last appeared, in 1817-18, in London. In this edition the autobiography was printed from Le Veillard's copy, in which, as Ben Bache made it, the wording had been changed in many places. You will remember also that this copy was sent before the fourth part was written, and so did not include it. The Temple Franklin edition became the accepted version of the autobiography and remained so for fifty years; it was copied, reprinted, and translated hundreds of times.

When John Bigelow was American Minister to France in 1865 and 1866, he started inquiries that resulted in the location of the original manuscript, which he finally purchased. Bigelow was greatly excited over what he found. A comparison of the manuscript with the Temple Franklin version showed many variations, and revealed, also, the neglected fourth part. He at once started to prepare what he believed would be the definitive text of the autobiography, and it was published in 1868. The entire autobiography was printed in English for the first time seventy-eight years after Franklin's death.

Bigelow intended to copy the manuscript carefully and exactly—at least he so declared. He left the spelling just as it was because he thought it showed the handicap under which Franklin had labored in the lack of early education. Spelling, however, in the eighteenth century, especially in the early part of the century, was a matter in which it was permitted to be temperamental. One might spell words very much as one chose. On the other hand, Bigelow took the liberty—and what is still more inexcusable according to our standards, without saying so—of changing both punctuation and capitalization, points upon which Franklin as a printer was very particular. Furthermore, the copying must have been entrusted to an incompetent or inexperienced secretary. The results were appalling.

Bigelow retained possession of the manuscript of the autobiography for some thirty years and then disposed of it to Dodd, Mead and Company, who in turn sold it to E. Dwight Church. In 1911 the manuscript passed, with the rest of the Church library, into the collection Henry E. Huntington was making.

All four parts of the original manuscript were written on folio leaves of approximately uniform size. Many years later these were mounted on guards and bound in boards, with a red-leather back. The binding is evidently of French workmanship—an inference that is confirmed by the spelling, "Francklin," in the title on the back of the cover. The mere transcription of the text is not an easy task, because of numerous corrections and interlineations, but that difficulty is insignificant in comparison with the uncertainty as to what Franklin wished the final wording to be. It is doubtful if he himself knew. When he sent the copies to Vaughan and Le Veillard, he made the "earnest request" that they should read them critically. He asked them to advise him as to whether or not the memoirs should be published and, if so, what changes should be made, for, he added pathetically, "I am now grown so old and feeble in mind, as well as body, that I cannot place any confidence in my own judgment." The changes of wording in the "fair copies" prepared by Ben Bache were made, I am inclined to believe, under his grandfather's instructions. Temple Franklin's text was based on one of these copies. We also have two French translations that bear directly on the problem. One of them is of the first part only and was evidently taken from a copy and not from the original. The other is of the entire autobiography, and the translator made use of both the original and a copy.

The Huntington Library is preparing what Van Doren properly calls a variorum edition, in which all the several possible readings will be placed together upon the same page. But let me put your minds at rest upon one point. None of these uncertainties affects anything of real importance. They relate only to questions of style, occasionally touching the picturesque wording of a phrase or sentence—nothing more.

The Memoirs will stand as we know them—an unsurpassed story of how a printer and shopkeeper in Philadelphia rose to be one of the world's great figures, and "the most complete representative of his century that any nation can point to," while underlying the whole narrative runs a dispassionate self-analysis that only could be made by an impersonal, impartial scientist or scholar, and has never been excelled, if it has ever been equalled.

EDITOR'S NOTE

Max Farrand assumed that when Franklin began writing his autobiography at Twyford in 1771 he was telling his son the little known facts of his life, probably expecting that through his son those facts would be made known to the world. What Franklin meant in the letter to his son at the beginning of Part One of the *Memoirs* has been controverted by recent historians. His only son, William, was then in his early forties and had been the royal governor of New Jersey since 1763. In 1771 the relationship between father and son was already strained. Claude-Anne Lopez and Eugenia W. Herbert, believing that Franklin's letter to his son was intended for William, suggest that Franklin's intention was to recapture the intimate relationship that had once existed between them.[1] Melvin H. Buxbaum points out, however, that William knew his father's past well and hardly needed to be reminded. J.A. Leo Lemay, with Buxbaum concurring, interprets Franklin's letter to his son as a literary device which enabled Franklin to create the illusion of an intimate relationship between himself and the

---

[1]Claude-Anne Lopez and Eugenia W. Herbert, *The Private Franklin: The Man and His Family* (New York: W.W. Norton & Co., Inc., c1975), p. 2.

reader.[2] A. Owen Aldridge suggests that Franklin intended the autobiography for his grandson, William Temple Franklin, who was eleven years old in 1771, attended school in England, and saw more of his grandfather than of his father, William Franklin.[3]

The first part of the *Memoirs* may have been intended for members of Franklin's family, as Franklin wrote, and his purpose may have changed when he resumed writing the story of his life in 1784. Some scholars are not sure about that. It is suspected that Franklin's purpose remained the same throughout. The only question is what the purpose was. Buxbaum offers the thesis that in 1771 Franklin sought to defend his character from the many political attacks which he had suffered through the years. His purpose remained an *apologia pro vita sua* when he wrote the rest of the *Memoirs* in 1784, 1788, and 1789-90. At the same time he created an image of America as a country of virtuous people.[4] The image of virtuous America pitted against corrupt Europe was popular in the writings of American patriots during the Revolutionary period — for example, Dr. Benjamin Rush and David Rittenhouse. Franklin offered the story of his own life as an illustration of the progress of a virtuous American. As David Levin has written, in the *Memoirs* Franklin "not only creates an attractive image of himself but uses himself as a prototype of his age and his country."[5] The portrayal of a poor boy who made good reflected an America where virtue was its own reward and where opportunities for vertical mobility were more abundant than in the decadent Old World. In a sense the *Memoirs* were not only a defense of Franklin and his America but a precursor of the nineteenth-century literature of the self-made man.

When Franklin resumed writing his autobiography in 1784 he wrote a list of thirteen virtues as basic to his plan of "arriving at

---

[2]Melvin H. Buxbaum, *Benjamin Franklin and the Zealous Presbyterians* (University Park: The Pennsylvania State University Press, c1975), p. 10; J.A. Leo Leman, "Franklin and the *Autobiography*: An Essay on Recent Scholarship," *Eighteenth-Century Studies*, I (December 1967), 200.

[3]A. Owen Aldridge, *Benjamin Franklin, Philosopher & Man*(Philadelphia: J.B. Lippincott, c1965), p. 219.

[4]Buxbaum, *Benjamin Franklin and the Zealous Presbyterians*, pp. 10, 17, 26-27, 34-35.

[5]David Levin, "The Autobiography of Benjamin Franklin: The Puritan Experimenter in Life and Art," *The Yale Review: A National Quarterly*, 53 (December 1963), 261.

moral perfection.'' That passage has led Farrand and many other scholars to believe that the major purpose of the *Memoirs* was the instruction of youth. Franklin used himself as an example of how one can evaluate his moral conduct each day of the week. John G. Cawelti sees the thirteen virtues ''as techniques for the development of self-discipline'' and the *Memoirs* as a whole as illustrating individual self-improvement and the cultivation of the virtues so that one could assume a ''responsible role in the general progress of society.'' Widespread imitation of Franklin's project would improve society and raise its standards.[6] A.B. England interprets Franklin's system of moral bookkeeping as an attempt ''to achieve in his own personality a degree of order'' which significantly contrasted with the disorder he often confronted in the world around him.[7] Some scholars, among them David Levin, attribute Franklin's ethics to his Puritan background. Seventeenth-century Puritans had sought, through self-evaluation, evidences of saving grace in their lives. The prudential virtues catalogued in Franklin's *Memoirs* were among such evidences. Some scholars, however, are doubtful of the extent of Puritan influence on Franklin's ethics. The orientation of the ''art of virtue'' in the *Memoirs* was secular rather than religious. Norman S. Fiering asserts that Franklin's moral thought had more in common with the later utilitarianism of James Mill than with the earlier Puritanism.[8] J.A. Leo Lemay, on the other hand, suggests that the plan of ''arriving at moral perfection'' described the *Memoirs* was a satire, because Franklin did not believe in the possibility of moral perfection.[9]

There were others in Franklin's time who speculated on methods of improving, not only individual moral conduct, but the moral standards of the society in which they lived. Some colonial intellectuals, for example James Logan and Cadwallader Colden, wrote unpublished essays on moral philosophy. More important, however, was the Rev. Samuel Johnson's *Ethices Elementa. Or, The First principles of moral philosophy* (Boston, 1746), reprinted

---

[6]John G. Cawelti, *Apostles of the Self-Made Man* (Chicago: University of Chicago Press, 1965), pp. 21, 23.

[7]A.B. England, ''Some Thematic Patterns in Franklin's *Autobiography,*'' *Eighteenth-Century Studies*, V (Spring 1972), 425.

[8]Norman S. Fiering, ''Benjamin Franklin and the Way to Virtue,'' *American Quarterly*, XXX (Summer 1978), 199-223.

[9]J.A. Leo Lemay, *op. cit.*, p. 203.

by Franklin and Hall in 1752 as part of Johnson's *Elementa Philosophica*. Johnson intended his book for young readers to the end of raising "the Mind gradually to its highest Perfection and Happiness." Franklin was so impressed by Johnson's work on ethics and logic that he intended to use it as required reading in the English School he planned for an Academy in Philadelphia. In a letter to Johnson he wrote: "I think also, that general virtue is more probably to be expected and obtained from the *education* of youth, than from the *exhortation* of adult persons; bad habits and vices of the mind, being, like diseases of the body, more easily prevented than cured."[10]

---

[10]Franklin to Johnson, Philadelphia, August 23, 1750, *The Papers of Benjamin Franklin*, ed. by Leonard W. Labaree *et al.*, (New Haven: Yale University Press, 1961), IV, 41.

Franklin's "Unfinished" Autobiography

RALPH KETCHAM

Ralph Louis Ketcham (1927-   ) is a Professor of American Studies, Political Science and History at Syracuse University. He served as an associate editor of Vols. V and VI of *Papers of Benjamin Franklin* from 1961 to 1963, and was a co-editor with the late Leonard W. Labaree of *The Autobiography of Benjamin Franklin*, published by the Yale University Press in 1964. Since then he has published several books on Franklin, including a biography, *Benjamin Franklin* (1965). He is also the author of *From Colony to Country: The Revolution in American Thought, 1750-1820*, published in 1974.

The following essay was especially written for this edition of *Meet Dr. Franklin*.

Benjamin Franklin's *Autobiography* is in one obvious sense an unfinished work; it does not describe the last thirty years of his life when in England, France, and America he earned fame as a statesman and diplomat. It thus has nothing to say about the American Revolution—just a few reflections on the relevance of early episodes of Franklin's life to that climactic event. Yet the life recorded, even including the portions Franklin wrote in 1771 while still a subject of George III, is profoundly revolutionary both in its own context and in projection to other times and places. Its "unfinishedness," that is, seems not the least troublesome because its direct implications are so evident, and because its lasting thrust is so clearly to open opportunities and set events in motion rather than to finish or conclude.

Had one charged Franklin during any part of his life covered in the *Autobiography* with being anything other than a loyal Englishman living in North America, he would have been both dumbfounded and insulted. His earliest boyhood memories were of the sense of salvation in New England because of the glorious victories of *old* England over Louis XIV. Franklin thought of his voyages to England before 1776 as "going home," as did nearly all colonials during that period. When he was a bookseller in

19

Philadelphia he took pride in the eager market for Pope, Addison, and other English writers, who were more admired there, Franklin thought, than in London itself. In 1751, he wrote of the British Empire as an harmonious family, growing in power, prosperity, and freedom on both sides of the Atlantic. He grieved at Braddock's defeat before Fort Duquesne and gloried in Wolfe's victory at Quebec as much as William Pitt himself. During the 1760's Franklin praised the British Empire as "the greatest political structure human wisdom ever yet erected," and wrote that in England there were "in almost every neighborhood, more sensible, virtuous, and elegant Minds than we [in America] can collect in ranging 100 Leagues in our vast Forests."[1] The revolution in loyalty, the first conscious phase of the American Revolution, came very gradually for him as English arrogance, narrow-mindedness, and social injustice loomed ever larger in his mind. Finally, in 1775, he declared from London that "the extream corruption prevalent among all Orders of Men in this old rotten State" was so great that he could not "but apprehend more Mischief than Benefit from a closer Union" between colonies and mother country.[2] It was this change that caused John Adams to declare that the important American Revolution, the revolution in the hearts and minds of the people, took place before 1776, and before a shot had been exchanged between redcoats and continentals.

Equally missing from Franklin's *Autobiography* are more than fleeting glimpses of the more deliberate second phase of the American Revolution, that in national purpose, which had its culmination in the Declaration of Independence, in the Federal Constitution, and in the inauguration of a new government under President Washington. Franklin's plan at Albany in 1754 for a partially self-governing union of the colonies, his resistance to proprietary prerogative in Pennsylvania, and his stunned objection in London in 1757 to Lord Granville's doctrine that "the King is the legislator for the Colonies," all described in the *Autobiography,* foreshadow the revolutionary purposes that preoccupied the country in 1776 and afterward. Generally,

---

[1]Franklin to Lord Kames, Jan. 3, 1760, and to Mary Stevenson, March 25, 1763; L.W. Labaree and others, eds., *The Papers of Benjamin Franklin* (21 volumes to date, New Haven, 1959—), IX, 7; X, 232-233.

[2]Franklin to Joseph Galloway, Feb. 25, 1775; A.H. Smyth, ed., *The Writings of Benjamin Franklin* (10 volumes, N.Y., 1905-07), VI, 311-312.

however, in the *Autobiography* Franklin accepts political principles, structures of government, and even national goals long
familiar to him as a Briton. Like most of his revolutionary colleagues, he gave serious attention to reformulations of national
purpose only in 1775 when he came "home" (by then meaning
North America) bent on independence. His work on the Pennsylvania and Federal constitutions, and his defenses of them, were
likewise declarations of purpose, as were his statements from
France of the foreign policy guidelines of the new nation. The importance of this phase was so obvious to participant and observer
alike that, then, and ever since, these formal, structural acts have
often seemed to embody the Revolution by themselves.

Less apparent, however, and initially at least, less self-
conscious, was the need for a new sense of national identity and
character. What special qualities would distinguish the citizens of
the United States? What would be the habits and attitudes and
characteristics of its people? What would they epitomize or stand
for in the world? Under the influence of Montesquieu, the Abbe
du Bois, and others, the eighteenth century placed great emphasis
on delineating national character. The Spanish, for example, were
said to be brave, mystical, and cruel; the English practical,
phlegmatic shopkeepers; and the French refined, artistic, and im-
moral. Each nation was thought to have a special character, evident in its history, the impression it made on travelers, its climate,
and in the features of its land. Most nations possessed long,
mysterious pasts from which their characters had simply come into
being. The new United States, on the other hand, could see its
origins clearly and explicitly. Moreover, its people were largely
British with minorities of Germans, Dutch, French, and others in
some of the provinces. Yet, in curious, unselfconscious ways these
transplanted Europeans, even in early colonial days, seemed
somehow a different breed of people. The open land, the fact of
migration across the Atlantic, the impulse to leave home, or
something else, was giving them a new character. As the former
colonists achieved independence they joined with Europeans in
asking, with increasing insistence and sophistication, Crevecoeur's
famous question: "What then is the American, this new man?"
Franklin's *Autobiography*, more than any other work, answered
this question and thus helped to explain and ultimately to further
define the revolutionary elements in the national character.

In 1783 Franklin's Quaker friend, Abel James, found the
rough manuscript of the first part of the *Autobiography* among
Franklin's papers, scattered by British troops during the Revolution. James read it with "great Joy," he said, and urged Franklin
to finish "so pleasing and profitable a work, . . . which would be
useful and entertaining not only to a few, but to millions."[3] Benjamin Vaughn, a young English friend, thought the manuscript
revealed "the internal circumstances [of America]. . .the manners
and situation of a rising people," and therefore would offer a clear
picture of the new ways of the New World.[4] Men on both sides of
the Atlantic sought to know what life was, or might be like, in the
new United States. And Franklin's life in Boston and Philadelphia
during his first fifty years seemed somehow to bear a remarkable
stamp, to inaugurate a new epoch in human history. It embodied
the characteristics Franklin himself explained in 1782 would be
useful "to those who would remove to America."[5] When published, Franklin's *Autobiography* became at once a model and an inspiration for young men anxious to achieve the new way of life.
Thomas Mellon, Irish immigrant and founder of the great banking
dynasty, read the "Autobiography" in 1827 on the meager acres
worked by his father in western Pennsylvania. It was, he later
wrote, "the turning point in my life."[6] For Jared Sparks, growing
up on a Connecticut farm, the *Autobiography* "first aroused my
mental energies...prompted me to resolutions, and...taught me
that circumstances have not a sovereign control over the mind,"
views that led Sparks to a career as an author and president of Harvard College.[6] A leading Florentine printer once explained that "at
the age of 35 I was a lost man...I read again and again the
Autobiography of Franklin, and became enamored of his ideas
and principles to such a degree that to them I ascribe my moral

---

[3]Abel James to Franklin, 1782; L.W. Labaree and others, eds., *The
Autobiography of Benjamin Franklin* (New Haven, 1964), p. 134.

[4]Benjamin Vaughan to Franklin, Jan. 31, 1783; *Ibid.*, pp. 135-40.

[5]Franklin, *Information to Those Who Would Remove to America*, Sept. 1782;
Smyth, ed., *Writings of Franklin*, VIII, 603-614.

[6]Mellon's comment is quoted in Harvey O'Connor, *Mellon's Millions* (N.Y.,
1933), pp. 4-5; Sparks' remark is from his letter to Miss Storrow, Oct. 16, 1817 in H.B.
Adams, *The Life and Writings of Jared Sparks* (2 volumes, Boston, 1893—6; and the
statement of the Florentine printer, Gaspero Barbera, first printed in 1869, is quoted in
Antonio Pace, *Benjamin Franklin and Italy* (Philadelphia, 1958), pp. 195-199. These
comments, and many others on the influence of the *Autobiography*, are gathered in
Labaree, ed., *Autobiography of Franklin*, pp. 9-12.

regeneration....Now at the age of fifty-one, I am healthy, cheerful and rich."[7] Franklin's *Autobiography*, translated into dozens of languages and reprinted hundreds of times, more than any other document revealed and propagated the new character which alone could fulfill the American Revolution and give the new United States a significant place among the nations of the world.

The revolutionary quality of the *Autobiography* is most evident implicitly, in its nature and style. The autobiographical form was popular in the eighteenth century, but the subjects were principally military exploits, court intrigue, and spiritual quests. Generals of the War of the Spanish Succession wrote of strenuous campaigns, grand strategy, and gory battles. The memoirs of Louis XIV's great commander, the Prince of Condé, for example, thrilled thousands in Europe and America. Also widely read were the "inside stories" of the scandalous, clandestine doings of the great European courts. The memoirs of the Cardinal De Retz, telling of the Machiavellian intrigues of the French government during Louis XIV's minority and of the cabal behind the election of a Pope, captivated a wide audience. Even more titillating were personal accounts of the boudoir escapades of noblemen and their mistresses. Nell Gwyn, Madame Pompadour, and even the fictitious Fanny Hill were legends if not idols in their day. More edifying but no less marvelous were the autobiographies of spiritual pilgrimage—graphic accounts like those of St. Theresa, John Bunyan, and the Quaker George Fox. Their mystical experiences and miraculous deliverances filled readers with awe and wonder.

Franklin's story, on the other hand, dealt with no heroics in the conventional sense, spilled no blood, told of no backstair trysts, and chronicled no mysterious path to sainthood. Rather than telling of a courtly world foreign and remote to most people, Franklin described a life begun in a humble station easily recognized by millions, not hundreds. Furthermore, he rose not by superhuman strength, seductive liaison, or even amazing grace, but by application of character traits accessible to anyone. His *Autobiography* is deliberately plain and homely. The picture throughout is not that of events most men could know only from the outside by fantasy, but of a world familiar to them and with which they could readily identify. His language, moreover, suited

---

[7]Franklin to David Hartley, Dec. 4, 1789; Smyth, ed., *Writings of Franklin*, X, 72.

the life he described; simple, direct, down-to-earth, and vernacular. Though Franklin's story is in its own way marvelous and majestic, like any account of human dignity and potentiality, it nonetheless meets its reader on his own ground, accepting on every page that what the author had done anyone else might do by forming the habits he describes. If life in the new world was indeed like this, then a most profound revolution had taken place that somehow depreciated every courtly life story ever told.

Critics of Franklin's *Autobiography*, and of life lived according to "Poor Richard's tags" as D.H. Lawrence put it, often find it mundane, unaesthetic, and bourgeoise. In one sense, though, they miss the point that Franklin intended to emphasize precisely those qualities as most likely to show the common man, mired in his workaday world, the way to prosperity and dignity. The *Autobiography* meant to teach practical first steps and then—in describing Franklin's retirement from business at age forty-two, devotion to science and literature, and long service to the public—to indicate the vast potentiality of the *means* exemplified by Poor Richard. Despite the almost scheming calculus of Franklin's little dots-in-squares method of achieving virtue, and even its ultimately shallow assumptions about human nature, the overall quality of the life described in the *Autobiography* is neither mean, ignoble, nor insensitive. It was to countless people uplifting, challenging, relevant, and therefore revolutionary.

The youthful reading Franklin records in the *Autobiography* as influential further suggests both the parts of Western culture that formed his character and their special meaning in the new world. Bunyan's *Pilgrim's Progress*, for example, despite Franklin's early repudiation of Puritan theology, was for him a graphic dramatization of the habits and qualities that made life meaningful and good, that would serve an earnest person in a secular as well as a religious pilgrimage. Vanity, sloth, dissipation, timorousness, and hypocrisy were to be shunned, while intrepidity, honesty, prudence, and charity were worthy. From Plutarch's *Lives* Franklin gleaned more lessons about virtuous character. In addition to extolling such personal earnestness as Demosthenes' learning to speak with pebbles in his mouth to cure stuttering, or shouting while running uphill to give volume to his voice, Plutarch gave greatest praise to men who served the public well. Pericles,

Publicola, Fabius Maximus, and Cicero, lawgivers and builders of the commonweal, were held up as model leaders. Alexander the Great and Julius Caesar, though praised for their courage and vigorous leadership, were condemned finally for becoming tyrants who deluged the world in blood. In remembering Bunyan and Plutarch as he did, Franklin took from his heritage precepts that he hoped would have special meaning in the new nation he helped found.

Of more particular relevance were works by Daniel Defoe and Cotton Mather on methods of community self-improvement. Living in London and embodying the ebullient bourgeois spirit, Defoe wrote an *Essay upon Projects* to offer practical ways to cure social ills. Cooperative effort and simple organization could save sailors' widows from destitution, make English roads the best in the world, and take money squandered on beer to provide old-age security. Defoe, in many respects an English Franklin in background, talents, and outlook, assumed always that reason and common sense could serve community needs. Cotton Mather's *Essays to do Good* applied Defoe's methods to encourage habits of piety and altruism in small neighborhood groups. Young men, by associating together, concerning themselves with each other's weaknesses and problems, accepting responsibility for community welfare, and resolving to practice Christian charity, could improve their own lives and induce remarkable social progress.

Then, as Franklin read the new, rational thought of his day, he found further encouragement to come to grips with the world in which he lived. Locke's empirical philosophy, insisting that *each man's knowledge was the product* of his sense impressions and therefore a unique individual response to the world around him, heightened Franklin's interest in his environment. Locke's belief that education should be personal, practical, and down-to-earth, and his insistence that the unique character of each man's spiritual experience made religious toleration not only right but necessary for social peace, became cornerstones of Franklin's own philosophy. Then, when he read *The Spectator*, described in the *Autobiography* as so influential, his world-view came into focus. Seeking to temper Puritan fanaticism with Augustan urbanity and to root out Restoration degeneracy with a new moral earnestness, *The Spectator* seemed to tell Franklin that he could have the best of his father's world and Locke's as well, joined in a way of life

both suited to him temperamentally and of clear meaning as he
landed penniless on Market Street wharf in Philadelphia. The
traditions and philosophy of the Old World, sifted in Franklin's
creative mind and tempered by the unsettled opportunities of the
New World, had achieved a new synthesis and a new relevance.
Though the *Autobiography* underscores Franklin's connection
with the past, it dramatizes as well new implications and revolutionary projections. Unselfconsciously, Franklin had acquired a
character so pregnant with meaning that in old age it called for a
wholly novel autobiography in both style and content.

When Franklin began his career as a printer, the lessons of
Defoe and Mather were immediately useful. Furthermore,
Philadelphia, a growing city less than fifty years old, stood ready
to be guided and organized by eager, able young men. The Junto,
Franklin's club of young tradesmen, did exactly what Defoe and
Mather suggested, and soon its members had not only greatly improved their own fortunes but had provided Philadelphia with an
array of useful institutions: a lending library, a fire company, a
learned society, a college, an insurance company, a hospital, and
an efficient city watch. Though the direct, visible results were impressive in their own right, the implications in personal terms were
even more remarkable. Somehow the environment of the New
World and the enterprising qualities Franklin had come to ex-
emplify, when brought together, created unprecedented prospects.
Social problems long thought insoluble suddenly seemed to yield
to amazingly simple stratagems. Books could be made available to
thousands, medical care furnished to all, and education made relevant to community needs. Fire loss, fear on the streets, and death
by plague could be sharply reduced, apparently, by human effort
and organization. Set beside fatalistic bromides hallowed from
time immemorial about the grim prospects of human life,
Franklin's story showed how practical effort, individually and by
civic-minded groups, could have a transforming impact in the New
World. The concrete example of his life, that is, revealed implicitly
the growth of a compelling character that would increasingly,
especially to foreigners, seem distinctively American.

Franklin's *Autobiography* also conveyed a sense of relevance
to everyday life in its easy movement from the personal to the
social to the political. Great questions of public affairs, instead of
appearing in a separate realm remote and inaccessible to most

men, are dealt with through the skills and attitudes Franklin had taught common men how to achieve. Values impressed upon Franklin in his youth proved highly useful as he began his ascent in life. The sober, honest, industrious ways of his father and of the Puritan catechisms were, Franklin showed, just the qualities a tradesman needed to prosper. Poor Richard's aphorisms and little schemes, like the plan for virtue, were practical, meaningful advice for rising young men. This obvious connection was the compelling message of Franklin's life story. Then, as Franklin looked beyond his own affairs, and considered community problems with like-minded men, it seemed apparent that the same virtues, practiced cooperatively, were exactly the prescription needed. There is nothing the least bit mysterious or miraculous about the Junto projects. Franklin's tone throughout emphasizes how obvious and simple all the enterprises were. Witness, for example, the manifest benefits of systematic, cooperative efforts to keep the streets clean or to maintain a sober, zealous night watch.

Part of the ease of success, of course, arose from the relative absence in a new city of the ancient prerogatives and vested interests that always oppose innovations. No foot-dragging guilds of firemen or academicians were there to resist Franklin's plans for a fire company or a college. He could succeed as a printer, and even expand his business the length of the Atlantic coast, because monopoly franchises or other hoary devices to keep out newcomers were not yet generally established. Everywhere Franklin and his friends turned their restless energy they found opportunity rather than opposition. Comparison with Defoe is instructive. He as much exemplified the enterprising spirit as Franklin, had at least as much originality in proposing projects, and was the more skillful writer, but London confronted him at every turn with immovable establishments. The very nature of the New World itself, unformed, indeterminate, and beckoning, encouraged ideas to become realities.

Franklin's gradual, unpremeditated entrance into politics was a simple extension of his personal and community activities. He became public printer and clerk of the Pennsylvania Assembly to advance his business. Then, as described so graphically in the *Autobiography*, he organized a militia in a Quaker province. He was unimpressed with pacifist dogma and felt that sharing the burden of self-defense had obvious utility: it would, probably with little bloodshed, keep French or Spanish warships from destroying Philadelphia. Then, he easily gained a seat in the Assembly in order to further the plans for the hospital and academy by attracting public support and funds. His intention was straightforward: to use the government of the province itself, as the most broadly effective agency, for promoting institutions of public benefit. That, after all, he had learned from Locke and others, was the only legitimate purpose of government.

This laid the groundwork for Franklin's opposition to proprietary privileges and ultimately set him on the course to political revolution. In entering politics, Franklin had no thought, of course, of resisting the mother country, but the *Autobiography* reveals that the habits and values he had acquired living in the New World were not always going to suit the authorities. The governor of Pennsylvania could not understand why Franklin sided with "these damned Quakers" when the proprietor was perfectly willing to give him, in the usual practice of British government, a lucrative office in return for his support. To Franklin it was equally unthinkable to turn against a group he thought had given Pennsylvania "good and useful" government. Having in mind privileges common in Europe, the proprietors sought unashamedly to exempt their vast lands in Pennsylvania from taxation. Franklin thought it "incredible meanness" for them to place the whole burden of defense on smaller landholders. Franklin told another governor who tried to bribe him that he would support zealously measures for "the Good of the People," without sweeteners, but that otherwise he would have to oppose, whatever the rewards or inducements. Franklin and a British Army commander in North America, Lord Loudoun, found themselves in a hopeless misunderstanding in 1757 when Loudoun insisted, wrongly, that of course Franklin was profiteering on war supplies like everyone else in His Majesty's service. For Franklin, simple precepts and habits of life were beginning to have fateful implications for the very nature of the British Empire. There is no more instructive insight into the origins of the American Revolution than the contrasts in Franklin's *Autobiography*, in accounts set side by side, between the means of his rise to prosperity, and the means proprietary governors and Royal commanders assumed would be used to manage the public business.

Though it took Franklin twenty years or more (until 1776) to realize the ultimate meaning of these impasses with proprietary and royal officials, he had in fact been leading a revolutionary life almost from the moment of his birth. The great public deeds of Franklin's later life, not described in his *Autobiography*, fulfill the commitment and promise of his first half-century. His indignation at Lord North's highhandedness would be expected from one who had left Boston rather than suffer the petty tyranny of a brother. His tactical skill in diplomatic negotiations in Paris would not have surprised Philadelphia neighbors who had seen him carry through a dozen civic projects. Marvelously effective and witty essays defending American rights were second nature to Poor Richard, who had learned from boyhood how to use words to propound plain precepts of justice and common sense. A full understanding of the life-style of Franklin's first fifty years, the point of the *Autobiography*, makes the events of 1763-1789 much less startling than they appear otherwise. Once the life Franklin had lived in Boston and Philadelphia was a reality, not only for him but less only in degree for thousands of others, revolt against hereditary privilege and the impulse to found a new nation were not only possible but probably inevitable.

The very character of the *Autobiography* itself, a perfectly credible, dramatically simple life story, enhanced its meaning, of course, beyond anything a mere abstract statement of revolutionary principles could do. Franklin had been reared in a family whose status and material well-being, at least, were indistinguishable from the common lot. In Philadelphia he was a runaway of unknown origin who nonetheless found the resources within himself, and a sufficiently open society, to make a decisive impact. The confidence this experience produced and the way of life thus implanted were the prime revolutionary forces behind both the dramatic events of 1776 and the only slowly realized identity of the new nation thus created.

As American writers after 1783 struggled self-consciously to bring into being a national literature and to convey to the world a sense of the national character, the popularity of Franklin's *Autobiography* played a key role. Reading it, people around the world, and Americans themselves, sensed the answer to Crevecoeur's question, "What is an American?" In a twinkling, apparently timeless and eternal patterns of life seemed outmoded. If one wanted to know what Americans were like, what their national aspirations were, one had but to read Franklin's *Autobiography*. Utterly swept aside were dynastic or mystical conceptions of national purpose. America's purpose was to nourish lives like Franklin's, and her character was that embodied in his life story. Systems of government and foreign policy, as Franklin showed in the last fifteen years of his life, were to be framed to serve that purpose and that character. The measure of the United States' uniqueness was the contrast between his life-style and that prevalent in the rest of the world. The mission of America was to offer itself as an example to mankind. Though critics at home and abroad, from Mark Twain to D.H. Lawrence, would expose scathingly the limitations of this way of life (or at least the limitations of their caricatures of it), it has remained worthy and compelling to millions. It has been as well a persistent reminder, whenever American society tends to stratify and stagnate, of what is being lost or betrayed. To say, then, that the *Autobiography* is unfinished is true both in a narrow, literal sense, and in that its meaning in the United States and around the world has been to see human potential as often unfulfilled and human society as capable of order and cooperative achievement it has seldom attained. But it is also a "finished" account of the values and habits than can in some ways transform life and revolutionize nations.

Indeed, in a world of new nations and of peoples struggling for self-determination the *Autobiography* has had a sustained appeal and relevance. Franklin himself sensed the universality of his view of life when he asked, near the end of his life and as he heard of the beginnings of the French Revolution, that "God grant... not only the Love of Liberty, but a thorough Knowledge of the Rights of Man, may pervade all the Nations of the Earth, so that a philosopher may set his Foot anywhere on its Surface, and say, 'This is my Country.'" Such an aspiration, of course, was central to the European Enlightenment, which Franklin embodied, and in some form it characterizes great philosophies and religions around the world, most of which he knew very little about.

The universal appeal of the *Autobiography* is evident in countless incidents. Goethe and his friends in Weimar, for example, clubbed themselves together according to the values and model of Franklin's Junto. A century later, in Meiji Japan, Franklin became something of a cult figure as stories from his *Autobiography* were put in school texts to teach lessons of striving

for success and of cooperative endeavor. More recently, it is un-
canny that values V.S. Naipaul writes of in describing Muslim-
Indian shopkeepers and aspiring African schoolboys in an isolated
African town at *A Bend in the River* (1979) are in many respects
those of the industrious, ledger-keeping, school-founding
eighteenth-century Philadelphian. In each case, of course, there
are also vast differences in attitudes and beliefs, and there is no
need to calculate the amount or direction of "influence." Rather,
everywhere the implication is that peoples and communities have
their deepest and most accountable being in the texture of everyday
lives, and that nations would thus do well to shun metaphysical,
vainglorious, or imperial notions of their destinies. The plain, credible, yet simply marvelous story in the *Autobiography,* of the poor
boy from Boston who through hard work, increasing wisdom, and
social responsibility made his way in the world, became a challenge
to his countrymen and dramatized for them their bonds with
peoples around the globe. It will not surprise us, then, at a time
when 40% of the earth's population are children and when we increasingly recognize the formativeness of the early years, that the
"unfinished" *Autobiography*, telling of Franklin's youth and early manhood, is not incomplete in its revelation of vital human
qualities nor the least indeterminate in its message to humankind.

Benjamin Franklin as a Scientist

ROBERT A. MILLIKAN

Robert A. Millikan (1868-1953) received the Nobel Prize for Physics in 1923 for his researches on the elementary electronic charge and the photoelectric effect. His contributions to physics also included verification of Einstein's photoelectric equation and determination of the precise value for Planck's constant. He was director of the Norman Bridge Laboratory of Physics at California Institute of Technology from 1921 to 1945, and served as chairman of the board of directors of the Henry E. Huntington Library and Art Gallery, San Marino, California. As the following essay shows, his work on electron theory followed the discovery by J.J. Thomson in 1897 "who himself pointed out that this electron theory was in essential particulars a return to the theory put forth by Franklin in 1749."

Benjamin Franklin is perhaps the only American in that relatively small group of men of any time or country who, without having been either the head of a state or a military hero, have yet gained so conspicuous a place in history that their names and sayings are known the world over. Although he lived two hundred years ago in what was then a remote corner of the earth, far from any of the centers of world influence, yet his name and traits are still so widely known that the following incident could happen. Of what other American names, save possibly those of Washington and Lincoln, could anything like this be said? Franklin would have found it as interesting and amusing as will this audience.

One evening about two and a half months ago I was being shown by a devout Brahmin through the great Hindu temple at Madura in Southern India. There were many hundreds of Indians wandering about through the scores of rooms in the huge structure. Occasionally one of them would fall prostrate on his face before the image of the elephant god or the monkey god, or one or another of the multitudinous forms assumed by Krishna or Siva or their wives. In one of the rooms an expounder of the Yogi philosophy was passing around a printed page of directions for

33

"the Yogi way of life" to a score or more of pupils. As I was looking on in the back of the room he approached and put one of the sheets into my hand. I glanced through it and saw that it was in English and consisted merely of a set of rules for physical exercise (mystically interpreted, however), for eating and sleeping and early rising, etc., etc. As I glanced down the page I read the injunction, "You are to spend some time each day, morning and evening, in reflection, as Benjamin Franklin did."

But while that incident reflects Franklin's world-wide fame it is quite clear that it has nothing to do with Benjamin Franklin as a scientist. May I introduce the consideration of that side of Franklin's character by quoting a paragraph from a short biography of Michelson which I published in the *Scientific Monthly* for January, 1939:

"It will probably be generally agreed that the three American physicists whose work has been most epoch-making and whose names are most certain to be frequently heard wherever and whenever in future years the story of physics is told are Benjamin Franklin, Josiah Willard Gibbs, and Albert A. Michelson. And yet the three have almost no characteristics in common. Franklin lives as a physicist because, dilettante though he is sometimes called, mere qualitative interpreter though he actually was, yet it was he who, with altogether amazing insight, laid the real foundations on which the whole superstructure of electrical theory and interpretation has been erected. Gibbs lives because, profound scholar, matchless analyst that he was, he did for statistical mechanics and for thermodynamics what Laplace did for celestial mechanics and Maxwell did for electrodynamics, namely, made his field a well-nigh finished theoretical structure. Michelson, pure experimentalist, designer of instruments, refiner of techniques, lives because in the field of optics he drove the refinement of measurement to its limits and by so doing showed a skeptical world what far-reaching consequences can follow from that sort of a process and what new vistas of knowledge can be opened up by it. It was a lesson the world had to learn. The results of learning it are reflected today in the extraordinary recent discoveries in the field of electronics, of radioactivity, of vitamins, of hormones, of nuclear structure, etc. All these fields owe a large debt to Michelson, the pioneer in the art of measurement of extraordinarily minute quantities and effects."

In that paragraph I have tried to appraise Franklin's place

among American scientists. Let me now express my personal judgment as to his place in world science. If I were asked to list by centuries the fourteen most *influential* scientists who have lived since
Copernicus was born in 1473, I should bring forward the following
names by centuries:

Century	Name	Nationality.
15th Century............Copernicus (1473-1543)		Polish
16th Century............Galileo (1564-1642)		Italian
17th Century............Newton (1642-1727)		English
	Huyghens (1629-1695)	Dutch
18th Century............Franklin (1706-1790)		American
	LaPlace (1749-1827)	French
19th Century............Faraday (1791-1867)		English
	Maxwell (1831-1879)	English
	Darwin (1809-1882)	English
	Fresnel (1788-1827)	French
	Pasteur (1822-1895)	French
	Gauss (1777-1855)	German
	Helmholtz (1821-1894)	German
	Volta (1748-1827)	Italian
	Willard Gibbs (1839-1903	American

There will doubtless be those, especially among Europeans,
who will say, "Why do you give Franklin so high a place when
there were but seven of his eighty-four years, namely, from 1746 to
1753, in which he pursued science at all, also when he wrote, so far
as I can discover, not a single scientific paper designed for publication in a scientific journal?" His private letters to his friend Peter
Collinson which he never expected to be published at all, are practically the sole source of our knowledge of his scientific work.
Even his own estimate of his scientific achievement was so small
that in his autobiography he makes but casual reference it.

    The answer to the foregoing inquiry is that I have been guided
in the placing of Franklin and all of the others on the above list
primarily by the significance of their contributions as measured by
the influence they exerted in the development of our modern
world. I have not been concerned at all with the erudition of the
candidates, the profundity or extent of their scholarship, nor even
by the magnitude and difficulty of the problems which they solved.

    No one, however, can read these letters to Peter Collinson—I
have had access to the fifth edition published in 1774—without being amazed by the fact that Franklin without any previous training

whatever in either the technique or the history of physics and with almost no contact with what others were doing or had done, within two years of the time of his first experiment had acquired a keener insight into the fundamental nature of electrical phenomena, not merely than any one had acquired up to his time, but even than any of his successors acquired for the next hundred and fifty years, when, about 1900, the scientific world returned essentially to Franklin's views.

To justify this statement and to bring to light the extraordinary quality both of Franklin's physical insight and of his power of induction I shall make most of the remainder of this lecture consist of a few direct quotations from the Peter Collinson letters which the editor informs us were being printed "without waiting for the ingenious author's permission to do so."

The first letter, dated March 28, 1747, reads:

"To Peter Collinson, Esq; F.R.S. London

Philadelphia, March 28, 1747

"Sir,

"Your kind present of an electric tube,[1] with directions for using it, has put several of us on making electrical experiments, in which we have observed some particular phaenomena that we look upon to be new. I shall therefore communicate them to you in my next, though possibly they may not be new to you, as among the numbers daily employed in those experiments on your side of the water, 'tis probable some one or other has hit on the same observations. For my own part, I never was before engaged in any study that so totally engrossed my attention and my time as this has lately done; for what with making experiments when I can be alone, and repeating them to my Friends and Acquaintance, who, from the novelty of the thing, come continually in crouds to see them, I have, during some months past, had little leisure for any thing else.

"I am, etc.

"B. Franklin."

Now as to some of the experiments themselves. The very first one of them, done within a few months of the time he first heard of electricity, contains the key to his invention of the lightning rod. Note from the following how skillfully and strikingly he arranges

---

[1] A straight three-foot glass tube as big as your wrist.

his electrostatic experiments by making the length of the suspension of the cork ball very long. After two hundred years of the development of electrostatics these experiments cannot be made more tellingly today than by setting them up and performing them *exactly* as Franklin directed nearly two hundred years ago.

He writes, "The first is the wonderful effect of pointed bodies, both in *drawing off* and *throwing off* the electrical fire. For example,

"Place an iron shot of three or four inches diameter on the mouth of a clean dry glass bottle. By a fine silken thread from the cieling, right over the mouth of the bottle, suspend a small cork-ball, about the bigness of a marble; the thread of such a length, as that the cork-ball may rest against the side of the shot. Electrify the shot, and the ball will be repelled to the distance of four or five inches, more or less, according to the quantity of Electricity. . . . When in this state, if you present to the shot the point of a long, slender, sharp bodkin, at six or eight inches distance, the repellency is instantly destroyed, and the cork flies to the shot. A blunt body must be brought within an inch, and draw a spark, to produce the same effect. To prove that the electrical fire is *drawn off* by the point, if you take the blade of the bodkin out of the wooden handle, and fix it in a stick of sealing-wax, and then present it at the distance aforesaid, or if you bring it very near, no such effect follows; but sliding one finger along the wax till you touch the blade, and the ball flies to the shot immediately."

"To show that points will *throw off* as well as *draw off* the electrical fire, lay a long sharp needle upon the shot, and you cannot electrise the shot so as to make it repel the cork-ball. . . . Or fix a needle to the end of a suspended gun-barrel, or iron-rod, so as to point beyond it like a little bayonet; and while it remains there the gun-barrel or rod cannot by applying the tube to the other end be electrised so as to give a spark, the fire continually running out silently at the point."

I can find no evidence that prior to Franklin the electrical properties of points had been discovered at all. He continued:

"The repellency between the cork-ball and the shot is likewise destroyed, (1) by sifting fine sand on it; this does it gradually; (2) by breathing on it; (3) by making a smoke about it from burning wood; (4) by candle-light, even though the candle is at a foot distance: these do it suddenly. . . the light of a bright coal from a wood fire; and the light of a red-hot iron do it likewise; but not at so great a distance.

"The light of the sun thrown strongly on both cork and shot by a looking-glass for a long time together, does not impair the repellency in the least. This difference between fire-light and sunlight is another thing that seems new and extraordinary to us."[2]

The insight shown in the three lines of the footnote below, in which he correctly makes particle carriers (ions, we now call them) from the match do the discharging while sunlight produces no ions and therefore does not discharge, is unbelievably penetrating for a date two hundred years back, though the conception of neutral particles being first attracted and then repelled is of course definitely wrong.

The next experiment, with its interpretation, is probably the most fundamental thing ever done in the field of electricity. Get it exactly in Franklin's words:

"1. A person standing on wax, and rubbing the tube, and another person on wax drawing the fire, they will both of them (provided they do not stand so as to touch one another) appear to be electrised, to a person standing on the floor; that is, he will receive a spark on approaching each of them with his knuckle.

"2. But if the persons on wax touch one another during the exciting of the tube, neither of them will appear to be electrised.

"3. If they touch one another after exciting the tube, and drawing the fire as aforesaid, there will be a stronger spark between them than was between either of them and the person on the floor.

"4. After such strong spark, neither of them discover any electricity.

"These appearances we attempt to account for thus: We suppose, as aforesaid, that electrical fire is a common element (we now call 'electrical fire' electrons), of which every one of the three persons abovementioned has his equal share, before any operation is begun with the tube. A, who stands on wax and rubs the tube, collects the electrical fire from himself into the glass; and his communication with the common stock being cut off by the wax, his

---

[2]"This different Effect probably did not arise from any difference in the light, but rather from the particles separated from the candle, being first attracted and then repelled, carrying off the electric matter with them."

body is not again immediately supply'd. *B* (who stands on wax likewise), passing his knuckle along near the tube, receives the fire which was collected by the glass from *A;* and his communication with the common stock being likewise cut off, he retains the additional quantity received. . . . To *C,* standing on the floor, both appear to be electrised: for he, having only the middle quantity of electrical fire, receives a spark upon approaching *B,* who has an over quantity; but gives one to *A,* who has an under quantity. If *A* and *B* approach to touch each other, the spark is stronger, because the difference between them is greater: After such touch there is no spark between either of them and *C,* because the electrical fire in all is reduced to the original equality. If they touch while electrising, the equality is never destroy'd, the fire only circulating. Hence have arisen some new terms among us: we say *B* (and bodies like circumstanced) is electrised *positively; A, negatively.* Or rather, *B* is electrised *plus; A, minus.* And we daily in our experiments electrise bodies *plus* or *minus,* as we think proper.—To electrise *plus* or *minus,* no more needs to be known than this, that the parts of the tube or sphere that are rubbed, do, in the instant of the friction, attract the electrical fire, and therefore take it from the thing rubbing: the same parts immediately, as the friction upon them ceases, are disposed to give the fire they have received, to any body that has less.''

The next two long letters are taken up largely with what he calls "M. Muschenbroek's wonderful bottle,'' accidentally discovered in Leyden one year earlier, 1746, now known as the Leyden jar, and with explaining all such effects just as we do today in terms of the opposite charges or the inner and outer coats.

Thus, to use his exact words, "At the same time that the wire and top (inside coat) of the bottle is electrified positively or plus the bottom (outside coat) of the bottle is electrified negatively or minus, in exact proportion: i.e., whatever quantity of electrical fire is thrown in at the top an equal quantity goes out at the bottom.'' And "Again, when the bottle is electrised, but little of the electrical fire can be drawn out from the top by touching the wire unless an equal quantity can at the same time *get in* at the bottom. Thus, place an electrised bottle on clean glass or dry wax and you will not, by touching the wire get out the fire from the top.''

These chapters, too, contain the uncannily clever experiment of showing, just as we do today, that the charge resides in or on the dielectric. How many of us realize that the familiar class-room experiment of removing the coats of a Leyden jar and touching each of them, then putting them back again, and after that getting a strong spark by connecting the replaced coatings with a wire was devised by Benjamin Franklin in 1749?

Again, he says, "There is one experiment more which surprises us, and is not hitherto satisfactorily accounted for; it is this: Place an iron shot on a glass stand, and let a ball of damp cork, suspended by a silk thread, hang in contact with the shot. Take a bottle in each hand, one that is electrified through the hook, the other through the coating: Apply the giving wire to the shot, which will electrify it *positively,* and the cork shall be repelled; then apply the requiring wire, which will take out the spark given by the other; when the cork will return to the shot: Apply the same again, and take out another spark, so will the shot be electrified *negatively,* and the cork in that shall be repelled equally as before. Then apply the giving wire to the shot, and give the spark it wanted, so will the cork return: Give it another, which will be an addition to its natural quantity, so will the cork be repelled again: And so may the experiment be repeated as long as there is any charge in the bottles. *Which shews that bodies having less than the common quantity of electricity, repel each other, as well as those that have more.* "

In that last sentence Franklin states clearly that matter which had lost its normal amount of electricity was self repellent. In modern terms the atom is neutral when it has its full complement of electrons. When any of these are removed the nuclei repel one another.

The next paragraph is added merely to illustrate the amusing and dramatic side of Franklin's character.

"Chagrined a little that we have been hitherto able to produce nothing in this way of use to mankind; and the hot weather coming on, when electrical experiments are not so agreeable, it is proposed to put an end to them for this season, somewhat humorously, in a party of pleasure, on the banks of Skuylkil. Spirits, at the same time, are to be fired by a spark sent from side to side through the river, without any other conductor than the water; an experiment which we some time since performed, to the amazement of many. A turkey is to be killed for our dinner by the *electrical shock,* and roasted by the *electrical jack,* before a fire kindled by the *electrical bottle:* when the healths of all the famous electricians in England,

Holland, France, and Germany are to be drank in *electrified bumpers,* under the discharge of guns from the *electrical battery.''*

In some of these letters, notably the fifth, Franklin goes off into long and incorrect speculations as to the difference between the terms "electric bodies per se" and "non electric bodies.'' But this adds to, rather than subtracts from my own appreciation of him, for no human being could possibly have seen correctly all the elements of a huge and thus far completely unexplored field, and his wrong steps give him opportunity to show his greatness by the way he goes to work to discover and to admit his error. Thus, he writes as follows:

"*Query,* Wherein consists the difference between an *electric* and a *non-electric* body?

"*Answer.* The terms electric *per se,* and non-electric, were first used to distinguish bodies, on a mistaken supposition that those called electrics *per se,* alone contained electric matter in their substance, which was capable of being excited by friction, and of being produced or drawn from them, and communicated to those called non-electrics, supposed to be destitute of it: For the glass, etc., being rubb'd, discover'd signs of having it, by snapping to the finger, attracting, repelling, etc. and could communicate those signs to metals and water. . . . Afterwards it was found, that rubbing of glass would not produce the electric matter, unless a communication was preserved between the rubber and the floor; and subsequent experiments proved that the electric matter was really drawn from those bodies that at first were thought to have none in them. Then it was doubted whether glass and other bodies called *electrics per se,* had really any electric matter in them, since they apparently afforded none but what they first extracted from those which had been called non-electrics. But some of my experiments shew that glass contains it in great quantity, and I now suspect it to be pretty equally diffused in all the matter of this terraqueous globe. If so, the terms *electric per se,* and *non-electric,* should be laid aside as improper: and (the only difference being this, that some bodies will conduct electric matter, and others will not) the terms *conductor* and *non-conductor* may supply their place.''

Without doubt the most profound paragraphs in all of Franklin's letters are the following, written in 1749:

"1. The electrical matter consists of particles extremely subtile, since it can permeate common matter, even the densist metals, with such ease and freedom as not to receive any perceptible resistance.

"2. If any one should doubt whether the electrical matter passes through the substance of bodies, or only over and along their surfaces, a shock from an electrified large glass jar, taken through his own body, will probably convince him.

"3. Electrical matter differs from common matter in this, that the parts of the latter mutually attract, those of the former mutually repel each other. Hence the appearing divergency in a stream of electrified effluvia.

"4. But though the particles of electrical matter do repel each other, they are strongly attracted by all other matter.

"5. From these three things, the extreme subtility of the electrical matter, the mutual repulsion of its parts, and the strong attraction between them and other matter, arise this effect, that, when a quantity of electrical matter is applied to a mass of common matter, of any bigness or length, within our observation (which hath not already got its quantity) it is immediately and equally diffused through the whole.

"6. Thus common matter is a kind of spunge to the electrical fluid. And as a spunge would receive no water if the parts of water were not smaller than the pores of the spunge; and even then but slowly, if there were not a mutual attraction between those parts and the parts of the spunge; and would still imbibe it faster, if the mutual attraction among the parts of the water did not impede, some force being required to separate them; and fastest, if, instead of attraction, there were a mutual repulsion among those parts, which would act in conjunction with the attraction of the spunge. So is the case between the electrical and common matter.

"7. But in common matter there is (generally) as much of the electrical as it will contain within its substance. If more is added, it lies without upon the surface, and forms what we call an electrical atmosphere; and then the body is said to be electrified."

In these paragraphs Franklin states with great succinctness what later became known as the Franklin one-fluid theory, and after 1900 was known as the electron theory. In his day, and for 150 years thereafter, it received very scant consideration in the old world, and the so-called two-fluid theory of Aepinus, put forward a little later, was universally taught in text books the world over up to the triumph of the electron theory in 1897 under the active leadership of J.J. Thomson, who himself pointed out that this electron theory was in essential particulars a return to the theory put forth by Franklin in 1749. For Franklin's electrical matter consisted of extremely subtle mobile *particles* (now called negative electrons), which in order to make matter exhibit its common or neutral properties had to be present in each kind of matter (we now say in each kind of atom; but the atomic theory had not been formulated in 1749) in a particular number, an increase in which number made it exhibit electrification of one sign, a decrease an electrification of the opposite sign. In Franklin's theory only one kind of electrical matter was mobile; the other sign of electrification appeared when the mobile kind was removed so that it could no longer neutralize the effect of the opposite kind *which inhered in the immobile part of matter* (i.e. in the nucleus).

The Franklin theory was mathematically identical with the two-fluid theory, but while the former was a definite and profound *physical* theory the latter was a hold-over from medieval mysticism. It came from the age of the so-called "imponderables"—an imponderable or weightless heat theory, the caloric—and the imponderable electric fluids. Such vague, tenuous, contradictory ideas were ill at home in the highly realistic, practical mind of Franklin. They were justified, like Faraday's lines of magnetic force, as analytical conveniences but not as physical realities. Franklin introduced a definite physical theory which rendered unnecessary such fantastic conceptions as two weightless and hence non-existent fluids introduced for purely *ad hoc* purposes, and then told to destroy each other, also for *ad hoc* purposes.

Let us now return to Franklin's discussion of points and their properties of throwing off or drawing off the electrical fire. He says, very modestly and wisely:

"These explanations of the power and operation of points, when they first occurred to me, and while they first floated in my mind, appeared perfectly satisfactory; but now I have written them, and considered them more closely, I must own I have some doubts about them; yet, as I have at present nothing better to offer in their stead, I do not cross them out: for even a bad solution read, and its faults discovered, has often given rise to a good one, in the mind of an ingenious reader."

In the next paragraph note how clearly he sees the necessity of eliminating unnecessary hypotheses, i.e., he adopts the scientific principle of "minimum hypothesis."

"Nor is it of much importance to us, to know the manner in which nature executes her laws; it is enough if we know the laws themselves. It is of real use to know that china left in the air unsupported will fall and break; but *how* it comes to fall, and *why* it breaks, are matters of speculation. It is a pleasure indeed to know them, but we can preserve our china without it."

He then describes some discharging effects of points conducted on a larger scale than he had before attempted, and in a later paper dated November 7, 1749, he enumerates all the known points of resemblance between lightning and electricity, and concludes with the comment:

"The electric fluid is attracted by points. We do not know whether this property be in lightning, but since they agree in all points in which we can compare them, it is not improbable that they agree likewise in this. Let the experiment be made."

In June, 1752 he made it, carrying out in a shed with his son the experiment which he describes as follows in his letter of October 18, 1752, to Peter Collinson.

"As frequent mention is made in public papers from Europe of the success of the Philadelphia experiment for drawing the electric fire from clouds by means of pointed rods of iron erected on high buildings, etc. it may be agreeable to the curious to be informed that the same experiment has succeeded in Philadelphia, though made in a different and more easy manner, which is as follows:

"Make a small cross of two light strips of cedar, the arms so long as to reach to the four corners of a large thin silk handerchief when extended; tie the corners of the handerchief to the extremities of the cross, so you have the body of a kite; which being properly accommodated with a tail, loop, and string, will rise in the air, like those made of paper; but this being of silk is better to bear the wet and wind of a thunder gust without tearing. To the top of the upright stick of the cross is to be fixed a very sharp pointed wire, rising a foot more above the wood. To the end of the twine, next the hand, is to be tied a silk ribbon, and where the silk and twine join, a key may be fastened. This kite is to be raised when a thunder-gust appears to be coming on, and the person who holds the string must stand within a door or window, or under some cover, so that the silk ribbon may not be wet; and care must be taken that the twine does not touch the frame of the door or window. As soon as any of the thunder clouds come over the kite, the pointed wire will draw the electric fire from them, and the kite, with all the twine, will be electrified, and the loose filaments of the twine will stand out every way, and be attracted by an approaching finger. And when the rain has wet the kite and twine, so that it can conduct the electric fire freely, you will find it stream out plentifully from the key on the approach of your knuckle. At this key the phial may be charged; and from electric fire thus obtained, spirits may be kindled, and all the other electric experiments be performed, which are usually done by the help of a rubbed glass globe or tube, and thereby the sameness of the electric matter with that of lightning completely demonstrated.''

In a further letter written in September, 1753, he says:

"In September 1752 I erected an iron rod to draw the lightning down into my house, in order to make some experiments on it." He carried on these experiments for some months to learn whether the clouds were positively or negatively electrified, and after many trials he says,

"I concluded that the clouds are *always* electrified *negatively,* or have always in them less than their natural quantity of the electric fluid.

"Yet notwithstanding so many experiments, it seems I concluded too soon; for at last, June the 6th, in a gust which continued from five o'clock P.M. to seven, I met with one cloud that was electrified positively, though several that passed over my rod before, during the same gust, were in the negative state."

The foregoing shows what most commendable scientific care he took in his experiments and what caution he used in drawing conclusions.

But he did not stop with making scientific experiments. His active and practical mind was not satisfied until he had applied it to the useful end of the invention of the lightning rod, as indicated in the first paragraph of the letter of October 19, 1752, quoted above.

After his definite proof of the identity of lightning and electricity he was recognized by the most distinguished English scientists by being elected to the Royal Society, and was presented for the year 1753 the Copley medal of the Society, the highest honor within the gift of the world's most illustrious scientific body.

After its presentation at the Franklin Institute I sent the article to Mr. I. Bernard Cohen of the Harvard Library, and received from him the following reply, which I am very glad to have presented along with the article because it enables the reader to gain a little better view of the breadth of Franklin's interests, and also to avoid some minor misunderstandings.

HARVARD LIBRARY
CAMBRIDGE, MASSACHUSETTS
November 30, 1940

PROFESSOR ROBERT A. MILLIKAN

Dear Sir:

Thank you very much for your kindness in allowing me to read your essay on Benjamin Franklin. I think it very interesting and I am very glad that it is to be published.

There is nothing wrong in any of your statements, although I think that two of them are misleading. First, you write of Franklin's work in electricity and only that. It is true, of course, that Franklin did his most significant work in electricity, but his scientific range was considerably broader. Thus, he did pioneer work in locating the position of the Gulf Stream, he discovered that northeast storms come from the southwest, i.e., they travel in the direction opposite to that in which they blow. He also made the first measurements of heat absorption with regard to colour, and was the first to investigate the conductivity of different substances with regard to heat. Similarly, he did other things in medicine (ventilation, the cause of colds, the invention of a flexible metal catheter) and advanced the cause of hospitals. And no small part of his contribution to science took the form of the advancement of it,—by forming the American Philosophical Society, by providing the means for publication of scientific works, by encouraging younger scientists (such as Priestley, etc.), and by spreading scientific information. This means only that in your essay you should, in my opinion, mention that you are concerned with Franklin and Electricity, and not write of Franklin and electricity as if it were Franklin and science.

Second, I cannot agree with your statement that Franklin wrote no article to be published in a scientific journal. We are misled by the form of his writing. An examination of the *Philosophical Transaction* of the eighteenth century shows that most of the articles were letters in form, addressed by a non-member of the society to a member, or by a member to the President. We know now that Franklin's letters were read at the meetings of the Royal Society and were discussed in various printed articles and pamphlets. This is one of my own finds, one not sufficiently brought out by any other writer. Thus the letters which Franklin wrote to Collinson were of two kinds: one was personal and never read to the Royal Society members, the other was public and was so read. This type of letter was the eighteenth-century equivalent of the "note" which one sends to a journal today. In this light, your statement is somewhat misleading. Further, there are some articles such as the "Loose Thoughts on a Universal Fluid" read at the American Philosophical Society and published in their Proceedings.

For the rest I found your article clear and refreshing. It is pleasant for me to find a first rank scientist like yourself stating firmly and definitely that Franklin was a scientist. If he did not give many years to science, that was not his fault; and we know that as he had to give more and more of his time to politics he lamented the fact more and more. He always considered himself a scientist doing necessary work in politics, and at eighty-one he could ask his friend Ingenhousz to rejoice with him that he was a "freeman" after fifty years of public service and that now he could go back to America and resume his experiments, if the English had not destroyed his equipment.

Besides, as you say so clearly, we judge a man by his achievement. What does it matter whether Franklin spent six years or twenty years at his work? Newton is not great because he put so many work-hours into his discoveries, but because his discoveries were of great importance. Thus, no one censures Newton because he gave most of his time to alchemy, theology, and affairs of the mind.

Yours sincerely,

I. BERNARD COHEN

EDITOR'S NOTE

Franklin won recognition in both Europe and America for his electrical discoveries. Despite his limited formal education he received honorary degrees from Harvard and Yale in America and from St. Andrews University in Scotland. He also received from the Royal Society of London its coveted Sir Godfrey Copley gold medal and congratulations from the King of France. He was elected to membership in the Royal Society of London and the Royal Academy of Science in Paris, as well as other learned societies in Edinburgh, Göttingen, Rotterdam, Padua, and Turin. His work in electricity — his one-fluid theory of electrical action and his research on lightning — made him an international celebrity.

In the late eighteenth century there arose a two-fluid theory which replaced Franklin's and continued to dominate electrical science until the end of the nineteenth century.

Scholars have explored the origins of Franklin's electrical theories and his knowledge of electrical experiments undertaken in Europe in the 1740s and earlier. I.B. Cohen has studied in detail Franklin's introduction to science and electricity and has shown that despite lack of formal training, Franklin was well educated in science, especially Newtonian experimental science, before he began his research on electricity.[1] Bernard S. Finn has argued that Franklin's acquaintanceship with European developments in electrical science was severely limited. Franklin was "ignorant of some important experimental evidence," and his writings on electricity betray an inadequate awareness of the literature of electrical science in the Europe of the 1740s. Franklin's isolation in America, Finn believes, benefited him in two ways: "he was limited in his knowledge and he was spared criticism."[2] J. L. Heilbron also finds that Franklin was ill-informed of the European literature on electricity in the middle 1740s. He points out that Peter Collinson sent with the glass tube the April 1745 issue of the *Gentleman's Magazine* which he believes Franklin must have read. That issue contained an imperfect English translation of Albrecht von

---

[1] I. B. Cohen, *Franklin and Newton: an Enquiry into Speculative Newtonian Experimental Science* and *Franklin's Work on Electricity as an Example thereof* (Philadelphia: The American Philosophical Society, 1956; Cambridge, Mass.: Harvard University Press, 1966, revised reprint 1981).

[2] Bernard S. Finn, "An Appraisal of the Origins of Franklin's Electrical Theory," *Isis*, 60 (Fall 1969), 362-369.

Haller's report on electrical experiments in Germany which had appeared in French in the *Bibliotheque raisonnee* for the first quarter of 1745. The translator, Heilbron shows, was ignorant of both French and electricity. Heilbron attributes Franklin's use of the word "electrise" to an inaccurate translation of the French word for "electrify" which appears throughout Haller's report in *Gentleman's Magazine*. Heilbron suggests that Franklin may have found the seeds of his idea of plus and minus electric charges and the first suggestion as to the identity of lightning and electricity in the translation of Haller's report.[3]

Millikan's essay on Franklin as a scientist is limited to his electrical experiments and theories. I. Bernard Cohen points out that Franklin had a much broader range of scientific interest than Millikan's essay implies. Cohen's note to Millikan remains timely. In addition to fugitive pieces in various journals on Franklin's interest in sciences other than electricity, a comprehensive and accurate study of Franklin's diverse scientific activities and speculations has been written by Cohen in his *Franklin and Newton*[4]

---

[3] J.L. Heilbron, *Electricity in the 17th and 18th Centuries: A Study of Early Modern Physics* (Berkeley: University of California Press, c1979), pp. 324-326, 329-330; J.L. Heilbron, "Franklin, Haller, and Franklinist History," *Isis*, 68 (December 1977), 539-549.

[4] See also I.B. Cohen, *Benjamin Franklin, Scientist and Statesman* (New York: Charles Scribner's Sons, 1975).

Benjamin Franklin and the Post Office

THOMAS COULSON

Thomas Coulson (1886–1971) was born in South Shields, England, and attended Balliol College, Oxford, and Sandhurst Military Academy. His distinguished career in the British Intelligence Service earned him the rank of Major and he played an important role in the capture of the German spy Mata Hari, for which he received the prestigious Order of the British Empire. Major Coulson's book about Mata Hari was the basis for a movie filmed after World War I. After coming to America, he held many positions at the Franklin Institute, and wrote a history of it entitled *The Franklin Institute from 1924 to 1950*. He served as Director of Museum Research at the Franklin Institute Museum for twenty-five years.

The following essay appeared in the September 1950 issue of the *Journal of The Franklin Institute*.

Franklin's original association with the American Post Office sprang directly from his interests as the publisher of a newspaper. At the time no law regulated the distribution of newspapers through the mail. Consequently, it was a decided advantage to a publisher that he should receive appointment as a postmaster. Tenure of this office enabled him to gather news cheaply and expeditiously through the post riders and, best of all, it enabled him to distribute his newspaper free of cost. If he had the courage to do so, he might forbid his post riders to carry any rival journal. This was the situation that irked Franklin. He found his newspaper, the *Pennsylvania Gazette,* excluded from the mails by Andrew Bradford, the postmaster of Philadelphia, who was the publisher of the rival *American Weekly Mercury.*

However, the application of this monopolistic tactic had nothing to do with Bradford's expulsion from office and the appointment of Franklin in his place. Franklin was doubtless getting around the difficulty by bribing the riders to carry his newspaper, which was the accepted practice. The trouble was that Bradford had unorthodox views about the keeping of accounts and the rendering of financial statements. For three years in succession he had neglected to make any returns or payments. As he was supposed to render semi-annual reports, the Deputy Postmaster General for American must have exercised much forbearance before he made up his mind to dismiss the delinquent. Franklin records his appointment to the office in his "Autobiography" as follows:

In October, 1737, Colonel Spotswood, late governor of Virginia, and then postmaster-general, being dissatisfied with the conduct of his deputy at Philadelphia, respecting some negligence in rendering and inexactitude of his accounts, took from him the commission and offered it to me. I accepted it readily, and found it of great advantage; for, though the salary was small, it facilitated the correspondence that improved my newspaper, increased the number demanded as well as the advertisements to be inserted, so that it came to afford me a considerable income.

The opportunity of pointing the moral was irresistible. Continuing on the subject of Bradford's dismissal, Franklin said: "Thus he suffered greatly from his neglect in due accounting; and I mention it as a lesson to those young men who may be employed in managing affairs for others, that they should always render accounts, and make remittances, with great clearness and punctuality. The character of observing such a conduct is the most powerful of all recommendations to new employments and increase of business." Although it is apparent that Franklin's main profit from the postmastership came from the prosperity it brought his newspaper, he was not unmindful of his official duties. The following advertisement appeared in the *Gazette* of October 27, 1737:

Notice is hereby given that the post office of Philadelphia is now kept at B. Franklin's, in Market Street; and that Henry Pratt is appointed Riding Postmaster for all the stages between Philadelphia and Newport in Virginia, who sets out about the beginning of each month, and returns in twenty-four days; by whom gentlemen, merchants, and others, may have their letters carefully conveyed, and business faithfully transacted, he having given good security for the same to the Honorable Colonel Spotswood, Postmaster-General of all His Majesty's Dominions in North America.

One would naturally suppose that Franklin, after his admonition upon the failure of Bradford, would discharge his duties diligently and that his accounts were scrupulously accurate and punctual. The conscientious manner in which his work was done induced the Postmaster General to appoint him Comptroller, a position which ranked as next in importance to that of the Deputy himself, and which gave him an intimate knowledge of the internal economy of the system that was to prove exceedingly valuable at a later date.

There is no reason to doubt that he found the position as postmaster a congenial occupation, apart from its effect upon his newspaper's circulation. Franklin enjoyed the companionship of his fellow men and it was his contact with people in every walk of life which gave depth and expanse to his philosophy. His position as postmaster greatly enlarged his acquaintance, for the delivery of the post was something of a social occasion, the significance of which has escaped the brush of the artist and the pen of the historian. Especially at times of crisis, such as the war in 1748, the arrival of the mail was the signal for the gathering of a crowd of anxious inquirers at his shop where, if they did not receive letters themselves, they could at least gather the latest news from those who were more fortunate. Franklin the editor was, therefore, at the fount of public opinion at such times.

Meanwhile, he prospered to such an extent that he was able to retire from active participation in his business as a printer, and began to exert himself more fully in public affairs. His retention of the Post Office would indicate that he regarded it less as a source of income than as a public service. He was to hold many offices but he sought appointment to very few. Yet, having acquired a perception of the value the Post Office could come to have as the unifying agent for the colonies, he deliberately sought appointment to the office of Deputy Postmaster General for America. The incumbent, Elliot Benger, was in ill-health and little hope was given for his recovery, whereon Franklin began to pull strings in order that he might secure the reversion of the office. To this end he wrote to his correspondent in London, Peter Collinson, soliciting his aid.

. . . The occasion of my writing this, via Ireland is That I have just receiv'd advice that the Deputy Post Master General of America (Mr. Elliot Benger, residing in Virginia) who has for some time been in declining Way is tho't to be near his End. My friends advise me to apply for this Post and Mr. Allen (our Chief Justice) has wrote the enclos'd to his Correspondent, Mr. Simpson, in my favor requesting his Interest and Application in the Affair and impowering him to advance a considerable Sum if it should be necessary.

I have not hithertofore made much scruple of giving you Trouble when the Publick Good was to be promoted by it, but 'tis with great Reluctance that I think of asking you to interest yourself in my private Concerns, as I know you have little time to spare. The Place is in the Disposal of the Post Masters General of Britain with some of whom or their Friends you may possibly have Acquaintance. Mr. Allen has desir'd Mr. Simpson to confer with you on the Affair and if you can without much Inconvenience to yourself advise and assist in endeavouring to secure the Success of this Application you will, whatever may be the Event, add greatly to the Obligations you have already conferr'd on me: and if it succeeds I hope that as my Power of doing good increases my Inclinations will always at least keep pace with it. I am quite a Stranger to the Manner of

Managing these Applications so can offer no particular Instructions. I enclose a Copy of the Commission of a former Deputy Post Master General which may be of some use. The Articles of Agreem' referr'd to in the Commission I have never seen but suppose they have always been nearly the same whoever is appointed, and have usually been sent over to America to be executed by the new Officer; for I know neither of the three last Officers went to England for the Commission. The Place has commonly been reputed worth about 150 pounds a Year but would be otherways very suitable to me, particularly as it would enable me to execute a Scheme long since form'd of which I send you enclos'd a Copy, and which I hope would soon produce something agreeable to you and to all Lovers of Useful Knowledge, for I have now a large Acquaintance among the ingenious Men in America. I need not tell you that Philadelphia being the Center of the Continent Colonies and having constant Communication with the West India Islands is by much a fitter Place for the Situation of a General Post Office than Virginia, and that it would be some Reputation for our Province to have it establish'd here. I would only add that as I have a respect for Mr. Benger I should be glad the Application were so managed as not to give him any Offense if he should recover. But I leave everything to you and Mr. Simpson referring you to Mr. Allen's Letter to that Gentleman for further particulars, and am dear Sir,

Your affectionate humble Serv'

B. Franklin

P.S. I have heard 200 pounds was given for this Office by Mr. Benger and the same by his Predecessor. I know not whose Perquisite it was. But lest that not be sufficient and there may be some contingent Fees and Charges Mr. Allen has ordered 300 pounds. However the less it costs the better as 'tis an Office for Life only which is a very uncertain tenure.

However, the solicitor was somewhat premature in his application for Benger refused to be accommodating. He clung to life and office and did not leave his post vacant until two years later. Finally, on August 10, 1753, the following order was issued:

Ordered that Mr. Benjamin Franklin, of Philadelphia in Pennsylvania, and Mr. William Hunter of Williamsburg in Virginia, be appointed Deputy Post Masters and Managers of all His Majesty's Provinces and Dominions on the Continent of North America, in the stead of Elliot Benger, Esq., Deceased, to commence this day, at an Allowance or Salary of 600 pounds p. Ann. to be paid out of the money arising from the Postage of Letters passing or repassing throughout the said Provinces and Dominions of North America.

The joint deputy, Colonel William Hunter, was publisher oi the *Virginia Gazette,* but he was in such poor health that he was not able to play an active part in the administration of the postal system at times. However, upon his appointment Franklin immediately visited him and the pair made a tour of inspection of the southern Post Offices. At first glance it might appear that the office of Deputy Postmaster General would be a lucrative post, for the salary of three hundred pounds was a respectable sum in those days when money had a much larger purchasing power, but it should be observed that the salary was to be paid out of the profits of the postal system and, as the system had never, as yet, managed to cover the cost of its maintenance, the hopes of a salary to be derived from it were somewhat visionary. However, Franklin had ideas for improving the service and he hoped by applying the principles of good management to make it not only self-supporting but profitable enough to pay the salaries. But in the meantime, Franklin and Hunter discovered that they had become speculators, for they had to dig into their own purses to pay the expenses of the innovations they adopted. Within the period of four years the Post Office owed them four hundred pounds.

Franklin was too sagacious to permit the office to become a drain upon his resources without receiving some compensation. He appointed members of his own family to salaried posts in a manner which would provoke howls of protest today. His son William succeeded him as postmaster of Philadelphia and later Comptroller. When William took over the latter office he was succeeded in the postmastership by Joseph Reed, a relative of Mrs. Franklin, and was followed in the course of time by Peter Franklin, who was brought from Boston to fill the post. The Post Office in Boston was given to Franklin's brother John, and when he died to his widow, who thereby became the first postmistress in America. However, it must not be supposed that Franklin was activated by selfishness in assuming the office of Deputy Postmaster General. It is characteristic of the man that he should take a large view of his duties and that his influence in their performance should extend far beyond the domain of the Post Office. His letter to Peter Colinson had indicated he had a wider view in prospect than the mere reform of a bankrupt system. His purpose became clearer as time passed.

He attended the Albany Congress in 1754 as a delegate from Pennsylvania and offered for discussion a plan which would draw the colonies into unified action, but the proposal only served to throw into sharper focus the variety and diversity of provincial prejudices and antipathies hindering a community of feeling. As Franklin acidulously stated: "Everybody cries a Union is absolutely Necessary, but when they come to the Manner and Form of the Union, their weak Noddles are perfectly distracted." There was nothing to be done at the moment but to accept the want of decision on the part of the other delegates, but it is a tenable supposition that a man of Franklin's political acuity should perceive not only the defects in the situation but also the means of providing a remedy. In brief, his remedy was an elaboration of the scheme hinted at in his letter to Peter Collinson. A more efficient postal system could be the means of drawing the colonies into a better understanding of their common interests and of knitting them into a homogeneous community. The breaking down of the separating barriers of thought was the only way in which the widely scattered colonists could be diverted from concentration upon local problems into thinking upon the major problems that affected them as a national entity.

Franklin was aware of the immensity of the problem confronting him. After he had founded the American Philosophical Society he had reason to deplore the lethargy of its members, but a little reflection must have convinced him that the absence of roads and the primitive means of communicating intelligence were grave handicaps for the members to overcome. Living in an age when the transmission of news is almost instantaneous, it is difficult for us to visualize existence in a community where the latest news was invariably stale. There were no daily newspapers, and those which were published weekly were often content enough to publish information of events which had taken place during the previous month. Letters were scanty in number because of the expense of their transmission. The scientists of the day, or philosophers as they chose to call themselves, to whom knowledge of what others were doing in their field was almost as necessary as the air they breathed, were always lamenting the delays in the diffusion of knowledge. To Franklin, with his questing mind, the need for quicker and cheaper transmission of intelligence, not only of a scientific nature but in every form of human activity, was imperative if the Colonies were to accept a recognition of their need for unity.

The letter to Collinson, in which he wrote that his appointment to the Postmastership "would enable me to execute a scheme long since form'd...and which I hope would soon produce something agreeable to you and to all Lovers of Useful Knowledge," undoubtedly had reference to his desire to quicken the correspondence among the "ingenious Men in America" united in the American Philosophical Society. The necessity for an enlargement of his plan and its more pressing urgency became apparent when he had to deal with an embryo nation. The manner in which the postal service could be applied would spring from his experience as Comptroller.

The postal system which Franklin and Hunter inherited in 1753 was still under the establishment of the Postal Act of 1710. This was the great charter of the British Post Office until the reforms introduced by Rowland Hill in 1840. It was of itself a reform act but like so many statutes of that nature its defects were as conspicuous as its good intentions. This Act consolidated the posts of the entire British empire and fixed the rates which could be charged. New York was intended to be the center of the system in North America (although it never did become so until many years later) and all rates were reckoned from that city with a fine disregard for the distances to the places named. To send a letter to the West Indies or to a point within 60 miles of New York cost four pence; to Perth Amboy or a point not exceeding 100 miles distant, six pence; to Philadelphia or New London, nine pence; to Boston or Annapolis, one shilling. The general rates from these places to way Post Offices was on the basis of four pence for 60 miles or six pence for 100 miles.

High prices were not the only deterrent to frequent use of the mails. The time consumed in transmitting letters was appallingly slow according to modern standards. Some effort was made to arrive at speed between the larger towns where roads existed, but even here the riders could encounter exasperating delays. It is needless to point out that the Colonies had developed along the Eastern shores, so that the post riders had to cross numerous unbridged rivers and creeks at their widest points. The Post Office Act instructed ferrymen to give the riders free and speedy passage, but what ferryman was going to row his cumbersome boat across the river and back without recompense for his exertions? The post riders were most often compelled to kick their heels in idleness until a paying load appeared, and this might mean a delay of hours.

This, be it remembered, was upon the better travelled highways. Along the roads that were less frequently used the speed was even slower. Here the post riders were frequently gray haired men whose days of activity were passed. They were content to travel at a more leisurely pace, dropping the reins on their horses' necks so that their hands might be free to knit socks or mittens as the animals ambled gently over the track.

In general, the worst feature of the Act was the toleration afforded private carriers of the post. They, and it must be confessed some of the official postmasters, allowed their riders to transport merchandise, carry money to pay bills, drive oxen, and otherwise display a delightful versatility for earning profit at the expense of the official post. They were willing to undertake any errand if only the delay to the mails it caused could be attributed to mischance, bad weather, or impassable roads.

This was the unsatisfactory situation which confronted Franklin and Hunter when they assumed office. Doubtless they would have gladly instituted reforms to put the post offices upon a self-supporting basis without delay, but Franklin had no sooner returned from Albany than he was compelled to give his attention to the Braddock expedition. This employment was not undertaken voluntarily. It was thrust upon him as the Deputy Postmaster General. His "Autobiography" makes this point clear:

> Our Assembly apprehending from information that he [Braddock] had conceived violent prejudices against them, as averse to the service, wish'd me to wait upon him, not as for them, but as postmaster-general, under the guise of proposing to settle with him the mode of conducting with most celerity and certainty the dispatches between him and the governors of the several provinces.

The outcome of this was that Franklin had to undertake a personal survey of the roads to establish communication between Philadelphia and Braddock's camp in Virginia, and to provide the transport wagons the General demanded. The journey was to give rise to an incident which was to cause Franklin no little trouble. He relates in his "Autobiography" that when he left Philadelphia he was accompanied by thirty or forty uniformed troopers of his regiment, who escorted him to the Lower Ferry. This was reported to the Proprietor who, offended by Franklin's usurpation of what he regarded as his privilege, demanded that the Postmaster-General be dismissed from office.

We see his solicitude for promoting better social intercourse among the outlying districts in his efforts to develop the initial impulse given to one territory by his survey of the route to Winchester for General Braddock. This survey was primarily of a military nature, but the post rider who travelled over it once a week could carry private letters to Lancaster, York, and the settlements in the Cumberland Valley. Franklin knew that a mail service over this route could not be self-sustaining, yet he urged the Assemblies to improve the road, well knowing that improvements in communication would result in the development of the country through which the road passed. He clutched at every chance of fostering intercolonial projects.

Meanwhile he was improving the mail service. There was not yet any attempt at delivering letters directly to the persons to whom they were addressed. Letters were delivered to the Post Offices along the post roads and remained there until called for. While postmaster of Philadelphia, Franklin had developed a means of facilitating delivery within the city and its immediate surrounding area by publishing in his *Gazette* the names of those for whom letters were being held in the Post Office. This example was quickly adopted in Boston, so that friends and acquaintances in both cities assisted in the delivery of the mail. The issue of the *Gazette* for July 26, 1753, contained the announcement of the first city delivery.

Whatever Letters for Persons living in Town, remain uncall'd for, on those days they are brought to the Post—Office, will the next morning be sent out by a Penny Post provided for that purpose.

While this was an innovation on the American scene, the practice had already been in operation in England, where it had been tried in London toward the end of the seventeenth century. It had proved to be such a boon that Franklin readily adopted it. He was soon employing three carriers to deliver his penny post.

Two years later he established the Dead Letter Office by instructing the postmasters that all letters remaining uncalled for at the end of three months were to be forwarded by the local postmasters to the central post office in Philadelphia.

One of Franklin's acts of magnanimity rebounded upon him. Aware from his own experience as a victim of the injustice of the actions of those postmasters who were also newspaper publishers and who excluded competing journals from the mails, he had, as soon as he was appointed a local postmaster, undertaken to accept for delivery all newspapers free of charge. This is additional evidence of his solicitude for the diffusion of information. Before many years had passed the number of journals began to increase to such an extent that their conveyance was burdensome to the carriers. The Deputy Postmasters had no authority to lower the rates, which would have done so much to increase the volume of business, but they had already spent so much out of their own pockets in maintaining the Post Office, that they now decided to impose a uniform rate for the transmission of newspapers through the mails.

No one will be surprised that the orderly and methodical mind of Franklin rebelled at the negligent manner in which the accounts were kept by local postmasters. He promptly instituted a more rigorous method of accounting by which one postmaster's accounts could be checked against another's. Still, this did not eliminate all the opportunities for the dishonest to profit, but beyond doing what he could to engage trustworthy men, Franklin could do very little to check the theft of money paid on letters gathered on the way and accepted for delivery by the riders. Nevertheless, superior management began to have its effect. For seven years Franklin and Hunter continued to cover the deficits of the Post Office from their own pockets. They did this hopefully, because each year they saw the revenues increase and they, naturally, entertained the hope that the receipts would sooner or later exceed the expenses. But it was seven years before the pair arrived at the point where they could recompense themselves and pay to the General Post Office in London the first profits to be derived from the American Post Office.

The revisions they had made in the postal service were sufficient to carry it forward while both Franklin and Hunter were out of the country. The latter had gone to England for reasons of health and, in 1757, Franklin had been employed by the State of Pennsylvania as their agent in London. During their absence the Deputies were represented by the Comptroller, James Parker, of New York, who had been a business partner of Franklin in the printing trade. Parker was a level headed business man and, if not much of a leader, was able to give a creditable account of himself in the direction of the Post Office. The correspondence conducted between them enabled Franklin to keep in close touch with affairs, and to give Parker a good deal of advice upon the management of the office.

His absence in England lasted until 1762, and when he returned home it was under a new commission. His former partner in office, Hunter, had finally succumbed to his ills, and his place had been taken by John Foxcroft, another Virginian. The next few years were a very busy period in Franklin's public life but his devotion to the duties of the Post Office was unstinted. In the spring of 1763 he set out upon another of his extensive surveys of roads and inspection of the local Post Offices. Not that there were so many offices, but the seventy-five in operation were scattered all the way from Maine to Virginia. South of the latter point practically all mail was carried by sea. On this particular journey Franklin drove a light two-wheeled vehicle, and was accompanied by his daughter Sally, who usually rode on horse-back. Altogether, he covered nearly 1600 miles on this journey.

We have made more than one allusion to Franklin's activities in the development of roads in the Colonies to promote intercourse and trade, and it was probably upon this occasion that he took another step in this direction. Certainly it was upon one of these journeys that he marked the distances by milestones. He had plac-ed on the axle of his carriage an odometer which is preserved in The Franklin Institute Museum. This instrument measured the distances he travelled and at every mile covered along the road from Philadelphia to Boston he caused a stone to be erected on which was cut the distance between one important place and another. These stones were also plentiful in the neighborhood of Philadelphia, being found on the Lancaster, York, Haverford, Gulph, Ridge, and Bristol roads.

There are reasons why we should think this journey was the oc-casion on which these stones were erected on the Boston Post Road. After he had completed the journey Franklin was able to give a very close measurement in miles of the distance he had covered, the only time when he was so detailed in the measurement of a journey. Another reason is to be found in the innovations which were soon introduced into the postal system. Franklin had been wooing and cajoling the British authorities in order to secure a reduction in the postal rates. The purchasing power of money was so relatively high in those days as compared to ours, that the rates discouraged the use of the mails. The post was a luxury too few people could afford. Franklin had long been convinced that lowering the rates would result in an increase of bulk in the cor-respondence carried and would increase the revenue.

Of greater significance than the prosperity of the Post Office, which was desirable in itself, was Franklin's political motive. The Colonies were separated by barriers of almost impenetrable wilderness and great distances. Franklin seemed to stand alone in his perception of the means by which these obstacles might be overcome. He was intent upon drawing the colonies together, upon developing a common understanding, and upon speeding the conviction that future welfare of the respective communities must all follow the same course. He held tenaciously to the view that a cheap postage and dependable service would speed the unification of the American people.

He dared not give public expression to his idea so long as the colonists were agitating for release from the control of British overlords, whose strength resided in the divisions among the colonists, but he worked indefatigably to improve the service so that his object might be achieved. Unconscious that they were aiding Franklin in his major scheme, those colonists who had only material gains in view were giving him support. The colonists were loud in their protests over the cost of carrying correspondence, and it must have been evident to everyone acquainted with the situation that a well-filled carrier's bag on the New York to Philadelphia road must have defrayed the cost of carriage several times over. The only argument which could be advanced against this practice was that the surplus gained on the popular roads helped to maintain service on the less popular.The general abuse of the franking privilege only served to inflame the denunciations of those who complained about the expense of using the official mails.

In spite of reluctance upon the part of the British authorities to grant the American Postmaster's request for a reduction of rates, the postal service was being steadily improved. Several years earlier, Franklin had proposed to run "a stage wagon" once a week to Boston for the purpose of carrying mail, but his more conservative contemporaries had shaken their heads in disapproval at such a radical suggestion to conquer space and time. The usual method of carrying mail was on horseback, but not at all in the strenuous manner of the later "Pony Express." The riders on the less prosperous routes were disinclined to maintain regular schedules. They preferred to wait until a paying load of correspondence had accumulated. Franklin struggled energetically against this feeling of inertia. He was continually urging greater speed and more frequent trips. He increased the number of riders on the northern roads which were under his immediate control. As the outcome of his inspection in 1763 he revised some of the routes so that the riders might save time. Not all his innovations met with universal acceptance.

There were, for example, five ferries to be used on the road between New York and Philadelphia. A new route was devised to reduce this number to three, thereby reducing the time wasted by the riders in waiting for paying passengers to arrive. But the road had been diverted from passing through Perth Amboy, where the Governor of New Jersey was in residence. Unfortunately, his British superiors reproved the Governor for neglecting his correspondence at the time, and the reproof had greater force since the same authorities had been at much pains to increase the packet service between Britain and America. The Governor eagerly grasped at the change in the post road as an excuse for the delay in his letters. Franklin handled the excuse expertly when it reached him. He pointed out that if the Governor would send his servant one mile away to meet the post rider he could save much time in the collection and delivery of mail, which was more frequent it had been when the road lay through Perth Amboy. Just how much the general situation had changed through the innovations and improvement is shown in a letter written by Franklin to Anthony Todd, the secretary to the General Post Office, in 1764.

I will now just mention that we hope in the spring to expedite the communications between Boston and New York as we have already that between New York and Philadelphia by making the mails travel by night as well as by day, which has never hitherto been done in America. It passes now between Philadelphia and New York so quick that a letter can be sent from one place to another, and an answer received the following day, which before took a week, and when our plan is executed between Boston and New York letters may be sent and answers received in four days, which before took a fortnight, and between Philadelphia and Boston in six days, which before required three weeks. We think this expeditious communication will greatly increase the number of letters from Philadelphia and Boston by the packets to Britain.

The improvement in the service and the increase of revenue derived from it had raised the opinion of Franklin held by the British authorities. They finally came around to his economic theory that a decrease in rates would so encourage the use of the mail that the bulk carried would increase rather than diminish the revenue. In 1765, an Act was passed to lower the domestic rates generally 30 per cent. The franking privilege was largely withdrawn and some minor provisions for regulating the carrying of the mails by ship captains who collected from and delivered to coffee houses were incorporated in the Act. This would have constituted a triumph for Franklin had the results of his wisdom and perseverance not been almost entirely obliterated by the passing of the Stamp Act in the following year.

Because the new rates, like the old, were based upon the mileage over which the letters were carried, more stringent measures had to be adopted in the calculation of the distances. The new Act required that the surveyors of the roads had to record the distances under oath. It was this new provision, prompted by the reduction of rates, which doubtless prompted Franklin to mark the Boston post road with milestones.

In September, 1765, a new commission was issued to Franklin as Deputy Postmaster General because of the enlargement of the postal service to Canada. Franklin and Foxcroft were confirmed in their offices with jurisdiction over the entire territory between Canada and Virginia. The Southern offices in North and South Carolina, Georgia, Florida, and the Bahama Islands, where the post was almost entirely water-borne, were created as a separate district under Benjamin Barons.

Franklin returned to England a few months before the passage of the Stamp Act. Naturally, he was strongly opposed to a measure which was so obnoxious to the colonists whom he represented. He was examined before the House of Commons when repeal of the Act was under consideration, and the position of the Post Office was the subject for much of his testimony. The astute diplomat arranged with a friend that the direct examination should be designed to enable him to offer evidence which would prove the impracticability of distributing the stamps through the Post Office, a task which he looked upon with the greatest disfavor. Later, when the supporters of the Stamp Act questioned him, Franklin refuted the suggestion that money paid for postage was a form of taxation. He stoutly maintained it was payment for a service rendered by the Post Office.

During Franklin's absence in England the Post Office underwent no change. Foxcroft continued to administer it (much to Mrs. Franklin's annoyance) from the Franklin home, where the headquarters remained despite the official designation of New York as the center of postal affairs. Parker continued as Comptroller and he maintained a steady flow of correspondence with Franklin. The burden of his letters had to do with complaints of his own misfortunes and the deterioration of the postal service. Franklin did what he could to remedy Parker's trouble but he was powerless to amend the situation which arose from the rapidly growing reluctance of the people to have anything to do with the agencies of the

British administration, of which the Post Office was one.

In the midst of a general dissatisfaction the post riders began to take advantage of their opportunities. There were widespread reports of corruption in the revival of the practice of carrying letters for personal profit. All manner of collusion was developed between the riders and businessmen to defeat paying the Post Office for the transmission of mail. Indeed, the riders were becoming so independent that they neglected to blow their post horns so that people who had letters for collection by the official channel might be warned of the rider's approach, and they discarded the locked portmanteaux with which they were provided, in favor of open sacks into which they could place letters or withdraw them without any accounting having to be rendered. Common carriers made their re-appearance as carriers of mail. Postmasters became careless in making returns and settling their accounts. It was evident that the controlling hand no longer existed.

Reports of the deficiencies in the service descended upon Franklin in a steady stream. He was profuse with advice, recommending that the negligent postmasters should be dragged before the courts. But he was having trouble of another sort. After his examination on the effects of the Stamp Act it became clear that he must clash with all those who were in favor of drastic action against the recalcitrant colonists. When Lord Sandwich, who supported the maintenance of the Stamp Act, was appointed Postmaster General it became evident that Franklin's tenure of office was in jeopardy. Those who argued that he should be relieved because his absence prevented him from fulfilling his duties to the Post Office were reinforced by malicious friends of the Penn family who were incensed by Franklin's efforts to reduce the Proprietor's powers in Pennsylvania. Thus Franklin became the center of an intrigue to have him dislodged as a Crown servant.

The Duke of Grafton conveyed a warning to him of the danger, suggesting that if Franklin desired to retain his office he should return to America. Grafton was one of those who had formed a high opinion of Franklin's talents, for he was later to suggest that if Franklin should be relieved of his Deputy Postmastership he should be given some other post. Reports of this new post reached America, where Foxcroft spoke of the proposed appointment of Franklin to the office of Under Secretary of State to Lord Hillsborough. For some little time, therefore, Franklin was in the position of not knowing whether he was to be discarded or promoted.

The uncertainty of his future did not prevent Franklin from indulging in a piece of impertinence which may have given him much glee but which certainly would have precipitated his departure from office had it been detected by responsible authorities. As the holder of the franking privilege he had customarily franked his letters with the words "Free. B. Franklin." He now changed the superscription on some letters home to read "B. Free Franklin." Perhaps it was a little too subtle for those who handled the letters.

Then, in 1774, came the affair of the notorious Hutchinson letters. The practice of interfering with letters entrusted to the mail was not such a rare occurrence as the furor raised over this incident would lead one to imagine, but a vast amount of animosity was manufactured against Franklin for his alleged violation of a private correspondence entrusted to the mail, for the prompt and secure conveyance of which he was responsible. What followed is best described in a letter he wrote on February 15, 1774.

I received a written notice from the secretary of the general post office, that his Majesty's postmaster-general *found it necessary* to dismiss me from my office of deputy postmaster-general in North America. The expression was well chosen, for in truth they were *under a necessity* of doing it; it was not their own inclination; they had no fault to find with my conduct in the office; they knew my merit in it, and that, if it was now an office of value it had become such chiefly through my care and good management, that it was worth nothing when given to me; it would not pay the salary allowed me and, unless it did, I was not to expect it; and that it now produces near three thousand pounds a year clear to the treasury here. They had besides a personal regard for me. But as the post offices in all the principal towns are growing daily more and more valuable, by the increase of correspondence, the officers being paid *commissions* instead of *salaries,* the ministers seem to intend, by directing me to be displaced on this occasion, to hold out to them all as an example that, if they are not corrupted by their office to promote the measures of the administration, though against the interests and the rights of the colonies, they must not expect to be continued. This is the first act to extend the influence of the government in this branch. But as orders have been some time since given to the American post-master-general, who used to have the disposition of all places under him, not to fill vacancies of value, till notice of such vacancies had been sent hither, and instruction thereupon received from hence, it is plain such influence is to be part of the system; and probable that those vacancies will for the future be filled by officers from this country. How safe the correspondence of your Assembly Committees all along the continent will be through the hands of such officers may now be worth consideration, especially as the post office act of Parliament allows a postmaster to open the letters, if warranted so to do by the order of the Secretary of the State, and every provincial secretary may be deemed a secretary of state in his own province.

Franklin's position in England had been a delicate one. As Deputy Postmaster General he was a Crown official but, as agent for various colonies, he was advancing interests opposed to those of the Crown ministers. If, in his course of actions, he had taken risks, they were calculated risks, and if he felt aggrieved for being dismissed after his long and loyal service to the Post Office, which he had brought from the stage of bankruptcy to one of prosperity, there should have been small reason for surprise.

In America he was replaced by Hugh Finlay, but Foxcroft was retained in his post. As the latter had now moved to New York, the headquarters of postal affairs was finally transferred to the city of the government's choice. The most significant feature of the change was that the Post Office was regarded as being placed safely under loyalist control. For the colonists objected to using what they called the "royal post" and before long a "constitutional post" was inaugurated by William Goddard of Baltimore. Thus, when Franklin returned to America he found the two postal systems openly competing for business. The newer enterprise soon wiped out the "royal post," and Franklin's name was once more associated with that of the Post Office.

On May 29, 1775, a committee of the Continental Congress was formed, comprising Benjamin Franklin, Thomas Lynch, R. H. Lee, Thomas Willing, Samuel Adams, and Philip Livingston, to consider the matter of the postal service. On July 26th, this committee presented its report, recommending the establishment of a Post Office for the various states. Letter rates were to be 20 per cent lower than those charged by the Act of 1765, but this recommendation was later rejected. Except for the payment of the postmasters, there was very little changed in the system as it had been under Franklin's administration. Franklin was unanimously appointed Postmaster General under the Confederation at a salary of $1000, but he generously applied the entire amount of his salary to those who were disabled in the war.

The most disappointed man in the series of changes was Goddard. He had anticipated being appointed Comptroller of the service, which was the office next in importance to Franklin's but this post went to the latter's son-in-law Richard Bache. Goddard was rewarded with an inferior post as surveyor of post roads, with a salary of $100. He thereon petitioned Congress for a commission in the army.

Franklin's service with the Post Office was now practically ended, although he retained the position to which he had been appointed. He was shortly to leave for France, entrusting the affairs of the system to Bache. When the United States Post Office was finally organized in 1782, President Washington appointed Samuel Osgood to be the first Postmaster General, but it was the cumulative contributions of Franklin to the service which were adopted and from which the present Post Office has been evolved. He has every right to be regarded as the father of the American Post Office.

Benjamin Franklin, Educator

On Education All Our Lives Depend and Few to That, Too Few,
With Care Attend .
Poor Richard's Almanac April,
1748

THOMAS WENDEL

Thomas Wendel (1924-   ) is a Professor of History and Social
Science Education at San Jose University. He has concentrated his
scholarly activity on the history of the Middle Colonies, and has
published numerous articles in history journals on politics in
eighteenth-century Pennsylvania. His biography, *Benjamin Franklin
and the Politics of Liberty*, appeared in 1973. Professor Wendel com-
bines his keen interest in the educational process and historical scholarship with a love of music (he is an accomplished musician).

The following essay was especially written for this edition of *Meet
Dr. Franklin*.

In 1783, Benjamin Franklin's old friend and literary colleague
Benjamin Vaughan urged Franklin to publish his autobiography.
"All that has happened to you," Vaughan wrote, "is connected
with the detail of the manners and situation of a *rising* people; and
in this respect I do not think that the writing of Caesar and Tacitus
can be more interesting to a true judge of human nature and society." Franklin's life story, Vaughan thought, "will in particular
give a noble rule and example of *self-education*." And finally,
"Your Biography will not merely teach self-education, but the
education of *a wise man*; and the wisest man will receive lights and
improve his progress, by seeing detailed the conduct of another
wise man."[1]

Vaughan's letter touches upon several themes underlying
Franklin's role as an educator. Franklin acted within a society
undergoing explosive population and economic growth; America
was indeed a *"rising"* people. He was, of course, America's
outstanding example of the self-educated man. And his life invited

---

[1]Leonard Labaree et al., eds., *The Autobiography of Benjamin Franklin* (New
Haven: Yale University Press, 1964), pp. 135-6. Hereafter referred to as *Autobiography*.

the emulation of others, an educational method highly regarded in his time.

Benjamin Franklin was never a school teacher, but he was nevertheless an educator. His *Autobiography* is but one aspect of his many activities that were at least in part educational in intent. Such activities spanned his entire life, a life long enough that he could enjoy those honors usually bestowed upon the great only after death.

He was the recipient, for example, of five honorary degrees from both colonial and European colleges and universities. He was associated, furthermore, with some sixteen learned societies, from his own American Philosophical Society to the Academy of Science, Letters, and Arts of Padua. In his last decades his name became the eponym for a fort, a tree, a county, a Philadelphia ward, a town in Massachusetts, the first state (short lived though it was) west of the Appalachians, and most fittingly, a college. The mission of this college reflected a longtime interest of Franklin: the Anglification, now Americanization, of Pennsylvania's German population through education.

As such, the college reflected one of Franklin's basic educational ideas: that education can be a primary means of acculturation. It was a belief that Franklin shared with many other educational thinkers of the Age of Enlightenment. It rested primarily on Locke's epistemology. According to the *Essay Concerning Human Understanding*, with which Franklin was familiar, ideas are formed from perceptions of the outside world conveyed to the mind by the senses. Since there are no innate ideas, the environment plays a crucial role in developing our understanding. Education, therefore, has great power to mold the minds of men.

Franklin College (now Franklin and Marshall) opened its doors in Lancaster, Pennsylvania, in 1787. The founders chose the name of the college from "a profound respect for the talents, virtues, and services to mankind in general, but more especially to this country, of his excellency, Benjamin Franklin. . ."[2] Franklin, then serving his third term as president of Pennsylvania, a position similar to today's governorship, contributed twice the amount donated by any of the other original subscribers.

True to its mission, Franklin College aimed at promoting, "an accurate knowledge of the German and English language, also of the learned languages, of mathematics, morals, and natural philosophy, divinity, and all such other branches of literature as will tend to make good men and useful citizens."[2] With the exception of "divinity," the curriculum reflected Franklin's educational ideals. While emphasizing "natural philosophy" (the physical sciences), the founders gave modern languages first place. Greek and Latin played distinctly minor roles.

Franklin's eager support of the college that bore his name reflects his longstanding desire that Pennsylvania's ethnic minorities be assimilated into the dominant culture. Here, Franklin anticipated the philosophy of Horace Mann and later American educators. These founders of the American public school system viewed education as a principal vehicle for the Americanization of an heterogeneous immigrant population. Franklin frequently expressed the fear that Pennsylvania's large German population "will Germanize us instead of our Anglifying them." The solutions he suggested in 1753 were "to distribute them more equally, mix them with the English, [and] establish English Schools where they are now too thick settled...."

In pursuit of the latter goal, Franklin joined with a number of interested persons in England and America who formed a society for the purpose of founding German charity schools. Despite some success—there were nine such schools by 1760—many German colonials bitterly resented the school movement. Franklin and his associates, they believed, were more interested in neutralizing the Germans' political power than in educating them.

Franklin himself had not helped matters by publicly referring to Pennsylvania's Germans as "Palatine Boors." By 1769, the Society disbanded, having failed in its mission of Anglification, an effort that succeeded mainly in uniting the Germans in defense of their own culture.[3]

---

[2]Saul Sack, *History of Higher Education in Pennsylvania*. 2 vols. (Harrisburg: Pennsylvania Historical and Museum commission, 1963), I, 114.

[3]Leonard Labaree et al.(eds.), *The Papers of Benjamin Franklin* (New Haven: Yale University Press, 1959-) [*hereafter Papers*], IV, 234,485; V, 203-206. Whitfield J. Bell, Jr. "Benjamin Franklin and the German Charity Schools," APS. *Proceedings*, XCIX (1955), 381-387. Franklin's much criticized "Palatine Boor" remark appeared in his *Observations on the Increase of Mankind*, which was published in Boston in 1755. He deleted the phrase from subsequent editions of this famous work. He may, however, have meant no more by "Boor" than farmer. Hector St. John de Crevecoeur in his celebrated *Letters from an American Farmer*, which appeared in 1782, uses the same term certainly without invidious intent.

Franklin's interest in "Anglifying" the Germans through education was paralleled by his more successful efforts on behalf of Black Americans. Here again, the chief instrumentality would be schools in which the freedmen and children of slaves would be taught those skills that would allow them to take productive places in colonial society.

Franklin's active support of such schools began as early as 1757 and lasted throughout his life. In 1760 in London he became a member of "Dr. Bray's Associates for Founding Clerical Libraries and Supporting Negro Schools," an organization dedicated to the continuation of the good works of Dr. Thomas Bray, who had served in Virginia as the commissary of the Bishop of London. Bray, who died in 1730, was noted for his philanthropic and missionary endeavors.

Deborah Franklin kept her husband informed of the progress of the Negro School which the Associates established in Philadelphia in 1758. Franklin, meanwhile, had been elected the Associates' chairman for 1761 and again for the following year. He advised the establishment of three more schools in addition to the one in Philadelphia. As a result, successful schools were founded in New York, Williamsburg, and Newport.

Franklin took pardonable pride in these activities. On his return to America in 1762, he included the schools while he toured the colonial Post Offices. "I have visited the Negro School here," Franklin wrote from Philadelphia. The children "appeare'd all to have made considerable Progress in Reading for the time they had respectively been in the school....I was on the whole much pleas'd," he continued, "and from what I then saw, have conceiv'd a higher opinion of the natural Capacities of the black Race, than I had ever before entertained. Their Apprehension seems as quick their Memory as strong, and their Docility in every Respect equal to that of white Children...."[4]

Franklin's observation, perhaps the first such statement by an American leader, indicates that the Negro children taught Franklin even as he helped teach them. He maintained his belief in the intellectual capacities of Blacks throughout his life, writing in 1774 to Condorcet that Negroes were "not deficient in natural Understan-

---

[4] *Papers*, X, 395-6; Ibid., 396; Richard I. Shelling, "Benjamin Franklin and the Dr. Bray Associates," *Penn. Mag. of Hist. and Biog.* LXIII (1939), 282-93.

ding, but they have not the Advantage of Education.''[5]In his last public act, Franklin signed, as president of the Pennsylvania Abolition Society, the Society's appeal for improving the condition of free Blacks. Among other ideas, the plan called for their education so that they ''shall receive such learning as is necessary for their future situation in life. . .''[6]

Education as ''preparation for life'' remained a constant theme with Franklin. It was a theme he applied not only to Blacks but to women as well. And again, as in the case of the Black children, it was observation—this time of a capable widow handling her deceased husband's business—that caused Franklin to urge

> that branch of education for our young females, as likely to be of more Use to them and their children in Case of Widowhood than either Music or Dancing, by preserving them from Losses by Imposition of crafty Men, and ennabling them to continue perhaps a profitable merchantile House. . . to the lasting Advantage and enrichment of the Family.[7]

Germans, Blacks, women, and finally poor children and orphans: the lot of all of these would be bettered by education. As for the last, a charity school became an essential part of Franklin's most significant educational venture: the ''College, Academy, and Charitable School of Philadelphia in the Province of Pennsylvania.''

From the beginning Franklin, in the words of provincial secretary Richard Peters, was ''the soul of the whole.''[8] As early as 1743, well-satisfied with his Pennsylvania career to date, he had two regrets: there being in the province ''no Provision for Defense, nor for a compleat Education of Youth; No Militia nor any College.''[9] As for the former, Franklin's pamphlet *Plain Truth* stirred the province to military preparedness. His contemporary proposal concerning education was stillborn, but six years later following the peace made at Aix-la-Chapelle, Franklin drew up and published his *Proposals Relating to the Education of Youth in Penn-*

---

[5]Albert Henry Smythe, ed., *The Writings of Benjamin Franklin*. 10 vols. (New York: The Macmillan Co., 1907), X, 66-68.

[6]John Bigelow, ed., *The Works of Benjamin Franklin* (New York and London, 1904), XII, 136.

[7]*Autobiography*, pp. 166-7; See also ''Dogood Papers'' #5, *Papers*, I, 18-21, wherein the young Franklin approvingly quotes Daniel Defoe on allowing women the advantages of education.

[8]*Paper*, IV, 35.

[9]Ibid., p. 181.

sylvania. This pamphlet, together with his *Idea of the English School* published two years later, spells out Franklin's remarkable design for education at mid-century.

The design was neither entirely utilitarian (as has often been alleged) nor entirely ornamental. It was both. It described, in a word, a liberal education for use. In contrast to the aristocratic educational practice of the time, Franklin proffered a classless education which is to say that it was designed as an instrumentality of that upward mobility of which he himself was already the archtype. Franklin's College, Academy, and Charitable School inculcated that love of learning which was the mark of the eighteenth century gentleman. But it also taught those useful subjects that when applied in the real world of America would make the gentlemanly life possible. As for the students' studies, Franklin wrote in a famous passage,

it would be well if they could be taught *every Thing* that is useful, and *every Thing* that is ornamental: But Art is long, and their Time is short. It is therefore propos'd that they learn those Things that are likely to be *most useful* and most ornamental, Regard being had to the several Professions for which they are intended.[10]

There is much that is modern in Franklin's proposals, even to the still startling thought that subject matter be relevant to the student's needs and interests. He recognized the interrelatedness of knowledge: history provided what we would today call the core curriculum. Students would be gently led on the basis of their own interests and needs, much in the spirit of the progressivism of a later age:

The History of Commerce...may also be made entertaining to Youth, and will be useful to all. And this, with the Accounts in other History of the prodigious Force and Effect of Engines and Machines used in War, will naturally introduce a Desire to be instructed in *Mechanicks*, and to be inform'd of the Principles of that Art by which weak Men perform such Wonders, Labour is sav'd Manufactures expedited, etc. etc. This will be the Time to show them Prints of antient [sic] and modern Machines, to explain them, to let them be copied, and to give Lectures in Mechanical Philosophy.[11]

Within this thoroughly integrated curriculum, students would also learn drawing "and some of the first Principles of Perspective". They would have actual experience in farming and gardening. They would be introduced to the physical sciences and

---

[10]Quoted in David B. Tyack, ed., *Turning Points in American Educational History* (Waltham, Massachusetts: Blaisdell Publishing co., 1967), p. 74.

[11]Ibid., p. 77.

mathematics. Above all, they would learn to express themselves clearly and succinctly in writing and speaking. Nor did Franklin ignore physical education: "To keep them in Health, and to strengthen and render active their Bodies," the students should be "frequently exercis'd in Running, Leaping, Wrestling, and Swimming, & etc." And finally, striking a refreshing note in the sober-sided world of colonial America, Franklin emphasized "delight" and "pleasure" in learning rather than hard discipline.

As for foreign languages, Franklin's preference for the moderns over the ancients is well known. Having taught himself French, Italian, and Spanish, he found that Latin followed easily enough. "From these Circumstances," he remarks,

I have thought that there is some Inconsistency in our common Mode of Teaching Languages. We are told that it is proper to begin first with the Latin, and having acquir'd that it will be more easy to attain those modern Languages which are deriv'd from it; and yet we do not begin with the Greek in order more easily to acquire the Latin. It is true, that if you can clamber and get to the top of a Stair-Case without using the Steps, you will more easily gain them in descending; but certainly if you begin with the lowest you will with more Ease ascend to the top.[12]

Or in a simpler metaphor, Latin before French put the cart before the horse. But more importantly, Franklin believed the ancient tongues to be relatively useless ornamentation in the mobile society of colonial America. Latin and Greek were the sign and symbol of an outmoded class-oriented education.[12]

Franklin's *Proposals* supplied the impetus for the chartering of the Academy and its evolution into the College of Philadelphia, the first nonsectarian institution of higher learning in the colonies. The college immediately took its place beside Harvard, William and Mary, Yale, and the College of New Jersey (later Princeton)—in the order of their founding—as a symbol of the growing maturity of colonial society. (The colonial period also saw the foundations of Columbia, Brown, Rutgers, and Dartmouth.) The College of Philadelphia could boast of Benjamin West in its first graduating class. In 1769, it established the first medical school in America. Some one-sixth of the signers of the Declaration of Independence were graduates of the College of Philadelphia; its distinguished faculty included James Wilson and Benjamin Rush; on its board of trustees were such luminaries as Thomas McKean, Francis Hopkinson, Thomas Mifflin, William Paca, and Jared Ingersoll,

---

[12] *Autobiography*, pp. 168-9.

all of whom contributed importantly to the era of the American Revolution and the nation building that followed.

During these years, however, the college curriculum, much to Franklin's distress, drifted back towards the classical model he opposed. Under the leadership of Anglican William Smith who, incidentally, introduced the term "provost" to American higher education, the Latin curriculum took precedence over the English school. Failing reelection as president of the board of trustees with a majority of whom he had political as well as educational differences, Franklin angrily expressed his resentment to his friend Ebenezer Kinnersly. "The Trustees," he wrote, "had reap'd the full Advantage of my Head, Hands, Heart and Purse, in getting through the first Difficulties of the Design, and when they thought they could do without me, they laid me aside."[13]

In spite of his resentment, however Franklin remained a trustee throughout his life. On his return from France, where he had served as American Minister throughout the War, he penned his blistering *Observations Relative to the Intentions of the Original Founders of the Academy in Philadelphia*. Here he defended the concept of the English school and fired his final volley at the classical languages: "they are as useless as the Europeans' hats which because of the modern wig, are carried on the arm. Latin and Greek are thus the '*Chapeau bras* of modern literature'."

Franklin's educational principles would ultimately flourish, of course, not only at the University of Pennsylvania, which in 1779 emerged from the College of Philadelphia. They would also come to characterize American education generally. One immediate source of this diffusion was the Military Academy at West Point, the first superintendent of which was Jonathan Williams, Franklin's grandnephew. Evidence suggests that President Jefferson, a profound admirer of Frankin, appointed Williams in order to fix upon the Academy a forward-looking philosophy. Williams had been devoted to his greatuncle, whom he resembled and with whom he had shared a love of science. The Military Academy, he wrote, was "a station favorable to the pursuits of science, for the foundation of which I am more indebted to the habits of intimacy

[13]Ibid., p. 96n.

and daily instruction of [Franklin] than to any other source whatsoever."[14]

The Academy's curriculum, accordingly, was definitely Franklinian: mathematics, natural philosophy, engineering, French, drawing, and practical experience in the field. From West Point emerged the engineers essential for carrying out the internal improvements called forth by the new nation. Its graduates, furthermore, filled many of the first professorships of scientific subjects in other institutions. They formed a direct link in the chain leading back to Franklin's *Proposals* of 1749.

Leonard Labaree in his classic *Conservation in Early American History* states that the colonials subscribed to the "widely held theory that an educational institution ought to exist primarily as a conservative influence on the community.[15] Franklin's educational thought is surely an exception to that rule. He broke away from the dominant components of Anglo-American education of his time. These were the ethical and religious traditions of Humanism and the Reformation, and the older scholastic approach to the rationalization of faith. It is true that educational theorists of the 17th and early 18th centuries had urged a more practical curriculum including modern languages and science. As for methods, Locke himself suggested reason and persuasion over "the schoolmaster's rod."[16] Franklin, however, has the distinction of creating through example and influence, through his writings and in deeds, the ultimate institutionalization of these ideas.

In his *Proposals Relating to the Education of Youth*, Franklin cites among others "the famous Milton," "the great Mr. Locke," David Fordyce, *Dialogues concerning Education*, which Franklin misattributed to Francis Hutcheson, "the learned Obadiah Walker," who authored a treatise on the education of a young gentleman, "the much admired Mons. Rollin," who was Charles Rollin, rector of the University of Paris, and "the ingenious Dr. George Turnbull," chaplain to the future George III and author of a work entitled, *Observations on Liberal Education, in all its Branches*, published in 1742 (*Papers*, III, 397-98).

---

[14]Dorothy Zuersher, "Benjamin Franklin, Jonathan Williams, and the United States Military Academy," (unpublished doctoral dissertation, University of North Carolina at Greensboro, 1974).

[15](Ithaca: Cornell University Press, 1962; originally published 1948), p. 91.

[16]James L. Axfell, ed., *The Educational Writings of John Locke* (Cambridge: Cambridge University Press, 1968), p. 254.

Herein lies a paradox, for Franklin himself had only two years of formal schooling, and these were during his early boyhood. Josiah Franklin had originally thought to devote his youngest son Benjamin "as the Tithe of his Sons to the Service of the Church."[17] The young man would attend Harvard College where he would be educated for the ministry. But the cost of a college education and the mercurial Benjamin's evident disinterest in matters theological changed Josiah's mind. Rather than serving as his alma mater, Harvard became the butt of the sixteen-year old Benjamin's sharp pen as he aimed the outsider's characteristic barbs at the dominant "Temple of LEARNING" of his day. Many of Harvard's graduates, "for want of Patrimony, liv'd as poor as Church Mice, being unable to dig, and sham'd to beg, and to live by their Wits it was impossible." They returned home "after abundance of Trouble and Charge, as great blockheads as ever, only more proud and self-conceited."[18] Thirty-seven years later, Franklin proudly received his first honorary degree from that same "Temple of LEARNING."

Franklin is not unlike self-made men of a later age who, following the "gospel of wealth," founded schools, colleges, and libraries out of genuine philanthropy or in some cases to salve guilty consciences. Like them, Franklin exemplifies that broader view of education recently set forth by such scholars as Bernard Bailyn and Lawrence Cremin.[19]

Education, according to this view, is not merely a matter of formal educational institutions. Rather, it is the entire process by which a culture is transmitted from the older to the younger generation. Fundamental to this process are the roles of family, church,. community, and apprenticeship. Formal educational institutions are relatively insignificant when these mechanisms remain stable. When they are weakened or undermined by rapid social and economic change, as in the eighteenth century, then formal institutions attain greater significance either as conservators of traditional values or as promulgators of new values more relevant to changing times. It is precisely this transformation that is reflected in the self-educated Franklin's activities on

[17] *Autobiography*, p. 52.
[18] "Dogood Papers #4, *Papers*, I, 14-18.
[19] Bailyn, *Education in the Forming of American Society* (Chapel Hill: University of North Carolina Press, 1960); Cremin, *American Education: the Colonial Experience, 1607-1783* (New York: Harper & Row, 1970).

behalf of the latter sort of educational institutions.

The most detailed study of the young Franklin is Arthur Bernon Tourtellot's massive and erudite *Benjamin Franklin: the Shaping of Genius, the Boston Years.* Franklin's genius was brought to fruition most certainly not by his two years of formal schooling. It was nurtured, instead, by his family. It was sharpened by his apprenticeship to the "Couranteers"—the group of bright young men around James Franklin, who published that cheeky paper, the *New-England Courant.* In sum, it was "Puritan Boston that planted in the young Benjamin Franklin the seeds of his character, his mind, and his achievement."[20] And it was in the conducive atmosphere of Puritan Boston that the boy Franklin established his own regimen of reading and writing that gave him the necessary tools to emerge, as he put it, "from the Poverty and Obscurity in which I was born and bred, to a State of Affluence and some Degree of Reputation in the World."[21]

Franklin was an intuitive pedagogue. He needed no schoolmaster to tell him the value of poetry in learning prose, nor to explain the virtues of emulation. Instinctively as it were, he went to school to Bunyan, to Locke, to Defoe, to the *Spectator*: in short to the best models of the English language available to him. He knew, too, the importance of incentives in learning. Desiring to learn Italian, he contracted with a chess-playing friend that the victor could assign to the vanquished a lesson in translation or grammar: "As we play'd pretty equally we thus beat one another into that Language."[22] His later prescription for an English school was in some sense the systemization of his self-education.

Franklin's Italian story is clearly meant to teach, a purpose that underpins the entire *Autobiography* in which it appears. In order to establish the proper pedagogical stance, Franklin composed the work as a letter from a father to his son. It does not matter that William Franklin was then some forty years old and royal governor of New Jersey. The *Autobiography* is instruction by emulation.

Franklin lived in a didactic age. His writings play a role in educating the public similar to that of Voltaire in France. The two

---

[20]Tourtellot, *Benjamin Franklin* (Garden City, New York: Doubleday & Co., 1977), p. 440.

[21]*Autobiography*, p. 43.

[22]Ibid., p. 168.

men on the occasion of one of their notable meetings in Paris in 1778 were hailed by an adoring public as "Solon and Sophocles"—both great instructors to their times. *Poor Richard* may not reach the literary heights of *Candide*, but both utilize satire and humor to instruct their readers in the ways of the world.

In the last year of his life, once more president of the trustees of the college (then temporarily severed from the University), Franklin could take satisfaction that during his long life he had founded the Junto ("the best School of Philosophy, Morals and Politics that then existed in the Province," he called it), the Library Company, and the American Philosophical Society—all of which were, at bottom, institutions of education.[23] All emerged in response to the rapid demographic and economic growth of colonial America.

Franklin, who unlike the majority of his contemporaries experienced both geographic and dramatic social mobility, was particularly sensitive to the social environment. His lifelong efforts on behalf of new educational and social institutions (the two functions were linked in Franklin's mind) is of a piece with Franklin, "the man of many masks." Franklin scholars have pointed to his "elusive personality" and the difficulty in finding the "real Ben Franklin." This "protean" character, however, is explainable as "a response to...rapid social change."[24] So is his penchant for clubs, scientific societies, libraries, and schools. These provided that sense of identity which the fluid society of America did not. The very mobility of which Franklin was the exemplar meant that formal institutions would provide that socialization which is at the heart of education. It is a function previously provided by such stable communities as "Puritan Boston."

Benjamin Franklin was consistent to the end. The town of Franklin, Massachusetts, mentioned earlier in this paper, wrote in 1778 to Franklin in France for a bell. The old pedagogue returned books instead, "sense being preferable to sound." Noting in his will that he owed his "first instructions in literature to the free grammar-schools of Boston," Franklin left a legacy to those schools for silver medals to be awarded annually to deserving pupils. In the next century, furthermore, both the Franklin In-

---

[23] Ibid., p. 118.

[24] John William Ward, "Who Was Benjamin Franklin?" *The American Scholar*, XXXII (1963), 541-553.

stitute of Philadelphia and the Boston Union, a technical school, would benefit from the interest on moneys he left as a legacy to those cities.[25]

The opening words of Franklin's will reveal the way he wished first to be remembered by posterity: "I, Benjamin Franklin, Printer..." Yet the works which brought him contemporary fame—*Poor Richard's Almanac, The Way to Health,* the scientific letters—provided a schooling for his times. "Franklin is dead," pronounced the Comte de Mirabeau before the French National Assembly. The great philosopher had not only "liberated America," but also "poured upon Europe torrents of light." Mirabeau was not alone in viewing Franklin as a kind of teacher to the world. Eulogies on both sides of the water utilized similar metaphors in describing Franklin's achievement. This contemporary assessment, together with his lifelong activities on behalf of education, indicates an equally appropriate epitaph to the one he penned: Benjamin Franklin, Educator.

Wealth [handwritten annotation]

---

[25]Carl Van Doren, *Benjamin Franklin* (New York: The Viking Press, 1964 [originally published 1938]), pp. 741, 762; Leonard Labaree, "Franklin and Education," in Helen Jordan, ed., *Benjamin Franklin's Unfinished Business* (Philadelphia: Benjamin Franklin Institute, 1956), 95-101. Franklin's will is conveniently reprinted in Van Doren's excellent *Benjamin Franklin's Autobiographical Writings* (New York: Viking Press, 1945), pp. 688-698.

Dr. Franklin as the English Saw Him

CONYERS READ

Conyers Read (1881-1959) was in active teaching at Princeton University and the University of Chicago from 1909 to 1920. From 1920 to 1933 he was a business executive in William F. Read & Sons, a textile manufacturing firm in Philadelphia. A non-resident professor of history at the University of Chicago from 1920 until the end of his life, he served as President of the American Historical Association in 1949. His published work was principally in the history of England.

The following essay was delivered in the Hall of The Franklin Institute on March 5, 1940 as one of the papers in the "Meet Dr. Franklin" Conference.

Benjamin Franklin during the greater part of a long life regarded himself as an Englishman. Up until the very verge of the American Revolution he insisted that America was a part of England, at least as much a part of it as Scotland was, and that any disposition on the part of either King or Parliament to deprive Americans of their rights as Englishmen was not only wrong in morals but wrong in law. His father was an Englishman born, and his interest in his English family connections is manifest throughout his life, even when he was a great fellow in London and they were poor country folk in Northamptonshire.[1] He spent two years in England before he was twenty, and nearly twenty years in England after he was fifty. His love for England was beyond question. His famous letter to Polly Stevenson on the subject in 1763 is almost too familiar to bear repetition,[2] and everyone knows his famous panegyric upon Scotland.[3] After he was fifty he travelled over a great part of England and visited Scotland and Ireland as well.[4] When he was close to sixty he seriously intended to move to

---

[1]On his visit to his ancestral home, cf. his letter to his wife of 6 September, 1768 in Smyth, "Writings," III, 451-4.

[2]Smyth, "Writings," IV, 193.

[3]In his letter to Lord Kames of 3 January, 1760. Smyth, "Writings," IV, 6.

[4]On this subject, of cf. particularly J. Bennett Nolan, "Benjamin Franklin in Scotland and Ireland, 1759, and 1771." (Philadelphia, 1938.)

England permanently[5]—and he was ready to consider a permanent appointment in England three years after the passing of the Stamp Act—though somewhat fearful that "old trees can not be safely transplanted."[6]

Franklin was not only English in his origins and in his sympathies, he was English also in his ways of thought and in his standards of behavior. And much which we call American in him was English by derivation, by translation—English, we might say, as modified by the frontier. Franklin was in his beginnings essentially a frontier type, an adventurer, a rebel against the conventional order. He declined to follow the pattern his father had set for him, he declined to subordinate himself to a less intelligent elder brother. He ran away from Boston to Philadelphia with a fine confidence in his ability to get on anywhere. And he had not yet got himself well-established in Philadelphia before he ran away again, this time overseas on a wild goose chase. There can be no doubt about his abounding physical vitality, the sound mind in the sound body. Indeed his superabundant physical vitality probably explains his many youthful falls from grace. But his interests even at the start were too definitely of the mind to succumb for long to the purely animal interests of the body. And there was besides a very definite and a very strong moral (I shall not call it religious) sense in him which I take to be one of the most important factors in his make-up.

It is to be noted that he had no formal schooling after he was ten. What else he learned he got as a printer's apprentice plus all he could pick up by indefatigable reading. And this lack of systematic education had clearly much to do with his habits of thought. It has something also to do with his social status in the cultured world of eighteenth-century Philadelphia. He was definitely not of the best Philadelphia families, definitely not received in the most select circles except in the condescending spirit with which the aristocrat accepts the brilliant *parvenu*. He was a craftsman, a self-made fellow, a producer rather than a consumer—a man who depended upon his achievements to exalt his status, not upon his status to magnify his achievements. And he was always more interested in

---

[5]Cf. his letter to William Strahan, 7 December, 1762 in "Writings," IV, 182.

[6]"Writings," V, 144. The quotation comes from a letter to Polly Stevenson written from Philadelphia 14 March, 1764, "Writings," IV, 217.

doing things than in speculating about them. What he thought was the by-product of what he did and almost all that he wrote has something of the character of observations made in a laboratory. It will not be forgotten that he was by training as well perhaps as by inclination a newspaper man with a keen nose for the news. But this is probably only another way of saying the same thing. For the newspaper as Franklin conceived it was by way of being a running commentary in the laboratory of developing social phenomena.

His moral sense attaches very definitely to his religious inheritance. His father was a rebel from the orthodox Anglicanism of the English Franklins—one of those non-conformists who met in secret conventicles under Charles II and found it expedient to leave the old country for the more congenial religious atmosphere of the new. He brought with him the later seventeenth-century version of the Puritan tradition, a rigid predestinarianism coupled with a stern Puritan code of morals, but with its adjustments already made to the plans and purposes of the diligent tradesman. Max Weber and Ernst Troeltsch and Richard Tawney have set forth very adequately the nature of these adjustments.[7] The fundamental difficulty which those who held to predestination had to face was the enforcement of a moral code when good behavior could have no possible bearing upon one's eventual fate. If you were elect you were elect—and nothing which you could do would damn you; if you were damned you were damned and that was the end o' it. They got round it by insisting that it was the business of the elect to manifest their election, to demonstrate that they were God's chosen by showing forth His praise in their lives. Good works, if not a cause, were a necessary consequence of election. And though no one could know for certain until the last trump who were chosen and who condemned, the major symptom of election was a fine self-confidence revealing itself in upright living. If I am indeed of the elect than I must behave as of the elect. In a sort of way the Puritan created his own salvation by his conviction of it. This looks like a reversal of the Catholic position of justification by works. The fundamental difference was that the Puritans

---

[7]Cf. Max Weber, "Die protestantische Ethik und der Geist des Kapitalismus" (1904-5); Ernst Troeltsch, "Die sozialen Lehren der christlichen Kirchen und Gruppen" (1912); R. H. Tawney, "Religion and the Rise of Capitalism" (1926). The first two of these are available in excellent English translations. Weber particularly has much to say about Franklin.

were not seeking salvation by good works, they were revealing salvation by a good life. Confession, repentance, absolution, played no part in their morality. The miraculous element was ruled out. It was not enough to do good sometimes and to win forgiveness for evil-doing at other times. The whole pattern of life was in question. Very likely the average fellow was not conscious of the distinction, but he could always fall back upon it to justify at once his belief in predestination and in righteousness of life.

This position explains that preoccupation of the Puritan with his state of grace, that periodical moral accounting which was so characteristic of Franklin himself. Out of it also the Puritan developed the idea of a calling, a vocation, the moral obligation of the Christian to work hard at his profession. Diligence in business became for him an evidence of grace, success in business the surest index of diligence. And so it came to pass, as Tawney puts it, that enlightened self-interest took on the attributes of an ornament to the spirit, and those very acquisitive instincts which had been denounced as vices in the Middle Ages became canonized as virtues.[8]

That there was no inconsistency between piety and prosperity was evident in the case of the Quakers in England and the Pietists in Germany, both of whom were notorious for both. And it is to be noted that the approval of diligence in business was very far from an approval of the mere accumulation of wealth for wealth's sake. The hoarding of money and its application to worldly display were definitely condemned—idleness was a moral sin in the rich as in the poor. John Wesley admitted that "we must exhort all Christians to gain all they can and to save all they can; that is in effect to grow rich."[9] But he added that the good Christian must also give all he can. There must be generous distribution as well as diligent acquisition. The Puritan position, while it condemned idleness and was disposed to condemn poverty as the offspring of idleness, nevertheless encouraged well-directed humanitarian impulses.

It must be observed also that diligence in business was not held to justify sharp practices in business. If lack of diligence, lack of sobriety, lack of thrift are the certain causes of ruination, as Hogarth has pointed out in his contrasted careers of the Industrious and the Idle Apprentice, so too, is dishonesty. You will

---

[8] From Tawney's foreward to Parson's translation of Weber's "Die protestantische Ethik," 2.

[9] Quoted by Weber, op. cit., Parson's trans., 175.

perhaps recall the lecture which Mr. Wiseman delivered to Mr. At-
tentive on this subject in Bunyan's "Life and Death of Mr. Bad-
man." "A man must have conscience towards God, charity to his
neighbors and ... moderation in dealing. ... Let the tradesman
consider that there is not that in great gettings and in abundance
which the most of men do suppose—for all that a man has over
and above what serves for his present necessity and supply serves
only to feed the lusts of the eye. ... Be thou confident that God's
eyes are upon the ways, ... that He marks them, writes them
down, and seals them up in a bag against the time to come. ...
Guilt shall go with thee if thou hast got it dishonestly.''[10] In
Richard Baxter's "Christian Directory" and by John Bunyan the
whole moral code of latter day Puritanism is set forth. And Bunyan's "Pilgrim's Progress" was the book Franklin remembered
first of all from the readings of his childhood and Bunyan's complete works his first book purchase.[11]

Franklin's code of morals has been described as essentially that
of the Puritans with the religious basis left out.[12] Without accepting the statement as sound we may at any rate concede that the
Puritan view of doing good irrespective of eternal salvation made
possible a Christian ethic without a Christian theology, particularly if we couple with it the prevalent notion that righteous living
gave promise of substantial terrestrial rewards. If honesty is the
best policy, then honesty along with the other business virtues of
diligence, thrift, prudence and sobriety was justified of her
children without the need of any divine sanction. Certainly in
Franklin's case his morality was self-sustaining. Yet it was undoubtedly the major interest in his life. No man was more given to
moralizing, no man more eager to demonstrate the validity of
righteousness of life. The book which he never wrote but which
most of all he wanted to write was a book on the Art of Virtue in
which he intended to show how virtue might be acquired—"To expect people to be good, to be just, to be temperate etc. without
showing them how they should become so seems like the ineffectual charity mentioned by the Apostle which consisteth in saying to
the hungry, the cold and the naked, Be ye fed, be ye warmed, be ye
clothed without showing them how they should get food, fire or
clothing.''[13]

---

[10]Bunyan, op. cit., G. B. Harrison, et. (London, 1928), 365-7.

[11]As he himself tells us in his Autobiography, "Writings," 1, 238.

[12]Weber, op. cit., Parson's trans., 180.

[13]Franklin to Lord Kames, 3 May, 1760, "Writings," Iv, 12-13.

What then was his religion? The answer to that question is hard to get at with certainty. It is to be remarked in the first place that Franklin never put much store in metaphysical speculations, and he definitely condemned what was generally called in the eighteenth century *enthusiasm,* that is to say ill-regulated religious emotion. He was not therefore prompted by his pragmatical habits of thought to pry very deeply into the sacred mysteries, nor was he in the least impelled by his calm and rational temper to abandon himself to any form of mysticism. With these attributes to start with he early became exposed to the rational philosophy of eighteenth-century England and that exposure made a deeper impression on him than he himself was disposed to admit. Franklin, indeed, to my thinking, is a curious and intricate blending of the pioneer American, the latter-day Puritan and the eighteenth-century rationalist.

While he was yet a boy he had read Locke on the Understanding and the works of at least three of the foremost leaders of the new school of rational theology—Shaftesbury and Clarke and Collins. Before he was twenty he had sat in a London tavern with Bernard Mandeville and listened to his ribald conversation and his cynical exposure of the so-called human virtues.[14] He had even himself composed a pamphlet in which he set forth the view that since God in His infinite wisdom had created all things and set all forces in motion, whatever *was* was right. And he had gone on to draw what seemed to him that inevitable conclusion that since nothing could possibly be wrong in a divinely ordered world "Virtue and vice were empty distinctions."[15] Forty years later when he

---

[14]"Writings," I, 243-4, for Shaftesbury, Collins and Mandeville. The sermons which Franklin refers to in his Autobiography, "sermons preached at Boyle's lectures" ("Writings," I, 295), were probably those delivered by Samuel Clarke as Boyle's lecturer in 1704-5 (Sir L. Stephen, "History of English Thought in the Eighteenth Century," I, 120).

[15]"A Dissertation on Liberty and Necessity, Pleasure and Pain," 1725, L. C. Wroth ed. (New York, 1930). The quotation is from Franklin's own summary of this work in his Autobiography ("Writings," I, 296). Smyth deliberately omitted this work from his edition of Franklin's "Writings" on the grounds that "it has no merit" and that Franklin "would have been distressed at its republication." On other grounds Smyth took it upon himself to omit also some of Franklin's more ribald utterances. It is a great pity that what is otherwise the best edition of Franklin's writings should have been emasculated by such impudent exercises of editoral prerogative. As a matter of fact, Franklin is no more Franklin without his philosophic doubts and his occasional indecencies than he would be without his lightning rod.

recalled and recorded his adolescent opinions he declares himself to have been "a thorough Deist."[16] It is not too clear just exactly what kind of Deist he had in mind when he made his comment. There were many such. But certainly the position which they all held in common was very much the position which Franklin had rather crudely stated in what was his first and virtually his only adventure in the realms of metaphysics.

To the Deists and to the eighteenth-century rationalists in general God was, as Paley put it, the great watchmaker, who fashioned the intricate machinery and set it going and then left it to operate according to the laws which he had imposed upon it. There was a grandeur in the conception—but it was a cold, mechanical sort of grandeur. The personal contact of the man with his Maker was gone, the possibility of any modification in the operation of the great machine in response to the prayers of the worshippers was gone. God retired behind a first cause. He was no longer God the Father, He became the Supreme Being, the Great Contriver, the Prime Mover, the Invisible Hand.[17] And this being so, the problem naturally presented itself to many thoughtful souls as it presented itself to young Franklin—if nature is good then there is no evil in the world, and if there is no evil in the world then good and evil are merely verbal distinctions. This conclusion may have satisfied a cynic like Mandeville, but it did violence to the moral sense of eighteenth-century Englishmen as indeed it did violence to young Franklin's moral sense. A good deal of eighteenth-century thinking was directed to the business of finding some way of reconciling a moral law with a preordained universe. It was in a sort of way the same problem which had faced the Puritans. Different thinkers followed different ways out. The way Franklin himself took was the way that most of his thoughtful contemporaries found satisfactory. "I began to suspect," he wrote, "that the doctrine, though it might be true was not very useful. . . . I grew convinced that truth, sincerity and integrity in dealing between man and man were of the utmost importance to the felicity of life. . . . Revelation had indeed no weight with me as such, but I entertained an opinion that though certain actions might not be bad because they were forbidden by it, or good because it commanded them, yet probably these

---

[16]"Writings," I, 295.
[17]On Deism in general cf. Sir L. Stephen, op. cit., I, passim.

actions might be forbidden because they were bad for us or commanded because they were beneficial to us."[18] In short he dismissed metaphysical considerations from his mind and accepted a moral law because it was "useful." The fact that it was divinely revealed had little weight with him, the fact that its validity in making for human happiness could be demonstrated was sufficient. He was indeed back to about the position of Richard Baxter, with the religious basis left out.

Now the interesting thing about Franklin's experience is that it had its counterpart in the spiritual history of the outstanding moralists of his time. He was not a freak, he was a type—so typical that he has been cited again and again to illustrate prevalent trends in eighteenth-century moral philosophy. The fact is that both in England and in France Franklin's thoughtful contemporaries were turning away from profitless metaphysical speculations to the practical business of useful and fruitful living. Whether Franklin's own transition was so sudden as he has himself described it is open to question. He was indulging in odd speculations about gods and demigods as late as 1728.[19] When a man writes of his youth after forty years he is apt to foreshorten much in perspective. Certainly Franklin clung resolutely to his gospel of good works and there is almost no evidence in his more mature life of a disposition to explore the sacred mysteries. "I think," he wrote to his father in 1738, "opinions should be judged by their influences and effects, and if a man holds none that tends to make him less virtuous or more virtuous, it may be concluded that he holds none that are dangerous.... I think vital religion has always suffered when orthodoxy is more regarded than virtue, and the scriptures assure me that at the last day we shall not be examined what we thought but what we did."[20]

When he was past seventy he set forth the essentials of his faith in a letter to Mme. Brillon, [21] and the famous letter on the subject he wrote to Doctor Stiles at the very end of his life does not differ from it in any essential particular. A God who made the world and governs it by His providence, a God who should be worshipped and served, served best by doing good to our fellows, the im-

---

[18]"Writings," I, 296.
[19]Cf. his "Articles of Belief and Acts of Religion," 1728 in "Writings," II, 91ff.
[20]"Writings," II, 215.
[21]"Writings," X, 419.

mortality of the soul, and a future life, in which vice would be punished and virtue rewarded—these were about all that mattered to him, and every one of them would have been endorsed by the Christian Deists with whom he had played in his youth. There is no essential change. His comments to Doctor Stiles with respect to Jesus of Nazareth familiar as they are will bear repetition: "As to Jesus of Nazareth, ... I think the system of morals and his religion, as he left it to us, the best that the world ever saw or ever is likely to see, but I apprehend it has received various corrupting changes and I have, with most of the present dissenters in England, some doubts as to his Divinity...I see no harm however in its being believed if that belief has the good consequences it probably has of making his doctrine more respected and better obeyed....I have ever let others enjoy their religious sentiments without reflecting on them for those that appeared to me unsupportable and even absurd. All Sects here, and we have a great variety, have experienced my good will in assisting them with subscriptions for building their new places of worship and as I have never opposed any of their doctrines I hope to go out of this world in peace with them all."[22]

The fact is that he attached little importance to theology, and much to righteousness of life. He would have endorsed Alexander Pope's couplet:

> For modes of faith let graceless zealots fight,
> He can't be wrong whose life is in the right.[22]

But he was discreet about making any public utterances on religion, and what he wrote to Stiles he wrote in strict confidence. His constant emphasis is not so much upon the truth of religion as upon the practical advantages of it. He criticized the position of the atheists not on the grounds that their conclusions were false, but that, false or true, they were likely to do more harm than good, that religion was serviceable in restraining ignorant men and women from vice and supporting them in virtue and that the lack of it would be socially more damaging than the fallacies of it.[24]

---

[22]Franklin to Stiles, 9 March, 1790. "Writings," X, 83ff.

[23]Franklin placed an advance order for a new edition of Pope with William Strahan in 1744. "That poet," he wrote, "has many admirers here." "Writings," II, 242, quoted in Van Doren, "Benjamin Franklin," 104.

[24]CF. on this Franklin's letter to an anonymous correspondent of uncertain date in "Writings," IX, 520ff.

This is substantially the position of what has been called the Common Sense School of eighteenth-century English thinking, the school to which Franklin's Scottish friends, Lord Kames and David Hartley and Francis Hutcheson and Adam Smith belonged, and to which, in his latter days at least, the most skeptical of them all, David Hume, gave formal adherence. Franklin once again conforms pretty closely to contemporary British patterns of thought.

And like these benevolent moralists Franklin came, in later life particularly, to lay the major emphasis upon the esteem attached to a man of virtue. It was, as Carl Becker has remarked, "both sufficient and efficacious, and likely to give one, without any painful searchings of the heart, the assurance of being in a state of social justification or even, if the esteem were general enough, of complete sanctification. I suppose Hume and Franklin when they were in France, for example, must have had this assurance as fully as any saint of the church ever did."[25]

Indeed I think we must all have been struck with the complete confidence with which Franklin faced his latter end. He makes no doubt that he will issue forth again in a new edition revised by the Author. His smugness is akin to the smugness of the latter-day saints, sure of their election. God had abundantly blessed him, the fact of that blessing was the guarantee of larger blessings to come. There were no final harassing doubts, no deathbed repentances. He had made his own salvation, and went forward to enjoy it unperturbed.

Franklin won his first recognition in England as a man of science. We can ignore the affair of the asbestos purse and his youthful contact with Doctor Hans Sloane, one of the great naturalists of early eighteenth-century England. We can ignore also his early desire to meet Sir Isaac Newton, a desire which was never realized—they are only significant as pointing to an interest in scientific matters of all sorts which became stronger and stronger as he grew older.[26] Had he been less of a man of business he would undoubtedly have been more of a man of science, at least he always believed that he would. Certainly his writings which are not political in character and more or less in the line of duty were

---

[25]C.L. Becker, "The Heavenly City of the Eighteenth-Century Philosophers" (1932), 49.

[26]On Sloane and Newton, cf. "Writings," I,278.

almost entirely concerned either with scientific phenomena or with moral philosophy. It is difficult to decide which engaged the greater part of his attention, scrutiny of nature or the moral improvement of man. I shall not attempt to appraise his scientific contributions, which ranged over the whole field of physics and biology from stoves and lightning rods to medicine and fertilizers. It is all of a definitely empirical character, and most of it has a definitely social implication. For all his contributions to electricity, his final interest in it took the form of a lightning rod. And he is perhaps better remembered for his Franklin stove than for his more recondite apparatus.

I need not pause to remind you how characteristic this interest in matters scientific was in eighteenth-century Europe, and even for that matter in the more enlightened regions of eighteenth-century America. The obvious proof of it lies right at hand in the reception which Franklin's scientific experiments were accorded. His recognition in the learned world—and this recognition, as you are well aware, took the form of honorary degrees in many of the great European universities and honorary membership in many of the very exclusive European learned societies—was based, first to last, upon his work as a man of science.

Anyone who reads his correspondence is struck, again and again, by his consistent interest in matters scientific. He will interrupt a letter to Lord Kames to tell him how to deal with a smoky chimney. He will fill his letters to his young lady friends with talk about the effects of evaporation upon temperature, he cannot keep it altogether out of his conventionally affectionate but normally quite superficial letters to his very worthy, but very pedestrian, wife. In any case he never really got down to it for any length of time. And his interest in it was always that of a man who was more concerned with making the truth manifest than in monopolizing the credit for its manifestation. Nothing can be more in accord with the true spirit of scholarship than his readiness to share at once any discovery, any observation which seemed likely to stimulate further discovery or further observation. It was his electrical experiments in the 1740's and particularly his experiments with lightning and electricity which first attracted English attention. Indeed they aroused universal attention, won him honorary degrees at both Harvard and Yale in 1753, won him the gold medal of the Royal Society in London the same year and membership in the society three years later. So when he reached London in 1757 on political business for Pennsylvania he was already a man of international renown.

Undoubtedly the dominating fact in his long stay in England, which with one brief interruption lasted seventeen years, was the developing conflict between England and her American Colonies. It is a long story and an entirely familiar one. The most striking thing about it from the point of view of Franklin as an American is that until the very verge of the Revolution he was very definitely not a rebel, very definitely working his hardest to bring about an accommodation, not a breach. So much so that he laid himself open to the suspicion that he was more English than American in his sympathies. He was even charged with suggesting the Stamp Act.[27] The fundamental issue was of course the right of the English Parliament to levy an internal tax in America. Franklin fought this in theory and in practice. In theory he insisted first of all that Englishmen in America were just as much Englishmen as Englishmen in England, and entitled to the same rights. He conceived of Parliament not as the legislative assembly of the whole Empire, but as the legislative assembly for Great Britain and he placed the colonial assemblies on a parity with it so far as the internal affairs of the Colonies were concerned. The bond of union he insisted was not in the Parliament but in the Crown. He definitely envisaged that dominion status for the American Colonies which turned out in the end to be the true solution of the problem. He was prepared to entertain an alternate solution, to wit, the direct representation of the Colonies in the mother parliament, but he regarded that as running counter to the actual historical development of the situation and no longer achieveable even if practicable. His loyalty to George III remained undiminished almost to the end, though he gradually awakened to the fact that the King was a broken reed to lean upon and that George derived such power as he had from the manipulation of Parliament. What finally led him to accept independence as the only alternative was his realization that, however England at large might feel about it, Parliament as it was then constituted was by and large representative of nothing but the corrupt and self-centered interests of the gang of politicians who controlled it, politicians who were more interested in lining their purses than in preserving an empire. He had hopes that he

---

[27]Van Doren, op. cit., 300.

might appeal to an enlightened self-interest, and he emphasized again and again the value of an American market to the commercial and the manufacturing interests. But though he did stir up some support for the American position among these interests, the politicians in the end commanded the field. There is very little in his actions or his attitudes in the nature of an appeal to abstract rights, and practically no foreshadowing of the arguments in the Declaration of Independence. His only real assumption was that the Empire should be preserved, and his one objective was to find the best way of preserving it. With the theoretical rights and wrongs, the constitutional issues, he was much less concerned than with the actualities of the situation—the brutal facts of the case. He saw clearly enough that America could not be coerced, but he insisted, as Lord Durham was to insist later in the case of Canada, that Americans were fundamentally loyal and could be depended upon to do their part if they were permitted to do it their own way.[28]

It is rather curious to discover, in view of the fact that he located the root of all evil in the composition of Parliament, that he displayed very little interest in contemporary movements for parliamentary reform. For example, he never saw in John Wilkes anything much more than a licentious, riotous, mischief-loving fellow, and referred to the riots in London in these terms, "Some punishment seems preparing for a people who are ungratefully abusing the best constitution and the best king any nation was ever blessed with."[29] No die-hard English Tory of the time could have put the case against political agitation more strongly.

Later, in his only recorded consideration of parliamentary reform, which shows by the way a rather amazing ignorance of parliamentary history, his recommendations were confined to the abolition of rotten boroughs by purchase. This he set forth in a memorandum to Christopher Wyvill, the assiduous promoter of

---

[28]Cf. on this whole subject V.W. Crane's excellent discussion of Franklin's attitude toward the British Empire in "Benjamin Franklin, Englishman and American" (1936), 72ff. I think Professor Crane does not make as much as he might have of Franklin's increasing despair of wringing any reasonable solution of the problem out of Parliament as it was then constituted. Cf. on this subject Franklin's letter to Ross in "Writings," IV, 133, and his better known letter to Galloway in "Writings," VI, 311ff.

[29]Franklin to John Ross, 14 May, 1768, "Writings," V, 133, quoted by Van Doren, op cit., 381.

parliamentary reform among the Whig gentry in general.[30]
Franklin seems to have fallen in with Wyvill's own views that the
thing chiefly wrong with Parliament was bribery and corruption,
that the center of bribery and corruption was in the boroughs and
that they should be done away with by buying them out. We cannot regard this proposal as a very penetrating one though it con-
formed to the current thinking on the subject among the liberal
statesmen of both Whig and Tory parties. It came from Franklin
after he had ceased to be an Englishman, after America had won
her independence. There is very little else in Franklin's writings on
the subject and very little indication of his support of, or even of
his interest in, a really liberal and democratic program of English
parliamentary reform.

And yet we cannot be too sure. One of the few independent
glimpses we have of him during his residence in London comes
from Josiah Quincy, Jr., a New England lawyer who visted
England late in the year 1774.[31] He was the son of one of
Franklin's good friends, and Franklin entertained him frequently
while he was in London—chiefly it appears at the London Coffee
House, in a group which Quincy called a club of friends of liberty.
Quincy speaks of meeting there Joseph Priestley, Richard Price,
Alderman Oliver, and eight or nine dissenting clergymen.[32]
Elsewhere the club is spoken of as the Honest Whigs. We know
relatively little about it, and but for the fact that the indefatigable
biographer James Boswell visited it on one occasion, we should
hardly know of it at all.[33] Quincy's designation seems to suggest
that it was concerned with liberty, and certainly there were some
radical reformers among its members, Priestley and Price particularly. But we cannot guess. Franklin, in the busy days of war,
looked back upon its Thursday evening meetings with particular
affection. "I only wonder how it happened," he wrote to Priestley
in 1782, "that they and my other friends in England came to be

---

[30]"Writings," IX, 339ff. On Wyvill and his activity in parliamentary reform, ct.
G.S. Veitch, "The Genesis of Parliamentary Reform" (1913), 54ff.

[31]Quincy's journal of his life in England is printed in "Memoir of Josiah Quincy Jr.
1744-75," by his son Josiah Quincy, first published in 1825. I have used the second edition (Boston, 1874).

[32] Quincy, op. cit., 204.

[33] Van Doren, op. cit., 402, 421, calls attention to Boswell's contacts with
Franklin, citing references in "Private Papers of James Boswell," G. Scott and F.A.
Pottle, eds., 18 vols. (1928-34), VII, 193-4, VIII, III, IX, 40.

such good creatures in the midst of so perverse a generation.'' [34] This kind of remembrance somehow does not suggest radical politics.

Indeed Franklin's contacts with English politics seem to have been very largely confined to the business he had in hand. He knew Shelburne and the great Burke and the greater Chatham. There are indications that he contributed his quota to Burke's notable speech on Conciliation and to Chatham's arguments in support of the American position in the House of Lords. But he probably felt it indiscreet to participate in purely domestic issues. It was characteristic of his pragmatical habits that he was not much inclined to talk about things which he was not in a position to do anything about.

His other contacts in England were mostly with a varied company. Among his closest friends he numbered a prosperous London printer, a Welsh bishop, two prominent dissenters and two distinguished physicians. He once went to Ireland with one of Charles Lamb's benchers of the Inner Temple.[35] He visited at the country house of the notorious Sir Francis Dashwood, leader of the still more notorious Monks of Medmenham—though elevated to the peerage as Baron Le Despenser and gone respectable when Franklin knew him. Of them all he got most pleasure out of the Scottish philosophers but most instruction out of the dissenters. Probably it was Priestley and Price who made a Unitarian out of him. It is rather curious to find none of the London wits or the London men of letters among his friends. He met Edward Gibbon, the historian, once by accident, and is accredited with a *bon mot* on that occasion almost too good to be true.[36] He met David Gar-

[34]"Writings," VIII, 453.

[35]I refer to Richard Jackson, of whom Lamb writes in his "The Old Benchers of the Inner Temple," "Jackson,—the omniscient Jackson he was called—had the reputation of possessing more multifarious knowledge than any man of his time." "Essays of Elia," Augustine Birrell, ed., 2 vols. (1902), I, 181. On Jackson's adventures with Franklin in Ireland, cf. Mr. Nolan's admirable account (op. cit., 123ff). I think Mr. Nolan is wrong (p.3) in speaking of Jackson as "Two Penny Jackson." Lamb himself distinguished clearly between Jackson and Twopenny who, according to Birrell, was not a bencher but a stock broker who had chambers in the Temple. (Lamb, op. cit., I, 181in).

[36] Van Doren (op.cit., 577) transmits the story from Horace Walpole. It is to the effect that Franklin, stopping by chance at the same inn with Gibbon, requested the pleasure of his company—to which Gibbon answered that, with all due respect to Franklin as a man and as a philosopher, he could have no commerce with a rebel. Franklin answered, with all due respect to a distinguished historian, that when Gibbon came to write of the decline and fall of the British Empire, Franklin would be happy to furnish him with material.

rick at a house party, and he met the indefatigable Boswell. To Boswell we owe one of the few intimate pictures we have of Franklin's London life, the picture of Sir John Pringle and Franklin over a chess board—Pringle very sour, Franklin "all jollity and pleasantry." "A prime contrast," Boswell observed, "acid and alkali."[37]It is to be regretted that he never met Dr. Samuel Johnson, though Franklin might have disappointed us if they had met. He was never much given to acrimonious controversy, and certainly Johnson and he were poles apart on the American issue. His most congenial intimates were Scotsmen, the most notable of them David Hume the philosopher, Lord Kames the advocate and William Robertson the historian. It is not surprising that he found himself more at home in their company than in any other. He had himself a Scottish mind, direct, clear, matter of fact. Later he confessed that the six weeks he spent in Scotland were "six weeks of the densest happiness I have met with in any part of my life." Adam Smith he certainly knew, though how well is a matter of controversy. In general it is to be observed that Franklin's English social contacts were normal friendly ones based upon community of tastes and a common interest in common problems. His life in England lacked the glamor of his latter adventures in France. He never became the fashion in England, and had no temptation to play to the galleries which later led him sometimes to make himself slightly ridiculous. There is a certain exotic quality about his whole French experience. In England he definitely belonged.

The problematical character of Franklin's connection with Adam Smith raises the issue as to the relation between Smith's economic philosophy and Franklin's.[38] Time does not serve to investigate the matter in detail. Certainly Franklin was a disciple of the laissez-faire philosophy. But equally certainly laissez-faire had received wide endorsement both in America and in England before ever Smith set pen to paper. We may surmise that Franklin arrived at his position through a somewhat different channel from Smith—not as the natural derivation from the rational philosophy of the times but as a practical protest against a system of economic control which at the moment was bearing with particular heaviness

---

[37]Van Doren, op. cit., 402.

[38]Franklin's economic views in general and his relations with Smith in particular are well considered in Lewis J. Carey, "Franklin's Economic Views" (1928), particularly 107ff.

upon America. To Franklin laissez-faire was born of the Naviga-
tion Acts. It was to him a specific remedy for a specific ailment.
But very likely he welcomed the classical expression of the princi-
ple in universal terms. Here again as in so many instances
Franklin's thinking seems to have run *pari passu* with progressive
English economic thought.

What I hope I have succeeded in demonstrating is that
Franklin in every department of his thought and action was profoundly influenced by his English inheritance and by his English
connections. He was to be sure an American, brought up in the
freer air of America and mercifully delivered from the inhibitions
of class and station and tradition which cramped the style of so
many of his contemporaries in the Old World. He was delivered
also from the inhibitions of a conventional education whose
crystallized patterns of thought often turn out to be more of a
liability than an asset in a rapidly changing world. But he was
nevertheless a typical eighteenth-century figure and he moved easily and naturally in an eighteenth-century world. There was nothing
abnormal about him—the difference between him and his fellows
was a difference of degree and not of kind. Indeed, one of his major characteristics was his adaptability to all sorts of situations, his
ability to get on well with all sorts and conditions of men. His mind
was singularly alert, but it was an eighteenth-century mind and in
the long run the positions which he reached in his thought and action were recognizable eighteenth-century positions. Getting on in
the world was his *metier* and though he comprehended in his
definition of getting on definite humanitarian purposes, get on he
did, in the American world, in the English world and in the French
world. He would have got on in any world. He accepted the
universe as it was, and his theories about it, scientific, political,
economic, religious, were little more for him than working
hypotheses, to which he gave no absolute allegiance and which he
was prepared to modify or to abandon when they no longer served
the needs of concrete situations.

He clearly belonged with those whom Becker gathered together
in the Heavenly City of the eighteenth-century philosophers. Like
them he accepted the world as a good world, his place in it as a
good place. He looked like them for the resurrection of the dead
and the life of the world to come. And yet one feels that he would
have been acutely unhappy in any celestial paradise where all the

crooked ways were made straight and all the awkward questions answered.

EDITOR'S NOTE

Conyers Read supposed that Franklin never met Dr. Samuel Johnson, the English author, while he was in London. It now appears that he did. On May 1, 1760 Franklin and Johnson attended a meeting of the Associates of Dr. Bray at Mr. Bird's bookshop on Ave Mary Lane in London. Franklin had been named chairman of the Associates on March 6, 1760, but he had been absent from the April 6 meeting when Johnson had been elected to membership. At the May 1 meeting there were only eight members present. Maurice J. Quinlan, who discovered the facts of his meeting, supposed that inasmuch as Franklin and Johnson "constituted two of the company of eight, they probably conversed with each other."[1] Unfortunately, there are no verbatim reports of discussion at the meeting. One can only speculate that Franklin and Johnson may have conversed about the education of Black children in the colonies.

---

[1] Maurice J. Quinlan, "Dr. Franklin Meets Dr. Johnson," *Pennsylvania Magazine of History and Biography*, 73 (January 1949), 36, 37.

Franklin's Experimental Religion

A. OWEN ALDRIDGE

Alfred Owen Aldridge (1915-   ) is a Professor of Comparative Literature at the University of Illinois. His biography, *Benjamin Franklin: Philosopher and Man*, was published in 1965 and his *Benjamin Franklin and Nature's God* in 1967. He is the editor of *Comparative Literature Studies* and Advisory Editor of *Eighteenth Century:Theory and Interpretation*.

The following essay was especially written for this edition of *Meet Dr. Franklin*.

For Benjamin Franklin, the topic of religion was a vital, compelling, and significant force during his entire life. Toward the basic problems of metaphysics and morality, he adopted the same experimental attitude which he followed in scientific inquiry. He investigated or personally participated in one or another of the activities of each of the dominant religious sects in his culture, including Anglican, Methodist, Congregational, Catholic and Jewish. As he says in his Autobiography, he offered support toward the construction of every church building erected in Philadelphia during his residence, and although he was not a member of any one sect, his "mite" was never refused.[1] Franklin was not an adherent of "experimental religion," however, as this phrase was used in the eighteenth century, referring to a personal emotional experience as advocated by adherents of the "Great Awakening" such as Jonathan Edwards and George Whitefield. He was in no sense a "born-again Christian" even though his name frequently appears in the records of Christ Church in Philadelphia, at that time a part of the Church of England. His religious experiments consisted in the devising of private schemes of worship and self-improvement as well as in active, although occasional, participation in the public worship of various sects in the communities in which he resided.

In his youth, Franklin experienced various doubts in the matter of religion and wavered between the extremes of atheism and

---

[1]Leonard W. Labaree and others, eds., *The Autobiography of Benjamin Franklin* (New Haven, 1964), p. 146.

polytheism in attempting to resolve them. "He that alters his Opinion on a *religious Account,*" he wrote in an essay before the age of twenty, "must certainly go thro' much Reading, hear many Arguments on both Sides, and undergo many Struggles in his conscience, before he can come to a full Resolution."[2] We have an incomplete record of Franklin's reading, but ample evidence of his use of reason or logic in attempting to resolve the nature of God as a metaphysical problem. While working in London as a printer, still before the age of twenty, he set type for a deistical work, William Wollaston's *Religion of a Nature Delineated* and proceeded to publish a pamphlet objecting to the form of reasoning it represented. In his pamphlet, *A Dissertation on Liberty and Necessity,* he put forth a contrary scheme of pure materialism in which man figures as a purely mechanical object. He admitted the existence of a benevolent God, but portrayed this divine force as so impersonal and rigidly determined that it was as mechanical as man. Among other propositions, Franklin observed that every event in life is preordained; that life is not preferable to insensitivity, for pleasure and pain counteract each other; and that there exists no distinction between virtue and vice. From the perspective of the twentieth century the pamphlet is remarkable for embodying a comment on space travel. "If we could take a Trip to the Moon and back again, as frequently and with as much ease as we can come and go from the Market," Franklin affirmed, "the Satisfaction would be just the same."[3] Franklin arrived at the conclusions in his pamphlet entirely by abstract reasoning; he later used abstract reasoning to refute them. He suggested "that if all things are ordained, prayer must among the rest be ordained. But as prayer can produce no change in things that are ordained, praying must be useless and an absurdity. God would therefore not ordain praying if everything else was ordained. But praying exists, therefore all things are not ordained."[4]

While establishing himself as a printer in Philadelphia, Franklin delivered a lecture to a group of fellow tradesmen, taking a middle position between determinism and free will. The supposi-

---

[2]Leonard W. Labaree and others, eds., *The Papers of Benjamin Franklin,* I (New Haven, 1959), 43.

[3]*Papers,* I, 69.

[4]Albert Henry Smyth ed., *The Writings of Benjamin Franklin* (New York, 1907), VII, 412.

tion of complete determination (that of his London pamphlet) Franklin repudiated as equivalent to making God responsible for all of the evil in the world as well as for deceiving mankind by creating the illusion of free choice. The supposition that everything in the universe is left to the operation of general nature or free agency, he rejected as equivalent to removing God from his creation and placing him in the position of an indifferent spectator. A third supposition that some events are determined and others left to general nature and free agency he also rejected since it effectively places God in the same position as the preceding supposition. Franklin, therefore, concluded "that the Deity sometimes interferes by his particular Providence, and sets aside the Events which would otherwise have been produc'd in the Course of Nature, or by the Free Agency of Men."[5] This is a position held by very few thinkers in the eighteenth century, even theologians, and Franklin himself did not adhere to it for very long, but fell back upon the assumption of the operation of general nature.

Two years before delivering this lecture, Franklin devised a private system of worship or "little liturgy" which incorporates the notion of polytheism. He assumed one "Supreme most perfect Being" who is the author and father of other beings or gods, vastly superior to man. "It may be," he speculated, "that these created Gods, are immortal, or it may be that after any Ages, they are changed, and Others supply their Places." As a result of contemplating the system of planets and fixed stars and stretching his imagination beyond the visible universe, Franklin conjectured that each sun or star with its attendant planets had been created by a different God, including "that particular wise and good God, who is the Author and Owner of our system."[6] And Franklin aspired to have the wise, good and powerful being of our system as his friend. His notion of the existence of many degrees of beings superior to man as well as many degrees of beings his inferior belongs to the concept known as the Great Chain of Being, which was expressed also by John Locke and Alexander Pope. The notion of polytheism, moreover, was not unique to Franklin, but shared by Newton and some others in the century.

One of the polemics of the time with relevance to atheism concerned the relationship between mind and matter. While Franklin

---

[5] *Papers,* I, 264-269.
[6] *Papers,* I, 102-104.

was contemplating plural gods in Pennsylvania, Voltaire and Frederick of Prussia were corresponding extensively and with great intensity on whether matter has the power of thought. Frederick, an atheist, assumed that if he could establish this position, he would have proved that a creator of the universe and, therefore, a divine being, was unnecessary. Franklin wrestled with essentially the same problem in correspondence with James Bowdoin, although taking a position opposite from Frederick's. In his opinion, the theory that mind or spirit could exist in inert matter would support rather than weaken the argument for the existence of God. In Franklin's words, "If God was before all things, and filled all space, then when he formed what we call matter, he must have done it out of his own thinking immaterial substance. The same though he had not filled all space; if it be true that *ex nihilo nihil fit.*"[7] Franklin soon after abandoned speculation concerning esoteric metaphysical topics, perhaps because he felt that the power of reason had limits beyond which it cannot penetrate the problems of existence. In regard to human relations, moreover, he was almost tempted in middle age "to wish we had been furnished with a good sensible instinct" instead of reason.[8] He, nevertheless, retained his interest in the interactions of matter and spirit from the scientific perspective.

In 1780 he allowed his imagination to take hold in a letter to Joseph Priestley on the heights to which the power of mind over matter might be carried. He speculated that large masses might be deprived of their gravity and given absolute levity for ease of transportation and that all diseases might be prevented or cured including that of old age.[9] Priestley reported these dreams to another clergyman, Richard Price, who was in turn so impressed that he confided them to his intimate circle of friends and Franklin was eventually quoted by William Godwin as conjecturing that "mind would one day become omnipotent over matter."[10]

Franklin considered the question of his personal faith so important that he expressed his creed twice in almost identical language in his Autobiography as well as in a personal letter in old age to one of his closest French friends, Mme. Brillon, and in a

---

[7] *Papers,* V, 486.
[8] *Papers,* XVI, 210.
[9] *Writings,* IX, 10.
[10] *Enquiry concerning Political Justice,* Book VIII, Chapter viii.

more formal letter to the president of Yale College, Ezra Stiles, the latter written three months before his own death. Stiles had particularly queried Franklin on his opinion of Jesus, and Franklin tactfully replied that he considered the religion and system of morals of Christ "the best the World ever saw," although probably corrupted by various changes, but he also admitted "some Doubts as to his Divinity; tho' it is a question I do not dogmatize upon."[11] In his Autobiography Franklin summarized his beliefs with no reference to Jesus. In the section written in 1784, he introduced his credo as merely "some religious principles," but concluded that he esteemed them to represent "the essentials of every religion." These principles consist of "the existence of the Deity; that he made the world and govern'd it by his Providence; that the most acceptable service of God was the doing good to man; that our souls are immortal; and that all crime will be punished, and virtue rewarded, either here or hereafter." Franklin added that he respected each of these doctrines, but with different degrees of respect since he found them in various sects "more or less mix'd with other articles, which, without any tendency to inspire, promote, or confirm morality, serv'd principally to divide us, and make us unfriendly to one another." Of special significance in this comment is the principle that religion should support morality, a principle which Franklin first expressed in his youth and reiterated constantly throughout his career.

In the section of his Autobiography written in 1788, Franklin added the principle that God "ought to be worshipped by Adoration, Prayer and Thanksgiving." Here he described his doctrine as both "an intended creed" and "the essentials of every known religion." More important, he indicated that he had devised the creed as early as 1734 and at that time had conceived of it as the nucleus for recruiting and organizing a religious and ethical sect of young, single men.

Franklin's creed can be characterized as deistical, and as such comparable to the beliefs of many other luminaries of the Enlightenment such as Paine, Jefferson, Voltaire, and Rousseau, but since there were many degrees of deism, Franklin's variety required clarification. Some deists accepted no more than Franklin's first article that a deity exists and others at the opposite extreme,

---

[11] *Writings,* X, 84.

known as Christian deists, not only assented to all of Franklin's articles but added others such as the divinity of Christ. Strangely lacking from any of Franklin's references to his creed is the cornerstone of all deistical systems, the affirmation that knowledge of God and the universe comes from the faculty of reason. The essence of the religion of nature is the belief that the existence of God may be discovered through reason alone without the aid of a supernatural revelation such as the Christian scriptures. Many Christians shared this belief, taking the revelation of nature and that of the Old and New Testaments as complementary. Franklin certainly believed that reason is a valid means of discovering the existence of a diety, and he unequivocally placed reason over Scripture authority, much as he respected the Christian tradition of the culture in which he was born.[12]

Deists offered two main proofs of the existence of God, the mechanical and the moral. According to the first, the universe as a marvelously complex mechanism must have had a maker; according to the second, a principle of virtue or the delineation of right and wrong seems to be ingrained in every human being, and this principle must have its source in a divine being. Franklin adopted both proofs at various periods of his life. According to his grandson, he once affirmed God to be "*notoriously the greatest mechanic in the universe*; having, as the Scripture testifies, made all things, and that by *weight* and *measure.*"[13] In a lecture which he delivered in his early years as a tradesman "On the Providence of God in the Government of the World," Franklin argued that the "physical perfection demonstrated by the physical universe could only be the product of infinite wisdom." After citing the "wonderful Effects" which mere human beings could produce through chemistry, he marvelled at the power which must be possessed by the one "who not only knows the Nature of every Thing in the Universe, but can make Things of new Natures with the greatest Ease and at his Pleasure!"[14] Much later in life, however, he gently satirized this mode of reasoning in a letter to a French deist, Abbe Morellet, explaining that God must have placed a stamp of approval upon the drinking of wine because he plac-

---

[12]A. O. Aldridge, *Benjamin Franklin and Nature's God* (Durham, N. Car., 1967), p. 97.

[13]*Nature's God,* p. 41.

[14]*Papers,* I, 266.

ed the bend in the elbow in such a way as to allow the glass to be raised to the mouth.[15] In a humorous statement also late in life, he seemed entirely to repudiate scientific deism. "Are there twenty Men in Europe at this Day, the happier, or even the easier for any Knowledge they have pick'd out of Aristotle?...The Knowledge of Newton's mutual *Attraction* of the Particles of Matter, can it afford Ease to him who is rack'd by their mutual *Repulsion,* and the cruel Distensions it occasions?"[16]

The contrary strain of moral deism is based in English philosophy on Lord Shaftesbury, who affirmed in 1699 that "whoever thinks there is a GOD, and pretends formally to believe that he is *just* and *good,* must suppose that there is independently such a thing as *justice* and *injustice, truth* and *falsehood, right* and *wrong*; according to which he pronounces that *God* is just, *righteous,* and *true.*"[17] Franklin never made a statement affirming virtue as a proof of the existence of God, nor did he rhapsodize over the beauty of virtue, but he utilized virtue as the foundation of his religious practice throughout his entire life. His doctrines and metaphysics varied, but his reliance on virtue remained undeviating. He was every bit as infatuated or obsessed with virtue as was Shaftesbury.

The emphasis on virtue is an important ingredient of nearly all religions, including those with which Franklin had most contact, particularly Puritanism, Methodism, Catholicism and Anglicanism, but Franklin's views on the motivation for virtue are unique. Most Christian sects in the eighteenth century inculcated virtue on the basis of authority. Whatever is commanded in the Scriptures, they maintained, had to be followed primarily because it is so commanded. Some clergymen, however, agreed with Shaftesbury that virtue is inherently beautiful and should be sought for this reason, that is, for its beauty as such. According to Shaftesbury, "The admiration and love of order, harmony and proportion, in whatever kind, is naturally improving to the temper, advantageous to social affection, and highly assistant to *virtue*; which is in it-self no other than the love of order and beauty in society."[18]

---

[15] *Writings,* X, 437-438.

[16] Richard E. Amacher ed., *Franklin's Wit and Folly* (New Brunswick, 1953), p. 69.

[17] *Inquiry concerning Virtue, or Merit,* Book I, Part I, Sec. ii.

[18] *Inquiry,* Book I, Conclusion.

Franklin, however, gave a purely utilitarian reason for seeking virtue. He summed it up in his Autobiography: "nothing so likely to make a man's fortune as virtue." In the original text this appears as a note.[19] Three paragraphs later he was more specific: "no qualities were so likely to make a poor Man's Fortune as those of Probity and Integrity." While he was writing this part of his Autobiography in Paris, he remarked to one of his young French friends, "If rascals knew all the advantages of virtue, they would become honest out of rascality."[20] In this sense, Franklin's *Way to Wealth,* a collection of proverbs inculcating industry and frugality, is an inherent part of his religion. As he explains in his Autobiography, these proverbs suggested "the Means of procuring Wealth and thereby securing Virtue."[21] Franklin even considered it possible for a sect to "regard Frugality and Industry as religious Duties."[22] He had also written in his newspaper *The Pennsylvania Gazette* in 1735, "Virtue is really the true Interest of all Men."[23] It is not difficult to understand why the French Theophilanthropists published a translation of *The Way to Wealth* under the title, *The Moral Thoughts of Franklin.*[24]

In his Autobiography Franklin attempted to join the sanction of Scriptural teaching with his private notion of utility. He explained that it had once been his intention to publish a work on morality designed to illustrate and enforce the doctrine "that vicious Actions are not hurtful because they are forbidden, but forbidden because they are hurtful, the Nature of Man alone consider'd: That it was therefore every one's Interest to be virtuous, who wish'd to be happy even in this World."[25] A somewhat more expanded version of this doctrine appears in an earlier section of Franklin's Autobiography in connection with his attitude toward the Scriptures. "Revelation had indeed no weight with me as such; but I entertain'd an Opinion, that tho' certain Actions might not be bad *because* they were forbidden by it, or good *because* it commanded them; yet probably those Actions might be forbidden

---

[19]Max Farrand ed., *Memoirs.* Parallel Text Edition. (Berkeley, 1949), p. 232.

[20]A. O. Aldridge, *Franklin and His French Contemporaries* (New York, 1957), p. 205.

[21]*Autobiography,* p. 164.

[22]*Papers,* IV, 232.

[23]*Papers,* II, 17.

[24]Aldridge, *French Contemporaries,* p. 24.

[25]*Autobiography,* p. 258.

because they were bad for us, or commanded *because* they were beneficial to us, in their own Natures, all the Circumstances of things considered."[26]

It seems almost certain that the French political scientist Alexis de Tocqueville drew upon this passage as the basis for his comment on American morality in his famous book *Democracy in America.* According to Tocqueville, "In the United States hardly anybody talks of the beauty of virtue, but they maintain that virtue is useful and prove it every day. The American moralists do not profess that men ought to sacrifice themselves for their fellow creatures *because* it is noble to make such sacrifices, but they boldy aver that such sacrifices are as necessary to him who imposes them upon himself as to him for whose sake they are made."[27] If it is true that Tocqueville did indeed find his source in Franklin, it follows that he transferred the latter's ideas on virtue to the American character in general.

Franklin himself realized "that the mere speculative Conviction that it was our Interest to be compleatly virtuous, was not sufficient to prevent our Slipping,"[28] and he devised in 1732 a system to enable himself and others to break vicious habits and to develop the contrary ones. The method described by Franklin as the Art of Virtue consisted of isolating thirteen specific moral virtues, entering each one of them on a separate notebook page, marking each infraction against any one of the thirteen in the appropriate place, and giving particular attention for one week to each virtue in succession. He used as an epigraph for his little book a passage from Addison's *Cato*:

Here will I hold: If there is a Pow'r above us,
(And that there is, all Nature cries aloud
Thro' all her Works) he must delight in Virtue,
And that which he delights in must be happy.

In another manuscript book of private devotions compiled at approximately the same time, he paraphrased this passage, but changed the emphasis: "I believe he is pleased and delights in the Happiness of those he has created; and since without Virtue Man

---

[26] *Autobiography,* p. 115.
[27] Alexis de Toqueville, *Democracy in America,* ed. by Phillips Bradley (New York, 1945), II, 129-130.
[28] *Autobiography,* p. 148.

can have no Happiness in this World, I firmly believe he delights to see me Virtuous, because he is pleas'd when he sees me Happy.''[29] Franklin variously described his Art of Virtue as ''for the benefit of Youth,'' ''adapted for universal Use,'' and ''a bold and arduous Project of arriving at moral Perfection.''[30] The concept of controlling behavior through the methodical development of proper habits was nothing unusual, however, in Franklin's day. George Washington at a much earlier age than Franklin, for example, copied out and presumably attempted to follow 110 ''Rules of Civility and Decent Behaviour.''[31] Franklin in a personal letter on the need for religion as a prop to moral behavior indicated his belief that the practice of virtue until it ''becomes *habitual*'' is the ''great Point for its Security.''[32] In his Art of Virtue, however, and nearly everywhere else where he addressed the subject, he considered morality independent of religion. Habit was paramount. Even in *The Way to Wealth* he stressed his technique of ''remembering and repeating'' his wise sentences.

Of Franklin's thirteen virtues, four have been categorized as bourgeois or Protestant capitalist (order, frugality, industry, and cleanliness); five as classical (temperance, justice, moderation, tranquility, and resolution) and two as equally Roman Catholic and Puritan (chastity and humility).[33] His definition of chastity was so far from rigorous, however, that it was omitted from some early printed editions of his Autobiography because of its alleged propensity to encourage something other than abstinence, that is, ''Rarely use Venery but for Health or Offspring; Never to Dulness, Weakness, or the Injury of your own or another's Peace or Reputation.'' The final virtue, sincerity, ''not the modern notion of authentic expression of self, but rather old-fashioned honesty'' has been termed ''unclassifiable.''[34] Some scholars in the light of Franklin's many literary hoaxes have speculated that this virtue may have been expressed with tongue in cheek[35] but if so, the hoax

---

[29] *Papers*, I, 103.

[30] *Papers*, I, 103; IX, 104, 105; *Autobiography*, p. 148.

[31] Claude-Anne Lopez and Eugenia W. Herbert, *The Private Franklin* (New York, 1975), p. 62.

[32] *Papers*, VII, 295.

[33] Norman S. Fiering, ''Benjamin Franklin and the Way to Virtue,'' *American Quarterly*, XXX (1978), 218.

[34] Ibid.

[35] Lopez and Herbert, *Private Franklin*, p. 26.

would have been on Franklin himself since he adhered to all parts of his scheme of attaining moral perfection throughout his entire life.[36] Literary hoaxes, moreover, have nothing to do with plain dealing in life. It must also be considered that in a succinct scheme of worship devised at the age of twenty, Franklin included the following injunction to sincerity among a total of merely four precepts: "To endeavour to speak truth in every instance; to give nobody expectations that are not likely to be answered, but aim at sincerity in every word and action—the most amiable excellence in a rational being."[37] With these words, Franklin anticipated William Godwin's theory in *Political Justice* [Book IV, chap. vi] that sincerity is "the most powerful engine of human improvement." Godwin carried the reliance upon sincerity to an extreme stage, by advocating "the habit of telling every man the truth, regardless of the dictates of worldly prudence and custom," and thereupon brought ridicule upon his entire system, but Franklin was not any less dedicated than Godwin to the practical applications of sincerity in the conduct of daily life.

In one of his early newspaper essays designed to show that "Virtue was not secure, till its Practice became a Habitude," he decried the Puritanical view that self-denial is good in itself. "The Truth is," he argued, "that Temperance, Justice, Charity, &c, are Virtues, whether practis'd with or against our Inclinations."[38] This concept seems to indicate that Franklin, like Shaftesbury, believed that intention rather than result defines the morality of an action, but elsewhere he took the pragmatic position that the result is paramount. In a discussion over the relative merit of virtue and Christian faith, he unequivocally declared, "Morality or Virtue is the End, Faith only a Means to obtain that End: And if the End be obtained, it is no matter by what Means."[39] When Franklin's mother learned that he had been professing heterodox doctrines such as this openly in Philadelphia, Franklin wrote a letter attempting to set her mind at ease. "Opinions," he declared, ";should be judg'd of by their Influences and Effects; and if a Man holds none that tend to make him less Virtuous or more vicious, it may be concluded that he holds none that are dangerous."[40]

---

[36]Aldridge, *French Contemporaries*, p. 206.

[37]*Papers*, I, 100.

[38]*Papers*, II, 21.

[39]*Papers*, II, 30.

[40]*Papers*, II, 203-204.

Franklin never set forth a table of vices or faults to contrast with the salutary qualities in his Art of Virtue, but he regularly took notice of the existence of vice both in humanity in general and in his private life. In his youthful system of worship he particularly prayed "That I may avoid Avarice and Ambition...Help me, O Father," and in an essay written three years before his death, he warned against the violent effects of "two Passions which have a powerful influence in the Affairs of Men. These are *Ambition* and *Avarice*; the Love of Power and the Love of Money.''[41] In his Autobiography he affirms that "there is, perhaps, no one of our natural Passions so hard to subdue as *pride,*" and admits that even if he had been able to overcome it during his life "I should probably be proud of my Humility."

Despite Franklin's warnings against avarice and ambition, some critics have accused him of promoting precisely these characteristics by means of the "rascal virtues" of his *Way to Wealth* and other prudential writings, but Franklin did not conceive of his admonitions of thrift as anything but salutary. He believed that freedom from want meant also freedom from the temptation to crime, that a minimum competency made acts of misappropriation unnecessary. In the words of one of his favorite proverbs, "it is hard for an empty Sack to stand upright." He illustrated his meaning from his own career in a letter to his sister: "What in my younger days enabled me more easily to walk upright, was that I had a trade, and that I knew I could live upon little; and thence (never having had views of making a fortune) I was free from avarice, and contented with the plentiful supplies my business afforded me.''[42] At the outset of his career, Franklin realized that there might be a conflict between his desire of attaining financial independence and that of living a moral life. He set forth the pertinent questions:

"Does it not require as much Pains, Study and Application to become truly Wise and strictly Good and Virtuous as to become rich?

Can a man of common Capacity pursue both Views with Success at the same Time?''[43]

---

[41] *Writings,* IX, 591.
[42] *Papers,* XVII, 315.
[43] *Papers,* I, 262.

Franklin wrote out no answers to these questions, but his Autobiography indicates that he was able to pursue both ends. In his quest for goodness, he similarly found no fundamental contradiction between altruism and the cultivation of private character considering them as complementary facets of the ideal human being, Franklin's acknowledged goal. He did not believe in unlimited perfection in the sense that the human species or any member of it may rise beyond physical or mental limits, but like French and English perfectibilians at the end of the century he assumed that any member of the species may aspire to the degree of perfection which that species is equipped to attain by its own nature. In his words, "if there may be a perfect Oyster, a perfect Horse, a perfect Ship, why not a perfect Man? that is as perfect as his present Nature and Circumstances admit?"[44] Franklin's perfect man would excel in both the private and the civic virtues. His theory of perfectibility could be construed as his answer to the Christian doctrine of original sin and also to the problem of whether man's original nature is good, as Shaftesbury and Rousseau maintained, or vicious, as La Rochefoucauld and Mandeville affirmed. Franklin throughout his life veered from one position to the other as far as mankind in general was concerned. In other words, his thought reflects a neutral position concerning the goodness or evil of the human race both in the abstract and in reference to situations personally affecting him. He, nevertheless, consistently believed that individuals, including himself, could undertake the "bold and arduous Project of arriving at moral Perfection," the words he used to describe his Art of Virtue.

So far in our discussion of Franklin's ethical goals we have confined ourselves primarily to personal morality and neglected the third of his religious principles "that the most acceptable service of God was the doing good to man." Such civic qualities as charity, compassion, forbearance and justice are notably absent from the Art of Virtue. We have already seen, however, that in an early essay he insisted "that Temperance, Justice, Charity, &c. are Virtues," and in various religious discussions throughout his life he constantly stressed the need for humanitarian activity. It is somewhat of a paradox that his constant doctrine in published writings and in correspondence is the imperative to do good to

---

[44] *Papers*, 1, 262.

one's fellow man, but his scheme of virtue is limited to personal qualities. His altruistic acts are part of the historical record and have been catalogued and properly remarked, but we have no insight except through his writings of his success or failure in living up to his goals of personal behavior. Even though he failed to make a systematic or comprehensive study of the altruistic virtues, he constantly referred to them in his letters and published works. In his early system of worship he specifically called upon God to enable him to "have Tenderness for the Weak, and a reverent Respect for the Ancient; . . . [and to] be kind to my Neighbours, good-natured to my Companions, and hospitable to Strangers; . . . rejoicing in the Good of Others."[45]

The term "religion of the heart" has been applied to deists such as Voltaire and Jefferson because of their warm and optimistic attachment to the world as they find it in contrast to purely rational deists who coldly expound deductive arguments for the existence of God.[46] Although Franklin occasionally considered God in terms of supermechanic, the social benevolence he advocated and practiced throughout his life derives from his opinion that virtue and love permeate the chain of being from God at the summit to the lowest mite at the base. This philosophical opinion, it must be added, did not prevent him in practical life from recognizing cynical motives of self interest when they appeared.

While Franklin included among his religious principles the doctrine "that the most acceptable service of God was the doing good to man," he did not introduce among these fundamental articles of belief any reference to personal morality. The evidence in The Art of Virtue that Franklin sought perfection in the pefectibilian sense of the word in his personal life does not lead by any means to the conclusion that he did not give equal or even more attention to the social or altruistic virtues. Benevolent deeds, carried out alone or in collaboration with others, characterized his entire life. His philanthropies were so widely known at the time of his death that Thomas Paine remarked, "All America, and more than all American knows Franklin. His life was devoted to the good and improvement of man. Let, then, those who profess a different creed, imitate his virtues, and excel him if they can."[47]

---

[45]*Papers,* I, 108-109.

[46]Gary Wills, *Inventing American* (Garden City, 1978), p. 283.

[47]Philip S. Foner, ed., *Complete Writings of Thomas Paine* (Garden City, 1945), II, 897.

When orthodox Christians challenged Franklin with the doctrine that salvation is achieved through faith, and not good works, he cited in rebuttal the parable of the foolish virgins, who were repudiated by Christ for their failing to provide oil for their lamps. In one of the several references to this parable in his works, Franklin wrote with some exaggeration "Our Savior...says nothing of *Faith,* but what he says against it, that is, that those who cry *Lord, Lord,* and profess to have *believed* in his Name, have no Favour to expect on that Account; but declared that 'tis the Practice, or the omitting the Practice of the Duties of Morality, *Feeding the Hungry, cloathing the Naked, visiting the Sick, &c.* in short, 'tis the Doing or not Doing all the Good that lies in our Power, that will render us the Heirs of Happiness or Misery."[48] It is significant that in his letter to Priestley referred to earlier in this paper, concerning the power of man over matter, Franklin followed his rhapsodic perspective of the future of physical improvement with the profound wish, "O that moral Science were in as fair a way of Improvement, that Man would cease to be Wolves to one another, and that human Beings would at length learn what they now improperly call Humanity."[49] Here Franklin speaks of moral science in reference to the social virtues, not to the personal ones. It would be a mistake, however, because of Franklin's vocabulary to assume that he considered personal morality an art and social morality a science. His emphasis on habit and the method of habit formation in acquiring the thirteen virtues indicates that he considered one type of morality just as much a science as the other.

The element of worship in religion like that of ethics has both a private and public aspect. Prayer and contemplation take place both in solitude and in formal church services, and both types of worship were essential to Franklin. In his early prayer book or "little liturgy" which he also called his "Articles of Belief and Acts of Religion," Franklin raised the question of the motives for worship. Deists such as Lord Shaftesbury argued that God was too remote from individual human concerns to wish for or to heed prayer or other forms of worship, but most Christians and some deists took the opposite position. Franklin succeeded in combining the two attitudes. In reference to "the one Supreme most perfect Being, Author, and Father of the God themselves," he admitted

---

[48] *Papers,* II, 30.
[49] *Writings,* IX, 10.

that it is great vanity to suppose that the "Supremely Perfect" would "in the least regard such an inconsiderable Nothing as Man." But the inferior gods, he felt, including the wise and good God who is the creator of our own system, would not be above being pleased with our praise or offended when slighted or neglected. In this sense, Franklin believed that human beings are made in God's image, that is, that they are endowed with some of the passions which the deity himself possesses. Franklin concluded his rhapsody with the self-admonition, "Let me then not fail to praise my God continually, for it is his Due, and it is all I can return for his many Favours." In regard to this deistical God, therefore, Franklin considered worship a religious duty. This is why he says in his creed that God "ought to be worshipped by Adoration, Prayer, and Thanksgiving." Nowhere in his writings, however, does Franklin indicate that he believed that the petitioning part of worship, whether private or public, would ever change the course of events; in other words, he had no faith that prayers would be answered. In his letter to Ezra Stiles at the end of his life, he wrote, "I do not perceive, that the Supreme takes it amiss, by distinguishing the Unbelievers in his Government of the World with any marks of his Displeasure." It may be that Franklin considered fasting as one of the means of private worship, although he may also have conceived of this form of self-deprivation as a means of discipline completely divorced from adoration, prayer, or thanksgiving. He may also have had in mind attaining physical benefit through dieting or revealing symbolically his affiliation to the Church of England. At any rate, he tells us in his Autobiography that he had several times kept Lent "most strictly" and had passed from the common diet to the reduced one without the least inconvenience.

Franklin was equally as insistent upon public worship as upon private, but he adduced somewhat different motives. He made a practice throughout his life of attending public worship, but he did not do so with consistency or regularity. In his youth, he deliberately evaded church attendance as much as possible in order to spend his time reading instead. In his early years in Philadelphia while still nominally a Presbyterian or Congregationalist, he stopped attending because the sermons were too heavily fraught with doctrine rather than morality. When he affiliated himself with the Church of England, however, he considered it a duty to attend as much as possible, and once particularly admonished his daughter Sarah to do the same. "Go constantly to Church, whoever preaches," he counseled. "The Acts of Devotion in the common Prayer Book, are your principal Business there; and if properly attended to, will do more towards mending the Heart than Sermons generally can do. For they were composed by Men of much greater Piety and Wisdom, than our common Composers of Sermons can pretend to be. And therefore I wish you wou'd never miss the Prayer Days. Yet I do not mean you shou'd despise Sermons, even of the Preachers you dislike, for the Discourse is often much better than the Man."[50] When Sarah had a child of her own, however, and asked her father's advice concerning the period when the child should be given instruction in religion and no longer be allowed to pray to Hercules as he had beem accustomed to do, he replied, "teach him . . . to direct his worship properly, for the deity of Hercules is now quite out of fashion."[51] Taken together, the two letters do not give a consistent view, but neither letter suggests, as Franklin does in his scheme for private worship, that prayer is a religious duty. Indeed the statement that praying is efficacious in "mending the Heart." suggests that it acts to form proper interior habits, exactly the same function served by his Art of Virtue. As Franklin once wrote to a religious doubter attempting to dissuade him from publishing a work against religion, the youth of both sexes "have need of the Motives of Religion to restrain them from Vice, to support their Virtue, and retain them in the Practice of it till it becomes *habitual,* which is the great Point for its Security." Franklin closed his argument with the question, "If Men are so wicked, as we now see them *with Religion,* what would they be if *without it.*[52] He had previously written in *Poor Richard,* "Talking against Religion is unchaining a Tyger; the Beast let loose may worry his Deliverer."[53] This reasoning supports a common attitude of many deists that men of superior intelligence and resolution may lead moral lives free from the sanctions of religion, but that the masses need the elements of religious fear and superstition to force them to adhere to virtuous principles.

---

[50] *Papers,* XI, 450.

[51] William Duane, ed., *Letters to Benjamin Franklin* (New York, 1859), 93.

[52] *Papers,* VII, 295.

[53] *Papers,* IV, 96.

Probably Franklin was thinking along these lines also when exhorting his daughter to engage in public devotion.

Apart from his attendance at church services, Franklin several times throughout his life directly advocated public worship. To encourage military action against French and Spanish privateers who were threatening the security of Philadelphia in 1747, Franklin, according to his Autobiography, called in "the Aid of Religion" by proposing the proclaiming of a Fast Day, "to promote Reformation, and implore the Blessing of Heaven on our Undertaking." Drawing on his New England religious heritage, Franklin himself wrote the formal proclamation, affirming that "it is the Duty of Mankind, on all suitable Occasions, to acknowledge their Dependance on the DIVINE BEING, to give Thanks for the Mercies received, and no less to deprecate his Judgments."[54] Franklin refers in his Autobiography to another occasion on which he encouraged group worship. In a later military operation against frontier Indians, the chaplain, a Presbyterian minister, complained to Franklin that the men seldom attended his prayers and exhortations. Franklin thereupon suggested that the chaplain appoint himself steward of the daily gill of rum allotted to each man and to disperse it immediately after prayers. The chaplain liked the idea, put it into practice, "and never were Prayers more generally and more punctually attended."[55]

Franklin's best-known commitment to public worship consists of his motion in the Constitutional Convention of June 1787 calling for prayers at the start of business each day, the prayers to be led by the various clergymen of the city. The motion was defeated, according to Madison because there were no funds to pay a minister, but a more probable explanation is that the majority of the delegates were fellow deists, but less convinced than Franklin of the utility of worship. Franklin's speech is a marvel of rhetoric, giving the impression that Franklin believed in orthodox Christianity, but avoiding any specific commitment. He refers to the divine being as "the Father of Lights" and as "that powerful Friend," both echoes of expressions in his private devotions.[56] He then refers to daily prayers which had been addressed for divine protection in the same room during the Revolutionary War and

---

[54] *Papers*, III, 228.
[55] *Autobiography*, p. 235.
[56] *Writings*, IX, 600-602.

assures his audience that these prayers "were heard" and "graciously answered." But instead of providing examples or revealing a direct connection between these prayers and specific events, Franklin merely affirms, "All of us, who were engag'd in the Struggle, must have observed frequent Instances of a superintending Providence in our Favour." Echoing Hamlet's pronouncement "there's a special providence in the fall of a sparrow," Franklin affirms, "The longer I live, the more convincing proofs I see of this Truth, *that* GOD *governs in the Affairs of Men.* And if a Sparrow cannot fall to the Ground without his Notice, is it probable that an Empire can rise without his aid?" Franklin follows Shakespeare with a quotation from "the Sacred Writings, that 'except the Lord build the House, they labour in vain that build it.' " Franklin adds, "I firmly believe this; and I also believe, that, without his concurring Aid, we shall succeed in this political Building no better than the Builders of Babel." The particular source of Franklin's passage in the Sacred Writings is the Old Testament. (Psalms 127:1) Two months after his motion in the Convention, he expressed to Joseph Priestley his opinion "that there are several Things in the Old Testament impossible to be given by *divine* Inspiration."[57] This skeptical attitude toward Christian Revelation is, nevertheless, not inconsistent with a belief that the new American government could not succeed without divine sanction or support. Franklin's assent to the Old Testament verse is also comfortable to his youthful supposition "that the Deity sometimes interferes by his particular Providence, and sets aside the Events which would otherwise have been prodc'd in the Course of Nature, or by the Free Agency of Men." Nothing in his advocacy of daily prayers, however, suggested that he believed these prayers, if instituted, would have had any effect upon subsequent events despite his assurances that earlier prayers during the Revolutionary War had been answered.

Franklin was fully aware of the salutary effect which prayer and worship have upon the individual even though he had no secure expectation that his own words of adoration and petition established a direct link between himself and the divine being. As we have noticed, he told Ezra Stiles, "I do not perceive that the Supreme takes it amiss, by distinguishing the Unbelievers in his

[57] *Writings,* IX, 267.

Government of the World with any peculiar Marks of his Displeasure." If Franklin recognized that private worship had a beneficial effect upon the individual, it is logical to assume that he also believed that public worship would be no less useful in raising both individual and social morale.

Franklin seldom deviated from his beliefs that there is a single God who made all things, that he governs the world through his providence, that he ought to be worshipped, and that the most acceptable service of God is doing good to man. We have seen, however, that Franklin made no connection between God's providence and man's worship. He had much less conviction, moreover, of the last two of his beliefs, that the soul is immortal and that God will reward virtue and punish vice, either here or hereafter. He was particularly dubious of the concept of personal immortality.

To be sure, in various letters of condolence to members of his family and others, he endeavored to give the impression that he was certain of a future life, and the same impression has been perpetuated by various *jeux d'esprit* such as his "Printer's Epitaph," in which he compared himself to a book which would reappear in a more perfect edition, corrected and emended by its author. Substantial evidence indicates, however, that he never completely abandoned the opinion expressed in his early pamphlet on *Liberty and Necessity,* that even though there may be a soul which acts upon the ideas in the brain, when death comes to the body, the thinking process ceases and "to cease to *think* is but little different from *ceasing to be.*" In August 1785, he confided to Jan Ingenhousz that he was not at all certain "if Consciousness and Memory remain in a future State."[58] Yet a mere three months previously he had written to George Whatley, paraphrasing his printer's epitaph and using the concept of the conservation of matter to bolster his hope for a future life. According to his reasoning, God has provided for the constant peopling of his world without the trouble of "repeated new Creations" and by the reduction of compound substances to their original elements has "prevented the Necessity of creating new Matter." Since in this process nothing is annihilated and not even a drop of water wasted, Franklin concluded, "I cannot suspect the Annihilation of Souls, or believe, that he will suffer the daily Waste of Millions of Minds ready made

---

[58] *Writings,* IX, 442.

that now exist, and put himself to the continual Trouble of making new ones.''[59] Franklin does not use the word *reincarnation* in this letter or elsewhere show great interest in the theory, but his parallel between the conservation of matter and that of minds seems to require a recycling of souls in the cosmic order as well as bodies.[60] In the letter to Ingenhousz, he seems to deny immortality; in that to Whatley, to affirm it; in actuality he maintains a future state in both letters, but in neither does he affirm the transference of memory or of consciousness.

In regard to the doctrine of rewards and punishments in a future state, Franklin is equally ambiguous. In both places in his Autobiography where he states his creed, he affirms that virtue will be rewarded and vice punished "either here or hereafter," certainly not a positive assurance that retribution will take place after death. That virtue will be rewarded in this life is an opinion consistent both with Franklin's ethical system and a skeptical attitude toward immortality. In revealing his creed to Ezra Stiles, Franklin changed emphasis in the direction of Christian orthodoxy by affirming that "the soul of Man is immortal and will be treated in another Life respecting its Conduct in this." Stiles as President of Yale College had particularly queried Franklin about his religion, and Franklin was reasonably sure, therefore, that his reply would be published. Probably he couched his answer in Christian terms both to avoid giving offense and to observe his own precept of publicly upholding the sanctions of religion.

Franklin also used the argument of some Christian polemicists that retribution in a future state is necessary to balance the inequities of this life, where many vicious men seem to prosper and virtuous ones to suffer. In reference to King George III, whom Franklin in company with many Americans in the Revolutionary Period considered an absolute fiend, he professed to be "convinc'd of a future State, in which all that here appears to be wrong shall be set right, all that is crooked made straight." The British monarch "from the number & extent of his Crimes" illustrated the impossibility "of giving equivalent Punishment to a wicked Man in this Life."[61] Franklin's use of this argument at this time, however,

---

[59] *Writings,* IX, 264.
[60] He does refer to a printed theory of transmigration in *Papers,* XVII, 315-316.
[61] *Writings,* VIII, 562.

should probably be considered political rhetoric rather than serious theology.

There is one doctrine which Franklin omitted from all statements of his creed, but which he, nevertheless, practiced regularly and uniformly throughout his life. This doctrine is tolerance. He supported financially in one way or another every sect in· Philadelphia, including the Catholic and the Jewish. In England, he participated in the establishment of a Unitarian chapel and cooperated in the drawing up of a deistical liturgy. Finally, after the Revolution, he served as an intermediary in the establishment of independent ecclesiastical government in the American branches of the Anglican and Catholic churches. In summing up his attitude toward the various sects in Philadelphia, he maintained that he had respect for all of them, but the greatest for those which inspired or confirmed morality, and the least for those which "serv'd to divide us and make us unfriendly to one another."[62]

A parallel may be drawn in regard to religious toleration between Franklin and the seventeenth-century Germany philosopher Leibniz. The latter, who was greatly impressed by the religion of China, suggested that Chinese missionaries be sent to Europe who would teach the principles of natural religion, and at the same time that Christian missionaries be sent from Europe to teach the Chinese the principles of revelation.[63] Franklin in his Autobiography describes his own efforts in Philadelphia to promote the construction of an interdenominational meeting house, "the Design in building not being to accommodate any particular Sect, but the Inhabitants in general, so that even if the Mufti of Constantinople were to send a Missionary to preach Mahometanism to us, he would find a Pulpit at his Service."[64] In the climate of opinion of mid-century Philadelphia, Franklin may have been the only promoter of the meeting house who would have made a Mahometan missionary welcome, and for this reason he has been accused of exaggeration for even referring to the possibility. One could quote in defense of his position, however, the words of Oliver Cromwell that "I had rather that

---

[62] *Autobiography*, p. 146.
[63] *Novissima Sinica*, 1699. English translation, 2d. ed., 1724. Preface.
[64] *Autobiography*, p. 176.

Mahometanism were permitted amongst us than that one of God's children should be persecuted."[65]

Toleration and humanitarianism were the fundamental criteria of Franklin's deism of the heart. Despite his varying portrayals of the deity, whether as father, friend, or even one among several superior beings, Franklin never wavered in believing and in acting upon his belief that "the most acceptable Service of God was the doing good to Man."

[65]W. C. Abbott ed., *Writings and Speeches of Oliver Cromwell* (Cambridge, Mass., 1934-1947), II, 521.

Franklin's Political Journalism in England

VERNER W. CRANE

Verner W. Crane (1889-1974) taught American history at the University of Michigan from 1916 to 1959. He was the author of *Benjamin Franklin: Englishman and American* (1936) and *Benjamin Franklin and a Rising People* (1954). His collection of *Benjamin Franklin's Letters to the Press, 1758-1775*, published in 1950, improved upon Benjamin Vaughan's edition of 1779 and more than doubled the number of anonymous and pseudonymous political writings previously recognized as Franklin's. The collection reveals Franklin as a master propagandist. As one scholar has written, Franklin was "a one-man Voice of America" who was less interested in accuracy than in shaping a favorable image of America in European minds.[1]

It is now one hundred and sixty years since Benjamin Vaughan published in London the first collection of Franklin's writings to include political as well as scientific essays. It would be hard to imagine less likely circumstances for such an undertaking. The volume was compiled in the midst of the War of Independence. Franklin at the time was in Paris as the minister of the rebel Congress to the court of Louis XVI; in the past year his first great diplomatic triumph, the treaty of alliance, had brought France also into the war with Britain. Meanwhile, his editor was in England: a nominal enemy, but actually an ardent admirer and a friend of the American cause. Since 1777 a number of letters concerning the project had crossed the channel between author and editor. From Paris Franklin forwarded to the enemy capital in 1779 the "Addenda and Corrigenda" which gave special authority to the Vaughan edition. Vaughan reprinted not only Franklin's imperialist essays of 1754 to 1760, and certain of his antiproprietary writings, but also—without apology to his English public—such caustic satires on the policies of Lord North's ministry as the "RULES by which a GREAT EMPIRE may be reduced to a SMALL ONE," and "An Edict by the King of Prussia." In his

---

[1] Willliam Randel, "The American Search for an Image Abroad," *Mississippi Quarterly*, XVI (1963), 16.

preface, indeed, Vaughan confidently asserted of the man whom some Englishmen called "Old Traitor Franklin," that "history lies in wait for him, and the judgment of mankind balances already in his favor." "No man," he declared, "ever made larger or bolder guesses than Dr. Franklin from like materials in politics and philosophy, which, after the scrutiny of events and of fact, have been more completely verified."

So far at least as concerns Franklin's reputation as a political writer on the causes of the American Revolution, the judgment of history to which Vaughan appealed rests even today largely upon the essays which he managed to assemble in the sturdy octavo volume of *Political, Miscellaneous, and Philosophical Pieces.* Later editors from William Temple Franklin to Albert Henry Smyth greatly extended the corpus of Franklin's writings in other directions, notably through the publication of the major part of his magnificent correspondence. But of his numerous political essays on the great cause between the colonies and the mother country, written during the busy years of his London agencies and printed contemporaneously in newspapers and periodicals in England and America, the last Franklin editor added only about a dozen items to those collected so long ago by the admirable Benjamin Vaughan.

Thus it has happened that while biographers and historians have tasted the quality of Franklin's political writing, they have never appreciated its scope during the very years of his maturity both as a man of letters and a politician. They have missed seeing how largely political journalism absorbed his energy at crucial moments. Unaware of the extent to which his writings were printed and reprinted in the English and also the American press, they have underestimated his influence upon political attitudes on both sides of the Atlantic.

The complaisance of modern editors with their fragmentary collections of the Franklin essays on politics is the more surprising in view of the fact that both author and editor were highly dissatisfied with what Franklin called the "very incompleat" edition of 1779. Vaughan had repeatedly urged Franklin to send him certain texts; but quite often he had been disappointed. The difficulty was that the two main sources from which they might have been furnished were inaccessible to Franklin in Paris. On his departure for France he had left his personal file of papers in Pennsylvania, in the keeping of Joseph Galloway, now a Tory. For many years, also, William Franklin had received from his father, as Benjamin later recalled, "sometimes the Rough Drafts, and sometimes the printed Pieces I wrote in London," but the last royal governor of New Jersey was at this time in patriot custody in America. "If I should ever recover the Pieces that were in the Hands of my Son," Franklin wrote to Vaughan, "and those I left among my Papers in America, I think there may be enough to make three more such Volumes, of which a great part would be more interesting." In 1784 Franklin sought to enlist the aid of his son, now in England, for an enlarged second edition of Vaughan, but the project fell through.

Franklin's own testimony that he had written many more essays in England than Vaughan had been able to assemble, seemed sufficient warrant, several years since, for undertaking a search for new Franklin essays in the London newspapers. This was pursued both in the so-called evening papers of the type of the *London Chronicle,* which had been casually but not thoroughly inspected before, and especially in the extant files of the London daily newspapers, never hitherto explored by any Franklin student. Difficulties were encountered: many issues have disappeared; and Franklin, in common with the other controversial writers of the age, had usually assumed the disguise of anonymity or pseudonymity.

Happily he left more clues than his great contemporary and fellow-contributor in the 1770's to the *Public Advertiser,* the mysterious Junius. Among the clues which proved useful are drafts and memoranda in the great manuscript collections, especially in the American Philosophical Society; allusions by Franklin himself, or by his correspondents; a helpful list which Franklin drew up in 1769 of those essays of his which Goddard had reprinted in the *Pennsylvania Chronicle;* contemporary identifications by his journalistic antagonists, some of which hit the mark, though others went far astray; his use of characteristic pseudonyms; and those other signs of authorship supplied by internal evidence, which in the case of so frugal a writer as Franklin are often highly convincing. Suffice it to say that it has been possible to recover what is probably the major portion of Franklin's political journalism in England; that this amounts in bulk to nearly the "three more such Volumes"—on the scale of the 1779 edition—which Franklin predicted; and that it is hoped that this belated "second edition" of Vaughan may shortly appear. Meanwhile the friends of Franklin may be interested in a brief analysis of the character and significance of this restored body of Franklin's political journalism, with sidelights upon Franklin's relations to the press.

As an old-time newspaper proprietor, trained in the rough-and-tumble of colonial politics it is not surprising that Franklin began to send in letters to the London papers at least as early as 1758, and that he continued to write on imperial politics all through the English period, even during the stormy final year of his London residence. Long before, in his "Apology for Printers," he had observed: "That the Business of Printing has chiefly to do with Men's Opinions; most things that are printed tending to promote some, or oppose other." Here is as neat a description of propaganda as one is likely to find—framed, moreover, by a master practitioner. It seems likely, indeed, that little in modern propaganda would surprise Franklin, except the name! The art, he understood, was an ancient if not always an honorable one: the eighteenth century had, as usual, introduced improvements. "To the haranguers of the populace among the ancients," he wrote in 1767, "succeed among the moderns your writers of political pamphlets and news-papers, and your coffee-house talkers." In 1782 he pointed out the great advantage of modern means of persuasion over ancient oratory: "The facility, with which the same truths may be repeatedly enforced by placing them daily in different lights in *newspapers,* which are everywhere read, gives a great chance of establishing them. And we now find, that it is not only right to strike while the iron is hot, but that it may be very practicable to heat it by continually striking."

To heat the iron in the controversies between colonies and mother country, Franklin himself had recourse both to pamphleteering and newspaper writing, and also to coffee-house oratory. Of his contributions in the latter sort, more important in forming opinion in eighteenth-century London than anything comparable today, little has survived. The recently reprinted dialogue on slavery of 1770 may well be what it purports to be, the dressed-up version of a coffee-house debate. But in any case Franklin was a more persuasive writer than talker. Two unidentified Franklin pamphlets, of 1766 and 1768, have been recovered, and there are traces of two others which were written but apparently not published. It was in the newspaper, however, that Franklin found his real forum in England.

A forum for debate the newspaper of the eighteenth century was intended to be. Especially was this true of London. There three great dailies circulated, and half-a-dozen so-called evening papers, printed thrice a week, which were carried by the post to Bath and Bristol and the provincial towns generally; they had, besides, their regular subscribers in America. In addition to news, usually stale, from the continent and the kingdom and even from the colonies, and advertising and literary notices—but as yet no editorials—a principal department comprised essays, largely controversial, on a wide range of political topics, in the form of letters to the printer, usually signed with a pseudonym. These contributed letters had an importance in the formulation of opinion far beyond that of letters from readers of today. It was the repeatedly asserted policy of the printers to open their columns without discrimination to writers on either side of any current debate; and in the best English papers, to a greater degree it would seem than in the colonial gazettes, this policy of impartiality was actually maintained. Henry S. Woodfall proudly described his daily, the *Public Advertiser,* as a "cockpit for Political Spurring." He strongly repudiated charges of partisanship, as in 1774, when one correspondent asked how he and his colleagues could justify to their consciences "the constantly printing Essays and Paragraphs, which accuse the Bostonians of Rebellion." Only a few weeks later, however, another writer—no doubt a ministerial hack—denounced the prostitution of the English press, under the guise of impartiality, to the cause of American Rebellion! On still another occasion Woodfall gave the following answer to a complaint: "The Printer does *not* plead guilty to the Charge of *Partiality.*—If twenty Gentlemen write Letters to answer One JUNIUS, the Printer inserts these Letters as quick as possible." It is obvious, however, that some among the score of anti-Junius scribes must wait upon the convenience of the printer. It was certainly an advantage, then, for a writer on political questions to have personal relations with the proprietors or shareholders of the principal papers. Such relations Benjamin Franklin amply enjoyed. It is therefore not surprising that only rarely do his letters appear to have been excluded: that commonly they were printed very promptly; and that often they were given special prominence. His newspaper connections are not far to seek. A good friend and neighbor in Craven Street was the wine-merchant Caleb Whitefoorde, himself a writer for the papers and also one of the proprietors of the *Public Advertiser*. But it was probably through his long-time printer friend, William Strahan, that Franklin first established his close connections with the London press. Strahan was not only the principal stockholder of the tri-weekly *London Chronicle,* with a one-ninth interest; he had important shares also in the *Public Advertiser,* the *Public Ledger* (another daily), and *Lloyd's Evening Post.* To each of these, as also to the third daily, the *Gazetteer,* Franklin was a contributor. Thirty-three of his essays have been discovered in the *Public Advertiser;* thirty-two in the *London Chronicle,* and eighteen in the *Gazetteer.*

By modern standards the circulation of these papers was absurdly small. The *Public Advertiser* is said to have printed about 3,000 copies; the *Gazetteer* in 1769 about 5,000. But they were certainly read much more widely than these figures would indicate, especially in the coffee-houses where they were also hotly debated. The public opinion which they helped to form was that of a minority, but of an influential minority in a country controlled by a minority ruling class. It was especially when Parliament was in session that political letter writers sharpened their quills, and among the rest Benjamin Franklin. It is significant of his purposes that most of his essays were printed in the months of the parliamentary sessions or of impending elections. Thus some twenty-four of his political pieces were printed in January issues of four years: 1766, 1768, 1769, 1770.

When letters caught on they were given wider currency through reprinting from the dailies into the evening papers—which also, as in the case of the *London Chronicle,* printed some essays for the first time—and in such monthly periodicals as the *Gentleman's Magazine.* This frequently happened with Franklin's essays; and indeed most of the texts presented by his editors have unfortunately been taken from these imperfect reprintings, or else from incomplete manuscript drafts. On this side of the Atlantic, colonial printers to fill out their sheets culled letters as well as old news from London papers and periodicals. Franklin fared especially well in the colonial gazettes, although it was rare that his authorship was asserted, and then sometimes incorrectly. The notable instance in which he was identified to American readers occurred in

1767. To offset malicious partisan attacks upon the agent's conduct in the affair of the Stamp Act, William Goddard reprinted in the *Pennsylvania Chronicle* a whole batch of Franklin essays from London papers. With his keen journalistic sense, and his wide connections among American printers, it is likely that Franklin himself saw to it that papers containing his essays came their way. Certainly it is true that most of his English writings were currently reprinted at least once and often many times in America; a thorough canvass would probably greatly extend the evidence. He wrote, then, for an audience both in England and America. And he wrote most often in the dual role of an Englishman and an American, seeking in the midst of bitter disputes to promote a more enlightened imperialism.

It was, however, as an imperial expansionist, and an advocate of royal government in Pennsylvania, that Franklin first addressed English newspaper readers in those years of his earlier agency which were also the climatic years of the Seven Years' War. His first contribution was probably the letter signed "A.B." in the *London Chronicle* for September 19, 1758, which was recognized as his by Cecilius Calvert: a piece of anti-proprietary propaganda in line with the original purpose of his agency.

But most of his journalism between 1758 and 1761 turned toward broader issues of the empire at war. When a peace movement arose in England—prematurely as it seemed to this expansionist American who hoped for great continental acquisitions from the French in North America—he addressed to Mr. Chronicle a series of letters which were Franklin war propaganda. As "CHEARFUL" he demonstrated in December how the supply of twelve millions for the next year might be raised not once but several times over, by the exercise of Poor Richard's stock virtues of "industry and frugality." And so might Britain avoid "a peace whch shall be either *unsafe* or dishonourable to the nation." As "New Englandman" he turned aside in May, 1759, to defend the colonial soldiery against the slurs of British officers serving in America whose letters he had read with mounting indignation in the London papers. (From this time on the defense of the Americans became one of his self-appointed tasks in England: defense of their customs as well as their opinions, of their diets even, as in his championing of American corn bread—a defense not so much against malignity, as against the dismaying ignorance of things American which he encountered in the mother country.) In November, 1759, he returned to his war propaganda to draw the portraits of those Englishmen who "wish for a peace with *France, let the terms be every so dishonourable, ever so disadvantageous...,*" as he did again in 1761, in the fictitious chapter "Of the Meanes of disposing the Enemie to Peace" which he alleged that he had drawn "from the famous Jesuit *Campanella's* discourses address'd to the King of *Spain.*" Here he listed among the pacifists: "All those who be timorous by nature, amongst whom he reckoned men of learning that lead sedentarie lives, using little exercise of bodie, and thence obtaining but few and weake spirits." In 1767, however, he reconsidered the case of the intellectuals when he found some of them clamoring for the use of force in America. He then wrote for the same *London Chronicle* (April 9, 1767) a curiously similar passage but to exactly the opposite effect:

It is remarkable that soldiers by profession, men truly and unquestionably brave, seldom advise war but in cases of extreme necessity. While mere rhetoricians, tongue-pads, and scribes, timid by nature, or from their little bodily exercise deficient in those spirits that give real courage, are ever bawling for war on the most trifling occasions, and seem the most blood-thirsty of mankind.

The climax of Franklin's political writing in the period of the first agency was, of course, the publication in April, 1760, of his famous Canada pamphlet, *The Interest of Great Britain,* arguing the case for a peace which should secure Canada and the trans-Appalachian West, rather than West Indian islands, for Great Britain. It is not so well known that Franklin had prepared the way for this pamphlet by printing in the *Chronicle* late in December, 1759, a letter signed "A.Z." which gave to certain arguments of the forthcoming tract a satirical turn.

When Franklin returned to England on his second Pennsylvania agency at the end of 1764, he returned to a land of many friendships and many useful connections—scientific, literary, and among others journalistic. Already he had his *entree* to Strahan's *London Chronicle.* Soon he was contributing also to the daily papers, as the successive crises over the Stamp Act, the Townshend Acts, the Tea Act, and the rest gave occasion. During the second agency even more than during the first the anti-proprietary campaign took an insignificant place in his writings among the larger concerns of the colonies in the era of imperial reorganization.

Franklin's letters to the newspapers appeared over a bewildering variety of signatures. Smyth listed some eighteen pseudonyms, but the list can be extended to about forty. Franklin's practice was thus quite unlike that of Junius, who made one signature immortal; or that of his own uneasy and suspicious colleague from Virginia, Arthur Lee, who dreamed of a like immortality as Junius Americanus. Thus far there has turned up among the new materials only one considerable Franklin series of a definitely periodical character: The Colonist's Advocate papers, eleven in number, which appeared in the *Public Advertiser* between January 4 and March 2, 1770. They marked the climax of Franklin's drive in the press for the repeal of the Townshend duties. The partial repeal by Parliament occurred March 5, and the series suddenly ended.

Better suited to Franklin's purposes in propaganda, as also to his temperament, was his more usual method of scattering a number of detached essays through the papers, over a variety of signatures, and in a great variety of modes. It would seem that he was deliberately seeking to create the impression that a numerous regiment of pro-American writers was in the field. If so, he was not altogether successful, for by 1774 ministerial paragraphers were tracing all such propaganda, sometimes quite erroneously, to what one of them called "Judas's office in Craven Street." Sometimes he chose to write in the character of an Englishman—several times over the actual signature of "A Briton." Franklin's methods reflect *ad hoc* nature of much of his political writing in England. Most often the letters were answers to writers who, he conceived, had misstated American facts or misrepresented American views. "Angry reflections on the Americans" were pretty certain to draw his fire.

The winter of 1765-6 saw him at his busiest, by testimony of such intimates as Strahan and Dr. Fothergill. "He is forever with one Member of Parliament or other," wrote Strahan on January 11, describing his activities as a lobbyist for the repeal of the Stamp Act. "All this while too," Strahan continued, "he hath been throwing out Hints in the Public Papers, and giving Answers to such letters as have appeared in them, that required or deserved an Answer.—In this Manner is he now employed, and with very little Interruption, Night & Day." Strahan was not exaggerating. In the newspapers that winter Franklin had challenged each of the prominent Grenvillite writers in turn. To "Tom Hint" he had replied over his favorite signature of "F.B."; to "Pacificus" as "Pacificus Secundus"; to "Vindex Patriae" as "Homespun" or "N.N." Not a little of the fencing skill which he exhibited on the great occasion of his examination before the House of Commons in February may be traced to his practice in these preliminary bouts in the London press.

In later years Franklin continued to reply to current "misrepresentations," as he called them, of the Americans. Thus in March, 1767, he read in the *Gazetteer* a satirical paper by some Grenvillite writer called "Right, Wrong, and Reasonable, according to American Ideas." In April he retorted in one of the most pungent of the newly discovered essays under this caption: "RIGHT, WRONG, AND REASONABLE, with regard to America, according to the Ideas of the Gentle Shepherd, and the genuine meaning of the papers and pamphlets lately published by him and his associates." Though here he deliberately borrowed the form of discourse set by his antagonist, he managed greatly to improve upon it. This was unhappily not the fortune of Francis Bernard, former royal governor of Massachusetts, when he rashly attempted a reply in the same kind to one of the most brilliant of Franklin's political satires. At least Franklin himself had reason for believing that it was Bernard who wrote the "labour'd, and special dull Answer" in the *Public Advertiser* to his own famous essay of September 11, 1773: "RULES by which a GREAT EMPIRE may be reduced to a SMALL ONE."

Franklin's political essays were timely, which is the essence of journalism; but his literary talent, and the wisdom which he managed to instill into even his slightest pieces, usually save them from being merely ephemeral. In his correspondence are passages which throw light on his careful timing of his press campaigns. Within ten days in April, 1767, he printed four considerable essays, three of them in two consecutive issues of the *London Chronicle*. In an unpublished letter to Joseph Galloway he confided the reasons for this special activity:

I have written several Papers to abate a little if possible the Animosity stirr'd up against us, and flatter myself they may be attended with some Success. I have taken that Method to answer all the groundless Charges, and state aright all the mistaken Facts that I heard urged in the Debates at the House of Lords, tho I durst not mention those Debates. I send you some of them. They have been reprinted here in several of the Newspapers.

Again in August, 1768, he wrote, once more to Galloway:

...a Party is now growing in our Favour, which I shall endeavour to increase and strengthen by every Effort of Tongue and Pen...

From August to December, accordingly, he printed some ten essays, only half of which have been preserved in his collected writings.

Franklin's strong literary bent is revealed in the variety of forms which he employed in his political writings, as well as in the familiar felicities of his style. There are allegories, hoaxes, imaginary colloquies, the Socratic discourse, as well as straight-out argumentation. Some of these forms Franklin had practiced since his salad days in the Junto, and throughout his early writing for the Boston and Philadelphia papers. Elsewhere it has been shown that in a piece printed in 1770 Franklin was pretty surely recalling the method he had employed in the *Pennsylvania Gazette,* so far back as 1755, in his dialogue between X, Y, and Z in defense of the Pennsylvania militia act. For he began in very much the same form another dialogue, "A Conversation between an ENGLISHMAN, a SCOTCHMAN, and an AMERICAN, on the Subject of SLAVERY," which Woodfall printed in the *Public Advertiser,* January 30, 1770. (This capital piece is obviously "the dialogue on slavery" which Vaughan asked Franklin to send over from Paris for his 1779 edition, but which he failed to get.) Another item also recently recovered which likewise exhibits Franklin's craft as a writer is the set of three fables dedicated to Lord Hillsborough.

Although Franklin did not altogether escape the vice of hasty writing which appears in even the more leisurely journalism of the eighteenth century, the surviving drafts show that he was still a vigilant reviser. His letters reveal that he set great store by certain pieces, especially his satires of September, 1773, and for literary reasons among others. On the while he preferred the "RULES by which a GREAT EMPIRE may be reduced to a SMALL ONE"—"as a composition for the quantity and variety of the matter contained, and a kind of spirited ending of each paragraph"—to the more spectacular hoaxing of "An Edict of the King of Prussia." It is a fact, possibly quite irrelevant, that an early draft of the favorite essay was jotted down on an invoice from Brown & Whitefoorde, Wine Merchants, for

6 bottles Sherry seal'd yellow Rose
6 D° Port seal'd yellow Cock
4 D° Claret seal'd yellow Star
2 D° Mountain seal'd red Cypher.

In the next year Franklin even suggested that the sting of these essays had brought about his public disgrace in the Cockpit, and the loss of his crown office as joint-deputy postmaster general for North America. The claim appears in a letter of February 19, 1774 which can safely be attributed to Franklin, although he concealed his authorship. It was published in the colonial press as a first defense of Franklin against the virulence of Wedderburn's attack. Written in the third person, the apologia points out:

When People give weak Reasons for Strong Resentment, one is apt to suspect they are not the true ones; so I fancy sometimes, that the Doctor's returning those Letters could not be the Foundation of all this Fury, and that possibly the Preface to the Boston Pamphlet, the Prussian Edict, and the Rules for diminishing a Great Empire, are suspected to be his, and yet not mentioned, lest the Attention of the Public should be more turned towards those pieces, which are thought to expose the late Measures too poignantly.

Franklin's work as propagandist-in-chief for the colonies in England was often, to be sure, of a routine sort. There were documents from America to insert in the London press: resolves of town meetings in Massachusetts, of merchants and mechanics in Philadelphia, letters from colonial correspondents to be abstracted. Usually Franklin wrote an adroit paragraph or so of introduction; he also wrote prefaces for several of those American tracts which he got reprinted in London. In the launching of still other pamphlets his part appears to have been that only of paymaster to the printer. Several such transactions are revealed by Strahan's ledgers and by Franklin's accounts, as agent, with Massachusetts Bay.

There is singularly little evidence of Franklin's collaboration with other political writers: in general he played a lone hand. Richard Jackson's supposed partnership in the writing of the Canada pamphlet of 1760 is now discredited, his share reduced to supplying of some materials for Franklin's use. Another aide was John Huske, member of Parliament for Malden, Essex, an American by birth who probably wrote an important anti-French pamphlet of 1755, *The Present State of North America.* Huske made himself useful to Franklin on at least two occasions. On Franklin's examination in 1766, by previous arrangement no doubt, he asked a number of the "friendly" questions which enabled the agent to shine so brilliantly before the House of Commons. And in 1768 Huske was the "merchant friend" who furnished the tables of British trade with the northern colonies and the West Indies which Franklin as "F.B." displayed and discussed for the readers of the *London Chronicle.*

Even Franklin's astonishing fertility was strained at times by the pressure to keep the American case before minister and members of Parliament, or at all events before the newspaper-reading politicos of the clubs and coffee-houses. In an emergency he did not hesitate to repeat himself. At the height of the campaign for the repeal of the Stamp Act he secured the publication in the *London Chronicle* of his letters to Governor Shirley, written as long ago as 1754, in which he had anticipated so many of the later American arguments against parliamentary taxation. In 1774, a year when Franklin's fortunes and those of America took a sad turn for the worse, the "RULES" of 1773 were reprinted in the *Gazetteer* from an "authenticated copy" furnished by "A Fidler," who was certainly Franklin. To be sure, he adopted a rather thin disguise:

Having lately had occasion to turn over some newspapers, published in the course of the last summer, in search of an advertisement, I accidentally stumbled upon a letter, containing many *excellent rules,* by which a *great empire* may be reduced to a *small one.*

As I apprehend this plan is at present under the consideration of the House of Commons, I think a re-publication of it, at this time, would not be improper. The rules appear to me to be admirably adapted to the end proposed; and tho' the experience which we have since gained may enable a *shrewd politician* to improve upon some of them, there are others perhaps which will serve to furnish *Lord North* with some ideas that possibly may not hitherto have occurred to him.

In 1774, also, the *Chronicle* reprinted Franklin's essay of 1768, usually called "The Causes of the American Discontents." But it was not printed without those deletions which had caused the author to complain in 1768 that the *Chronicle* editor had shown himself a Grenvillite. It is pretty clear, then, that it was Franklin who in 1774 furnished a true copy to the *Chronicle.* In December, 1774, Rivington brought out the restored essay as a pamphlet from his press in New York.

It was in the critical year of 1774 that there was also printed, apparently for the first time, the well-known "Answer" which Franklin had written back in 1769, to certain "Queries" on

American affairs which Strahan had raised in a letter to his American friend. Meanwhile, however, this document had been widely circulated in manuscript copies, as had been the case earlier with Franklin's "Examination." One copy of the "Queries and Answer" Franklin had sent to his Boston correspondent, the Reverend Samuel Cooper, and it eventually found its way with other Franklin letters into the possession of George III. Strahan himself had sent other copies to David Hall and William Franklin. Still another, he said. had been put in the hands of the Duke of Grafton and "the other Chiefs of the Ministry." Perhaps because of Franklin's pessimistic conclusion, that "Mutual Recriminations will. . . go on to complete the separation" between colonies and mother country, Strahan had warned Hall that it would be "highly improper to publish it, or risk its getting into the papers." But in 1774, as now appears, Franklin procured its printing in the *Public Advertiser,* and a little later in the *Gazetteer.*

Franklin's frugality had occasionally an amusing aspect. Several times, when writing anonymously or pseudonymously, he quoted himself with words of praise which no doubt concealed a private chuckle. Thus in 1770 as "The Colonist's Advocate" he cited a famous passage from his own examination with this admiring comment:

For, what their Disposition, with Respect to the Mother-Country, was, before the Year 1763, is well known to the Public, and justly described, in the following Words, by a Gentleman, who has done great Honour, and important Service to his Country by his Manly Defense of his Liberties.

Franklin practised another less obvious type of literary economy which throws light on his writing methods, and incidentally facilitates the search for the lost Frankliniana: the economy of ideas, of turns of exposition and argument, even of phraseology. Sometimes these echoes suggest that he was using certain well-thumbed notes and memoranda—notably one set of jottings which he seems to have prepared in advance of his examination in 1766. At other times it would appear that his tenacious memory was drawing up old treasure from a well-stored mind. In the margin of the notes just mentioned was a stray jotting which read: "Germany the Mother Country of this Nation." Seven years later, in an essay which appeared in the *Public Advertiser,* March 16, 1773, Franklin expanded this note to refute the annoying assumption by many Englishmen that America was somehow their property. "Britain," he wrote, "was formerly the America of the Germans."

> They came hither in their Ships; found the *Cream* of the Land possessed by a Parcel of Welsh Caribbs, whom they judged unworthy of it, and therefore drove them in the Mountains, and sat down in their Places. These Anglo-Saxons, our Ancestors, came *at their own Expense,* and therefore supposed that when they had secured the new Country, they held it of themselves, and of no other People under Heaven. Accordingly we do not find that their Mother Country, Germany, ever pretended to tax them; nor is it likely, if she had, that they would have paid it.

Here he dropped the theme for the time being. But he returned to it in the fall, to expand it further into the elaborate hoax of the "Edict of the King of Prussia." This famous essay Woodfall printed on the front page of the *Public Advertiser* (September 22, 1773) though he placed it under a Danzig date-line, with the editorial explanation: "The Subject of the following Article of FOREIGN INTELLIGENCE being exceedingly EXTRAORDINARY, is the Reason of its being separated from the usual Articles of *Foreign News.*" In a note to Franklin he explained more candidly: had it "been printed as a Foreign Article I feared it would have been lost, or at least not so much attended to as it deserved."

Among the many types of argumentation which Franklin used, one which most directly reflects his shopkeeping background was his practise of "stating an account." For instance, in the *Public Advertiser,* January 17, 1769, he itemized such an account for "The Right Hon. G.G. Esq; and Co.... with the Stockholders of Great Britain." Or rather he stated two accounts: one of the great losses already incurred from the American troubles, another of the immensely greater losses to be expected "if the Rupture hitherto only apprehended shall take place," and war ensure. He concluded: "Thus stand the Accounts; yet this same G.G. the Root of all the Evil, sets up for an Economist."

Franklin set up for something of an economist himself; and many of his arguments in the English press were directed at British folly in driving good customers away from the shop. These arguments were addressed more especially to the British merchants and manufacturers. Indeed, from 1767-1774 Franklin shaped most of his propaganda to reinforce in that quarter the successive colonial movements of economic pressure through withdrawal of trade. There is evidence that Franklin himself had a good bit to do with encouraging these non-importation, non-consumption, and home-manufacturing movements in America, from the early days when Poor Richard in his almanac for 1765 turned his preaching of industry and frugality into a political channel, to the later days when it was widely believed that Franklin's advice had helped to shape the Association of the first Continental Congress. However that may be, in England he was the press agent for non-importation, picturing again and again the losses of English trade already incurred, and the future losses to be expected; and in 1770, when the great non-importation league was breaking up, skillfully covering the American retreat. To this kind of propaganda belongs what appears to be Franklin's last important essay in the English press. In the *Public Ledger* for November 19, 1774, before news had come to England of the final action of the Congress, there appeared a sensational letter signed "An American" and addressed "To the Merchants of England." It contained a startlingly accurate prediction of the forthcoming restrictive measures of the Congress, with dire prophecies of their effects on the economy of England, Ireland, and the West Indies. Thomas Hutchinson read it, and in a letter to Thomas Gage fixed on Josiah Quincy, Jr., who had reached London just two days before on a mysterious mission for the Boston radicals, as the author. But this striking manifesto is not all in the younger Quincy's manner, and very much in Franklin's. In his two-hour talk with Quincy on November 17 Franklin had had ample opportunity to learn what was afoot in the Philadelphia Congress. It would therefore appear that this important forgotten letter was Franklin's last despairing attempt to turn the tide of British policy in America by underscoring the threat of economic pressure: his last attempt through propaganda to save from shipwreck the old British Empire.

Franklin's espousal of the tactics of economic pressure had meanwhile worked some modifications in his own conviction that the American people should remain so long as possible a farmer society. Economic retaliation—even at the price of a certain measure of industrialism—he preferred to violent measure of popular revolt, chiefly because he long believed that America needed no sudden revolution; that time and a rapidly multiplying population were shifting the balance of imperial power to the western hemisphere. His repeated denials in the English press that

Americans were seeking independence, as their opponents charged, were sincerely made. Until very late in the quarrel Franklin himself remained an Anglo-American Imperialist. But his imperialism was of a special sort, not to be understood by crown lawyers or even by English Whigs of the eighteenth century, though quite in the present-day temper of the British Commonwealth of Nations.

For fairly obvious reasons the search for Franklin's underlying constitutional views—his notions of the true character of the British Empire and of the basis and extent of American rights within the empire—should begin, not with his published political writings in England, nor even with his correspondence, but with the marginal comments which he wrote in his own copies of the controversial pamphlets of the period. These secret jottings reveal that as early as the winter of 1765-6 his private views ran to a claim of what would now be called dominion status, within an empire united by allegiance to a single crown but not by subordination to a single parliament. From 1768 on hints of these principles, even then in advance of most American opinion, began to appear in his letters and in such newspaper essays as the "American" and "Briton" papers of September-October, 1768.

On the whole, however, until very late in the controversy, Franklin conceived his role as that of the expounder in England of prevailing opinion in America—and even, to some degree, as the interpreter of British opinion to the colonies. Again and again the discourse in his essays follows such a pattern as this: "But perhaps it may be some satisfaction to your Readers to known what ideas the Americans have on the subject. They say... [etc.]" And of the American views thus introduced: "I relate them merely in pursuance of the task I have impos'd on myself, to be an impartial historian of American facts and opinions." At the same time he urged on the English government the importance of reckoning with American opinion, however perverse or heretical it might seem in the longitude of Westminster: "It has been thought wisdom in Government exercising sovereignty over different kinds of people, to have some regard to prevailing and established opinions among the people to be governed, wherever such opinions might in their effects obstruct or promote publick measures."

Indeed, the major impression which remains after reading the whole body of the Franklin political essays, is not so much of the cleverness of his propaganda devices, or of the sting of his satires, clever and even devastating as these essays often were, but of the statesmanlike sense of responsibility which on the whole they exhibited. If he deliberately suppressed the discussion of fundamental constitutional issues, it was not because he was intellectually lazy. Nor was it merely because as a prudent politician he realized that these issues were alarming to the "friends of America" in England, and might even disturb his comfortable status as an absentee crown official for America. The very fact that in his own theory of the empire he had early reached radical views made him the more hesitant to swing the debate in the direction of constitutional theory. For he understood that the hardening logic of the American case was irreconcilable with principles just as firmly held in England. And so as Francis Lynn he deplored, in 1768, "the public discussion of Questions that had better never have been started." But for "those unnatural and churlish-hearted Men...who, needlessly, wickedly, and madly sowed the first seeds of discontent between Britain and her Colonies," he wrote in 1770, "Peace and Harmony would have reigned between the different Parts of this mighty Empire from Age to Age, to the unspeakable and inestimable Advantage of both." In the passage that follows immediately after this nostalgic invocation of empire, he makes sufficiently clear the kind of empire that could hold his affections and those of his fellow Americans:

Those men make a mighty Noise about the importance of keeping up our authority over the Colonies. They govern and regulate too much. Like some unthinking Parents, who are every Moment exerting their Authority, in obliging their Children to make Bows, and interrupting the Course of their innocent Amusements, attending constantly to their own Prerogative, but forgetting the Tenderness due to their Offspring. The true Art of governing the Colonies lies in a Nut-Shell. It is only letting them alone. So long as they find their Account in our Protection, they will desire, and deserve it. This our Experience confirms. So long as they find their Advantage, upon the Whole, in carrying on a Commerce with us, preferably to other Countries, they will continue it. Nay, unless we compel them to the contrary by our unnatural Treatment of them, they will shew a Prejudice in our Favor. Whenever they find Circumstances changed to the contrary, taxing and dragooning will only widen the Breach, and frustrate what ought to be the Intention of both Countries, viz. mutual Strength, and mutual Advantage.

Benjamin Franklin: Student of Life

ROBERT E. SPILLER

Robert Ernest Spiller (1896-   ) taught in the Department of English at Swarthmore College from 1921 to 1945 and at the University of Pennsylvania from 1945 to 1967. At the latter university he was the Felix E. Schelling Professor of English from 1961 to 1967. He is an editor of several anthologies, including *The Roots of National Culture, American Literature to 1830* (1933 and a revised edition in 1949), *Literary History of the United States* (1948 and a fourth edition revised in 1974) and *The American Literary Revolution, 1783-1837* (1967).

The following essay was delivered in the Hall of The Franklin Institute on March 1, 1940 as one of the papers in the "Meet Dr. Franklin" Conference.

1.

So many aspects of Franklin's life, thought, and work have already been discussed by the preceding speakers in this series that there should be little left to say. But perhaps I have one advantage over the others. They have all been limited to specific subjects, whereas I am asked to talk about life—or at least, Franklin's reading of life, which might lead me into almost anything. But I shall try to limit myself to an attempt to define the point of view which seems to me to have been at the root of all his many and varied actions, and thereby provide one more comment on that sense of wholeness and unity of character which we all feel in his presence but which we all find so difficult to define. However many avenues of his thought and experience one follows out to their manifold expressions, the return trip brings one always to the same source. Franklin asked only one question of life and of the things in it: "Does it work?" The method of his thinking seems to me always to be pragmatic. He relies in every problem upon experience in the immediate sense as his final authority.

If this seems too simple a statement of the question and too easy an answer, my excuse is that I am not a philosopher, that I do not believe Franklin to have been one, and that I do not look to philosophy in the strict sense of the term to provide much more than some of the language of the discussion that I have undertaken. It is the habit of literary critics and historians to describe

143

people in terms of the main-springs of their actions and thought. Such a statement as I have made about Franklin is perhaps as much a comment upon myself and my tribe as upon him. We find ourselves constantly using such phrases as "philosophy of life," "reading of life," and "romantic and classic," to the alarm and disgust of more disciplined thinkers. Because literature involves the emotions as well as the mind, the terms which are usually applied to the definitions of thinkers are inadequate. They must either be abandoned or have their meanings stretched to include emotional attitudes as well as rational systems. When I call Franklin "pragmatic," therefore, I am attempting to describe his whole personality and the meaning of his attitude toward life. In this sense I am treating Franklin as a literary figure, which undoubtedly he is, rather than primarily as a philosopher, scientist, statesman, or social critic, even though I may give much attention to these aspects of his thought and pay little or none to the form and style of his writings.

The pigeon-holing of a great man in so summary a fashion must always imply the phrase "it seems to me." If you will consent to my calling his attitude "pragmatic," I shall try to define and to illustrate what the word may mean within the limits of this discussion. If we are satisfied that the elusive sense of unity which is so obvious to most students of Franklin has been thereby defined, we may raise the further questions of whether this attitude is characteristically, even though not exclusively, American, and whether it is a satisfactory philosophy of life in itself—in short we may ask whether pragmatism works.

2.

To say that Franklin was a pragmatist is not to imply that he would even understand the accusation were he alive today. As far as I know, the term has been in use in this sense for scarcely more than half a century. In 1907, William James called it "a new name for some old ways of thinking,"[1] and proceeded to put it into the

---

[1] William James delivered a series of lectures on Pragmatism at the Lowell Institute in 1906 and at Columbia University in 1907. These lectures were published in 1907 under the title: *Pragmatism: A New Name for Some Old Ways of Thinking*. Although *The New English Dictionary* gives seven earlier uses of the term, its use in philosophy was invented by C.S. Pierce in discussions with James, and its special meaning was expounded by him in an article "How to Make our Ideas Clear," *Popular Science Monthly*, January, 1878.

philosopher's every-day vocabulary as one more mystification for the layman. It is the same system of thought that has more recently been called instrumentalism because, in the words of James himself, in it "theories thus become *instruments*, not answers to enigmas." It is little more than a point of view, "the attitude of looking away from first things, principles, 'categories,' supposed necessities, and of looking toward last things, fruits, consequences, facts." The result is that "ideas (which themselves are but parts of our experience) become true just insofar as they help us to get into satisfactory relation with other parts of our experience."[2] Ideas, then, have no intrinsic value apart from experience; they are valid only insofar as they can be proved useful in practice. They therefore cannot form a philosophy in the usual sense.

If Pragmatism is not in the full sense a philosophy today, it was even less so in Franklin's time; and Franklin, who did not even have this term by which to describe his point of view, was not a philosopher. It was customary for his contemporaries to call him one, and he himself founded a society which he called philosophical. Recent biographers have continued to use the term in describing him, but it must be remembered that the word "philosopher" in the eighteenth century often meant "natural philosopher," or what we should mean by the term "natural philosopher." This was Franklin's own use of it when he names as resident members of the American Philosophical Society a physician, a botanist, a mathematician, a chemist, a mechanician, a geographer, and a general natural philosopher.[3] This last Franklin himself unquestionably was, and his membership in foreign scientific societies was fit tribute to his attainments in this field. But metaphysician or logician he was not.

The danger of attempting to explain Franklin's mind in terms of systematic philosophy is illustrated by a recent analysis of his thought by Chester Jorgenson who strives to attach him to what he calls "scientific deism," a metaphysical system based upon Newtonian physics and the rationalism of Locke. Mr. Jorgenson develops his thesis at some length and concludes: "To see the reflection of Newton and his progeny in Franklin's activities, be

---

[2] W. James, op. cit., Lecture II, "What Pragmatism Means," pp. 53,54-55.

[3] "A Proposal for Promoting Useful Knowledge among the British Plantations in America." Phila.: May 14, 1743. *Writings*, ed. by A.H. Smyth, New York:1905-07, II, 228-232.

they economic, political, literary, or philosophical, lends a compelling unity to the several sides of his genius, heretofore seen as unrelated." His *modus operandi* is best explained "in reference to the thought pattern of scientific deism."[4] This theory is undeniably suggestive if it be used merely as an explanation of the formative period of Franklin's thought, but Mr. Jorgenson has neglected to give full weight to Franklin's emphatic rejection of the naive system-building of his youth. His short period of philosophical inquiry, 1725-29, ended with his *Modest Inquiry into the Nature and Necessity of* [not Liberty, or God, but] *a Paper Currency*.[5]

Related in so formal a sense I do not believe that the sides of his genius were. To be sure, Franklin absorbed the spirit of inquiry and experiment from the intellectual atmosphere of his day and he may justly be thought of as a product of the eighteenth century enlightenment, but to assume from this that he formulated in his own mind and held to a philosophical basis for his actions is to push a half-truth too far. It would be difficult to document the statement that "Franklin was a disinterested scientist in the sense that he interrogated nature with an eye to discovering its immutable laws."[6] As far as I know, Franklin only once attempted an intellectual and systematic statement of his philosophy. This was in his early pamphlet, *A Dissertation on Liberty and Necessity, Pleasure and Pain* (1725), published when he was only nineteen. By following the logic of his own propositions through, he reached conclusions which seemed to him not to work. Among his surprising results are the statements that, "If there is not such Thing as Free-Will in Creatures, there can be neither Merit nor Demerit in Creatures," and that, "Pleasure is equal to Pain." "I printed a small Number," the old man wrote in looking back over the follies of his youth. "It occasion'd my being more consider'd by Mr. Palmer, as a young Man of some Ingenuity, tho' he seriously Expostulated with me upon the principles of my pamphlet which to him appear'd abominable. My printing of this pamphlet," he concludes, "was another Erratum."[7] That was the beginning and the end of the philosopher Franklin.

---

[4] *Benjamin Franklin, Representative Selections*, with an Introduction, Bibliography, and Notes, by Frank Luther Mott and Chester E. Jorgenson. New York: 1936. Introduction, p. cxli.

[5] *Writings*, II, 133-154.

[6] Ibid., p. cxi.

[7] "Autobiography," *Writings*, I, 277-78.

But another kind of sage was born at that moment, one who lived rather than formulated his thought. Fifty years later he explained to Benjamin Vaughan that "the great uncertainty I found in metaphysical reasonings disgusted me, and I quitted that kind of reading and study for others more satisfactory."[8] If we wish, therefore, to discover a "compelling organic unity" in his thought, we must seek it rather in his attitude and actions than in his expression of theories. The sense of wholeness with which he impresses us is perhaps more accurately attributed by Mr. Van Doren to the fact that "his powers were from first to last in a flexible equilibrium."[9] Where should we look for the secret of that poise?

3.

The first and most obvious field for our inquiry is of course that of scientific experiment, which he insisted in carrying out in spite of the protests of the good Mouse Amos, who lived, according to Robert Lawson, in Ben's fur cap.

"I shall tear the lightening from the skies." Lawson quotes him as saying, "and harness it to do the bidding of man."

"Personally," said the mouse, "I think the sky's an excellent place for it."[10]

The familiar stories of the Pennsylvania fireplace, or the electric kite, or any of the other examples of Franklin's investigative mind would any of them reveal the process of thinking in which I am here interested. Apparently he read the reports of investigations being conducted elsewhere and kept up a correspondence with other experimental scientists, but of theoretical reading there is little record except in his youth. His correspondence with Collinson, Kames, Hartley, and other European thinkers is full of discussions of scientific experiments and political and economic developments, with some practical morality, and no metaphysics. Phenomena themselves first attacted him—smoky chimneys, the common cold, oil on water, lightning striking barns and steeples. Then followed a few simple experiments to determine the conditions under which each operated. When he had satisfied his curiosity on this point, he did not, as would most experimental

---

[8] Passy, November 9, 1979. *Writings*, VII,412.

[9] C. Van Doren, *Benjamin Franklin*. New York:1928,p. 782.

[10] R. Lawson, *Ben and Me*. Boston:1939, p. 41.

scientists, formulate a law or hypothesis and push the problem further into theoretical regions. Rather, he turned about and sought to harness the lightning with rods and wires, make a ladder for his bookshelves, or work out a system of diet and exercise that would check the common cold. Such abstractions as atoms, calories, and vitamins would have had no interest for him. But he was tireless in the observation of phenomena. In a letter to Lord Kames, June 2, 1765, he observes that after wearing green spectacles the page he is reading appears reddish, but draws no conclusions except that here is a relationship between green and red "not yet explained."[11] In another letter, to the Abbe Soulevie, he expresses his preference for that "method of philosophizing, which proceeds upon actual observations, makes a collection of facts, and concludes no further than those facts will warrant." [12] He disciplined his imagination to discover only observable facts and then asked to what use his findings might be put to improve the lot of man, and more particularly of Philadelphians.

It would seem that Franklin's mind ran a similar course with reference to social thinking. His fire company, his postal service, his library, and his newspapers and magazines at home and in other colonies were developed to answer the public need rather than for personal profit alone. Experience in each case pointed out a situation which needed the exercise of his ingenuity, and his solution to the problem was so obvious, once it had been put into practice, that it immediately became public habit. Often it was a scientific discovery which was turned into a social channel and the two currents of his mind flowed together. He had no consistent view of the nature of society other than that dictated by his understanding of the needs of his own country. Rousseau's Sophie, the Comtesse d'Houdetot, made him the hero of a *fete champetre* at her house at Samois, but the social reformer Franklin seems to have shown more interest in the lady than in the theories of the social idealist Rousseau. Adam Smith's *Wealth of Nations*, which appeared in 1776, does not seem to have had much direct influence, although he had met its author in 1759 at the house of Dr. Robertson in Edinburgh. When he reached the conclusion that American independence was inevitable, he joined Jefferson in approving an

---

[11] *Writings*, IV, 380.
[12] Ibid, VIII, 601.

agricultural economy. "There seem to be but three ways for a nation to acquire wealth," he wrote. "The first is by war, as the Romans did, in plundering their conquered neighbours. This is robbery. The second is by commerce, which is generally cheating. The third is by agriculture, the only honest way, wherein man receives a real increase of the seed thrown into the ground, in a kind of continual miracle."[13] Such a simplification of Physiocratic doctrines could only be made by a man who had his eye fixed upon the practical problems of a young and unexploited country.

In the education of youth, he revealed the same lack of concern for abstract theory, the same practical and farsighted wisdom with reference to fact. In his several tracts on educational matters, he stresses the need for the establishment of academies in the colony and outlines a pragmatic curriculum in which facility in speaking and writing, and the reading of contemporary and recent English literature, share with history and natural science the places habitually assigned to logic, theoretical mathematics, and the classics. He even urges that, with this study, excursions might be made "to the neighbouring Plantations of the best Farmers, their Methods observ'd and reason'd upon for the Improvement of Youth."[14] The modern "activity" school which has developed from John Dewey's pragmatic theories of education, with its emphasis upon the study of the immediate environment, is largely a rediscovery of practices which Franklin advocated in 1749. Higher education, with its diversified vocational schools, has followed a similar pattern. To Franklin, it was enough that America needed young men to carry forward the material welfare of the colonies and their people.

A similarly pragmatic attitude is to be discovered in his political thought. Such men as Tom Paine and Jefferson were left to absorb the theories of the French political radicals and to draft the Declaration of Independence while Franklin sat back behind his square spectacles and merely helped it to do its work by writing perhaps his most stinging and famous satire, "Rules by Which a Great Empire may be Reduced." Conciliator that he had been up to this time, he was ready to add a barb to the shaft. Apparent inconsistencies in his position during the years when the revolu-

---

[13] *Writing*, V, 202.

[14] *Proposals Relating to the Education of Youth in Pennsylvania*. Phila.: 1849, Ibid, II, 386-396.

tionary movement in the colonies was taking shape are explained when reference is made to his fact-finding approach to the problem rather than to any systematic political philosophy. Professor Verner Crane has analyzed this problem so carefully and convincingly in the last of his Colver Lectures,[15] and doubtless again in his lecture in this series, that I shall merely agree here with his main point: that Franklin's first ideal was one of federated imperialism, but that colonial loyalty led him to alter his actions in terms of developing circumstances which were beyond his control. The really significant conclusion is not whether he held to this or that political philosophy, but that in the crisis he used his far-sighted understanding of men and events to lead rather than to follow colonial thinking into channels which brought the most satisfactory results, within the limits of possibility. He changed his plan for action with changing circumstances.

4.

When we turn from consideration of scientific, social, and political questions to the more subjective realms of ethics and human relationships, the problems become more difficult and more subject to misunderstanding. This is the real test of the theory I have proposed.

I once asked a loyal scholar of Franklin why he was so much interested in him, why he was willing to devote so much time to a study of him and of his ideas. The answer was immediate and spoken with firm conviction, "Because he knew how to deal with women." If I repeated my question here, I should probably receive a variety of answers, but I suspect that many of them would be variations on the theme, "Because he knew how to deal with life." We are attracted to many great figures of the past because of their ideas or their works; Franklin, I think, draws us because he so obviously worked out a rule of life which brought an unusual degree of satisfaction to him and to most people with whom he came into contact.

There are two kinds of sources which might be used in reformulating Franklin's attitude on personal experience and moral conduct: the record of his relationships with other people, and his own formulation of his ethical code. On a superficial view, the

---

[15]V.W. Crane, *Benjamin Franklin, Englishman and American*. Providence, R.I.: 1936.

conclusions derived from one of these kinds of sources do not agree with those based on the other. There appears to many people an inconsistency between the experimenter with life and people, who emerges from a review of the biographical facts, and the dogmatic moralist of the *Autobiography, Poor Richard*, and some of the letters. So great has this inconsistency appeared to some people that poor old Ben emerges from their studies as little more than a smug hypocrite. "Although I still believe that honesty is the best policy," writes the Englishman D.H. Lawrence, "I dislike policy altogether; though it is just as well not to count your chickens before they are hatched, it's still more hateful to count them with gloating after they *are* hatched. It has taken me many years and countless smarts to get out of that barbed wire moral enclosure that Poor Richard rigged up. Here am I now in tatters and scratched to ribbons, sitting in the middle of Benjamin's America looking at the barbed wire, and the fat sheep crawling under the fence to get fat outside and the watchdogs yelling at the gate lest by chance anyone should get out by the proper exit. Oh America! Oh Benjamin! And I just utter a long loud curse against Benjamin and the American corral.

"Moral America! Most moral Benjamin. Sound, satisfied Ben!"[16]

There has never been a more wrong-headed comment made on Franklin, yet it is easy to see why this romantic, mystical Englishman, who doubtless knew no other Franklin than that he extracted from the *Autobiography* and the *Almanacks*, should rebel against what seemed to him to be a self-appointed Chief Justice of Human Nature:

"Eat not to fulness; drink not to elevation.

"Lose no time, be always employed in something useful; cut off all unnecessary action.

"Avoid extremes, forebear resenting injuries as much as you think they deserve."

Do what you want to do, but don't do too much of it—a "Do" and a "Don't" in every sentence! No wonder that Lawrence found smugness here, and tried to free himself from the inhibitions he had learned from Poor Richard!

---

[16]D.H. Lawrence, *Studies in Classic American Literature*. New York: 1923, p. 21.

But he completely missed the fact that these moral dogmas were not set down for him. In their first forms, they were merely working guides for the young man Franklin, not a final statement of his ideal of perfection. They furnished a means of pinching himself in the arm when he found himself doing something of which he, in the long run, could not approve. And, from his own testimony, such occasions were not rare. Many a good New Year's resolution would make a bad law of the land. The most that the old man Franklin hoped was that some of these little instruments of conduct might be useful to some of his descendants as well. They had been sharpened by his own experience and were of value to him chiefly as a way of paring down his own excesses. He recorded the whole experiment with the detachment of a scientific observer, himself the student and himself the object of study. His proposed book, *The Art of Virtue*, which he never wrote, was intended, he explains, to help those who had lost the better support of Christian faith, to retain at least a working morality.[17]

The frankness of the *Autobiography* has charmed and troubled the critics from the start; charmed because, in simple Addisonian English, Franklin set to work like an honest tradesman to take an inventory of his life, its successes and failures; troubled because the tradesman included in his account the qualities of spirit which for some have an untouchable sanctity. Which is the prude: the man who can evaluate his impulses and measure their consequences or the man who looks upon his own ego as the mysterious, untouchable mystery of the eternal? The elements which make up conduct are no more exempt from Franklin's analysis than are those which control the phenomena of nature. The same scales must be used for weighing one's self that have proved their worth in the weighing of objective nature. Father Abraham's speech (*Poor Richard's Almanack* for 1758) preaches frugality and industry as practical answers to the question of high taxes.[18]

The difficulty of appraising Franklin's moral attitude lies, therefore, in this apparent inconsistency between his obviously experimental way of living and the codified system of controls which he attempts in the early pages of the *Autobiography* and which finds expression in the sayings of Poor Richard and elsewhere. In his writings, Franklin apparently states a theory of conduct first

---

[17] Letter to Lord Kames. *Writings*, IV, 12-13.
[18] *Writings*, III, 408.

and urges others to accept and apply it to themselves; in his own actions he seems to reverse the process, to work experimentally toward an inner equilibrium of desire and control without deliberate formulation of principles until after the fact. The inconsistency is a real one if his statements on moral questions be accepted primarily as an effort to guide others. Unquestionably he is himself to blame. He played the part of the moral teacher, he gave the appearance of wishing to pass on to others his own rules of conduct. But, at the same time, this impression of Franklin as a dogmatic moralist is misleading. Before he was twenty-three he had weighed pleasure against reason in the characters of Philocles and Horatio. The resulting rule of moderation was still his fifty years later when he wrote "The Whistle." It was a rule of living which would always allow a pragmatic test, always be flexible.[19] It is, therefore, important to judge him not so much by what he seemed to be or by what he thought himself to be, as by what he was, and I think it safe to say, even in the face of all the moral aphorisms that dot his pages, that in his own life he tested conduct as he did nature by the experimental method, balancing reason and pleasure anew in each new circumstance. In this view, his proverbs, epigrams, and rules become merely the laboratory note-book of a pragmatic moralist; not texts from a secular pulpit.

"He that falls in love with himself will have no rivals."

Franklin knew that he was very much in love with himself.

"The most exquisite folly is made of wisdom spun to fine." He had tried it himself and given it up.

"We can give advice but we cannot give conduct." He had seen his own admonitions disregarded, as were Father Abraham's.

Such aphorisms as these have the appearance of chemical formulae derived from the test tube. Even the moralistic passages from the *Autobiography* may be so interpreted because Franklin is as conscientious in reporting his failures as he is his successes in living up to his own ideals and rules of conduct. But this interpretation of his moral attitude can scarcely be avoided when the facts of his conduct are reviewed apart from the evidence of the *Autobiography*. It is his lack of dogmatism which charmed in all his personal relationships, his receptivity to the ideas of others, his adjustability to their moods. His comment on his two old Junto

---

[19] *Writings*, II, 157-170

friends, Potts and Parson, would suggest that he recognized things in human nature which wisdom could not alter: "Parson was a wise man that often acted foolishly; Potts a wit that seldom acted wisely. If *enough* were the means to make a man happy, one had always the means of happiness without ever enjoying the thing; the other had always the thing without ever possessing the means. Parsons even in his prosperity always fretting; Potts in the midst of his poverty always laughing. It seems, then, that happiness in this life rather depends on internals than externals; and that, besides the natural effects of wisdom and virtue, vice and folly, there is such a thing as a happy or an unhappy constitution."[20] This is indeed an admission for one who supposedly believed so fully in the correctability of human nature.

Not unlike the misunderstanding of Lawrence is that of those recent critics who have labeled Franklin "the first civilized American," and "the apostle of Modern Times," but the error is of a contrary sort.[21] Phillips Russell and Bernard Fay revolted, as did Lawrence, against the sanctimonious lay-preacher of the misread *Autobiography,* but instead of merely condemning him, they attempt apologies by playing up in a deplorably sensational fashion his wordliness, his cosmopolitan vices, his doubts, and his weaknesses. The resulting pictures are as distorted as that which they set out to correct. The chief value of these books, in spite of the superficiality of the one and the supposedly documented thoroughness of the other, is that they free Franklin from the clutches of Mrs. Grundy and restore him to the more congenial society of Madame Brillon. Ford[22] had allowed the latter lady's confession that she sat on the sage's lap, but other evidence even more damaging was as yet unrevealed. After the bad taste and the misrepresentation of the Russell book had opened the way, it was possible for Mr. Van Doren and others to discuss, without apology, the presence of illegitimacy in the Franklin family to the fourth generation, cut short there by untimely death. And after the Fay book, it was easier to appreciate Franklin's life as a struggle with himself and with circumstances. The starch was washed out of the bourgeois saint.

---

[20] *Writings*, III, 457.

[21] P. Russell, *Benjamin Franklin, the First Civilized American*. New York: 1926. B. Fay, *Franklin, the Apostle of Modern Times*. Boston: 1929.

[22] P.L. Ford, *The Many-Sided Franklin*. New York: 1899.

Such revelations and interpretations are in themselves of no moment except to prove once and for all that Franklin's moral aphorisms were expressed with conviction because moderation was for him an acquired art rather than a result of prudish inhibitions. They reassure us that he was a human being who developed character and kindliness by facing life squarely and evaluating it in its various and contradictory moods as it presented itself to him. The moralizing of the old man was the summary of a life which had been richly, if not always wisely or even admirably lived. *Poor Richard* was the note-book of a laboratory moralist.

It is hardly necessary to review for this audience the many evidences of Franklin's kindly interest in others, particularly in young people, throughout his long life. Mr. Stifler's[23] collection of his correspondence with Polly Stevenson and the Shipley girls, covering more than thirty years, is almost testimony enough. But to this may be added a list of all those young men whom he stimulated and aided to successful lives through the Junto, by means of letters of introduction as in the case of Tom Paine, and by setting them up in business for themselves after an apprenticeship with him. And if evidences of his tolerance be sought, his treatment of Arthur Lee and Silas Deane, both of whom he refused openly to condemn even when the tide of popular feeling was strong against them, might be sufficient. It may be argued that good business sense and self-interest led Franklin to set his partners up in the printing and publishing business in neighboring colonies, but no such explanation can be given for his willingness to accept the risk of public stigma rather than to denounce the weaknesses of his diplomatic associates.

These instances are taken from widely spread epochs in his life, and the latter ones reveal even more patience and kindliness than do the earlier ones. Franklin verified by experience his early belief that more flies are caught by molasses than by vinegar, that a world in which people get on with each other is happier and more comfortable than one in which they do not. Perhaps this point of view is sufficient explanation of the change in his political philosophy from a belief in British federation to one in American independence. His moral philosophy was as pragmatic and adjustable as was his political.

---

[23]J.M. Stifler, *My Dear Girl; the Correspondence of Benjamin Franklin with Polly Stevenson, Georgiana and Catherine Shipley*. New York: 1927.

5.

In no sphere of experience, however, is this trial-and-error method of Franklin's more dramatically revealed than in that of religion. Those who would accept his guidance for the whole of life must follow him through to this, and it is here that many of his warmest admirers are forced to stop. Because he was so nearly successful in depriving God himself of his mystery, he shocks many a potential disciple who admires his experimental approach to problems of science, society, and politics, and even those who are willing to apply with him the same methods to the problems of human conduct.

A careful analysis of Franklin's religious beliefs and practices would demand a review of 18th century Deism, but once more I shall be content with a discussion of his attitude alone. Again he is more interested in a workable practice of religion than in the formulated dogmatisms and skepticisms of his age. Brought up in a society which accepted a dogmatic Calvinism, the same revolt which took him to Philadelphia carried him over spiritually to the company of the religious doubters who owed their Deistic beliefs to Newton and Locke in the first instance. His first experiments in formulating a faith of his own show the traces of both influences, but they proved unsatisfying. He soon gave up the attempt to define the nature and scope of the power of God when his reasoning brought him to the conclusion that freedom of the will was a logical impossibility but a practical necessity. A system of living founded upon such premises would not work and was therefore not for him. Yet he felt the need of a God to whom he could pray. The resulting Deity was little more than a fellow-traveler, one who stood ready with his higher authority to sanction the actions which experience taught him were best. Franklin, I believe, never defined his Deity in these words, but in all his contacts with religious sects and religious people, he asked only that whatever God they might profess would prove his goodness by directing them into the wise and virtuous ways of living. He tells us that, religiously educated a Presbyterian, he attended no services for public worship with any regularity because he became impatient with theological discussion. Nevertheless he recognized the practical virtues of the churches as agencies for the public welfare, and was willing to contribute to any sect that would serve the civil interests as well as their own. For the same reason he welcomed and supported George Whitefield when he came to Philadelphia in 1739, and his justification for joining the Masons was that God judges men more for what they do than for what they think.[24] His *Articles of Belief and Acts of Religion*(1728),[25] written at the age of 22, posits a Deistic Christian God who has infinite power but is above using it arbitrarily, and a curious hierarchy of beings superior to man that is suggestive of pagan pantheism. The most important clause in this creed, however, is the statement that God is good and wise, and therefore Benjamin Franklin of Philadelphia sees every reason for making Him his friend. In this spirit of independence, he proceeds to his devotions as he would to a conversation with a superior moral adviser for whom he feels deep reverence. All of his later religious efforts, including his proposed abridgement of the *Book of Common Prayer*, were designed to make more easy and immediate the every-day intercourse between man, the superior of the animals, and God, the supreme in wisdom and judgment of all beings. But in his most religious moods, this intercourse was still in the nature of a conversation between one being and another. Surely no one has ever devised a more helpful God, but the experience of religious exultation is lacking in the relationship. It was for immediate and practical aid that he urged the Constitutional Convention of 1786 to turn to God, and the psychological effect of his suggestion was good.[26] Franklin's pragmatic attitude seems to stand this final test; he created and clung to a God who helped him discover how to live, and allowed him to make the discovery for himself. With other problems of the nature and function of the Deity he early lost interest. And when Ezra Stiles asked him a month before his death, to state his opinion on the Divinity of Christ, he replied: "It is a question I do not dogmatize upon, having never studied it, and think it needless to busy myself with it now, when I expect soon an Opportunity of knowing the Truth with less Trouble."

---

[24]Letter to Josiah Franklin, April 13, 1838. *Writings*, II, 214-16.

[25] *Writings*, II, 91-100.

[26]M. Farrand, *The Records of the Federal Convention of 1787*. Rev. ed. 4 v. New Haven: 1937, I, 450-52.

6.

Franklin's ways of thinking and living may be distinguished from those of his European contemporaries like Voltaire and Johnson in that they were so characteristically American. The particular form which his pragmatism took was a result of his participation as a principal actor in the greatest mass movement of civilization that history records. Lewis Mumford summarizes it in a sentence: "The settlement of America had its origins in the unsettlement of Europe."[27] Never before had man made so deliberate and so ambitious an effort to transfer a matured civilization to a primitive land. The movements of Greek culture to Rome and of Latin culture to England are trifling when compared to the gigantic task of transferring the culture of Western Europe to American shores. Nor was the contrast between the sophistication of the culture and the barbarism of the land ever so striking. Historians have labeled the effort "the frontier movement" and have more and more, since Frederick Jackson Turner defined it in 1893, come to realize that much in American cultural history can be better explained when referred to this basic factor. Franklin lived at a time when the frontier culture of the eastern seaboard colonies was reaching maturity through a painful adolescence. As a result, his pragmatism has a peculiarly American flavor, a vitality and aggressiveness which the tired skepticism of contemporary European thinkers lacked. Whatever his predilections may be toward a life of contemplation and dogmatic belief, the American philosopher from the earliest days has been forced out of his assumptions and into a mold of vigorous pragmatism by the very circumstances of his life. However sound his philosophy when kept in the realm of theory, and however admirable his love of security and retirement for contemplation, the immediate need for action has always been too great to allow any system of thinking which cannot justify itself by providing swiftly the needs and the minimal comforts of life. "America was promises," sings our latest Laureate Archibald MacLeish; but the American is pragmatist. He must make some of the promises work.

I should like to ask your indulgence for perhaps too long a digression at this point because I feel that we can only appreciate

---

[27]L. Mumford, *The Golden Day*. New York: 1926, p. 11.

Franklin's pragmatism by discovering the same trait in other Americans and seeing it as a dominant strain throughout the long history of our intellectual development.

It takes little argument to prove that the original settlers in this country were primarily concerned with practical problems. Those who were not, did not live to produce books or descendants. Even when they were motivated by religious ideals as were the Plymouth colonists and the Pennsylvania Quakers, their first acts were such common sense translations of their theories into workable practices as the *Plymouth Compact* and the classic treaty with the Indians. And even when the colonies were fairly settled, there was more debate on problems of economics and government than upon the abstractions of philosophy and the amenities of literature. In the famous *Bloudy Tenent* controversy itself, Roger Williams was protesting persecution for cause of conscience as a working principle of throttling free speech in a democracy rather than as a scholastic dogma. It was more than a century before the colonies produced in Jonathan Edwards a philosopher who is worthy to take rank among original and systematic thinkers, and almost two hundred years before that type of literature which is concerned with the pleasures and amenities of life took shape in Cooper, Irving, and Bryant. The great theorist of the Revolution, Tom Paine, had few original ideas and devoted his energies to applying the principles which he had learned in his reading to the problems which his adopted country faced in the fact.

This unusual phenomenon of a whole nation working in accord with a philosophy which it had not, in almost two centuries, had time to formulate is commented on some years later by the astute Frenchman, de Toqueville: "I think that in no country in the civilized world is less attention paid to philosophy than in the United States," he writes. "The Americans have no philosophical school of their own; and they care but little for all the schools in which Europe is divided, the very names of which are scarcely known to them. Yet it is easy to perceive that almost all the inhabitants of the United States conduct their understanding in the same manner, and govern it by the same rules. Each American appeals to the individual exercise of his own understanding alone. As it is on their own testimony that they are accustomed to rely, they like to discern the object which engages their attention with extreme clearness; they therefore strip off as much as possible all that covers it, they rid themselves of whatever separates them from it, they remove whatever conceals it from sight, in order to view it more closely and in the broad light of day."[28]

With this shrewd explanation of the American habit of pragmatic independence of mind, even such idealists as Emerson and Thoreau consent to fall into the pattern. Kenneth Murdock has pointed out that the Puritans themselves were men of affairs and tied their idealism closely into their daily lives.[29] By 1840, Puritanism had stripped itself of all the inhibitions and regimentations of theological dogma, and life could be defined and lived as a new testing of experience each day by each individual. Emerson came very near to formulating an ethical philosophy, even though he failed to systematize his metaphysics and esthetics. In *The American Scholar*, in 1837, he preached an idealization of the moral code of which Franklin was, in many respects, an example. Impatience with books as books is countered by a plea for closer communion with nature and for action. Franklin's nature was of the human variety, but we can easily imagine him, granted Emerson's gift of tongues, speaking the following lines: "If it were only for a vocabulary, the scholar would be covetous of action. Life is our dictionary. Years are well spent in country labors; in towns; in the insight into trades and manufactures; in frank intercourse with many men and women; in science; in art; to the one end of mastering in all their facts a language by which to illustrate and embody our perceptions. Life lies behind us as the quarry from which we get tiles and copestones for the masonry of to-day."[30]

I am fully aware that in calling Emerson a pragmatist, at least in some phases of his thought, I am flying in the face of much of the traditional interpretation of his attitude, although I am not alone among his recent critics in committing this crime. Frederick Ives Carpenter writes: "Emerson's philosophy may perhaps be described as a Pragmatic Mysticism. It is idealistic in that it puts the mystical experience first. It is dualistic in that it looks both ways from its position on the bridge between soul and nature. It is monistic in that it maintains that this bridge is the only reality. But

---

[28]A. de Toqueville, *Democracy in America*, trans. by H. Reeve. new York: 1898, II, 1-7.

[29]K. Murdock, "The Puritan Tradition," *The Reinterpretation of American Literature*, edited by Norman Foerster, New York: 1928, p. 105.

[30]R.W. Emerson, *Works* (Cent. Ed.), I, 97-98.

it is pragmatic in that it tests all truths (including the mystical belief in the value of life) by experience.

"It remains to suggest," continues Mr. Carpenter, "that this pragmatic mysticism is essentially *the* American philosophy."[31] With this conclusion I am inclined heartily to agree although it has been pointed out convincingly that Emerson, in his more mystical moods, rejects the experimental attitude toward physical facts which is characteristic of the pragmatism of Franklin and of other more practical people from William Penn to William James. But the discovery of pragmatism in any sense in Emerson is akin to the sensational. In him, and perhaps also in Thoreau, Whitman, and the other leaders of the mid-nineteenth century renaissance of idealism in literature and life, the mystical is more important than the circumstantial experience. But if we compare these idealists with European literary men and philosophers of the same general stamp, like Coleridge, Goethe, and Kant, the horns of the Yankee tradesman appear above the all-seeing eye.

Throughout the American experience, therefore, our chief problem has been the adjustment of an extreme form of pragmatic individualism, demanded by the circumstances of our civilization, to the fundamental hunger of human nature for something higher and better than it can obtain in this world. The purer forms of idealism have seldom taken root in our soil because of the urgency of the pragmatic challenge, especially in the early days. Franklin, more successfully than any other Colonial, faced this issue and was temperamentally able to make the adjustment which the circumstances of his time and country demanded. He reduced religion to practical ethics and he tested conduct by experience. Emerson, a mystic by temperament, found his ethics, as his Puritan forefathers had done before him, on the same pragmatic base. It was left for William James to return to the foundations which Franklin had laid by the pattern of his life and to formulate a theory which Franklin had lived without formulation. There is much reason to believe that this modern pragmatism is the characteristic American philosophy, the one which our experience had dictated from the start. We may not each of us accept it without qualifications for ourselves, but as a people we have learn-

---

[31]F.I. Carpenter, *Ralph Waldo Emerson, Representative Selections*, New York: 1934. Introduction, p. xxxvii.

ed it and applied it throughout our history. We may, like Emerson and many another American, feel the need for accepting the mystical experience and explaining the universe in terms of a polarity rather than of a single point of reference. But in Franklin's singleness lay his strength and his unity. It might prove a sanitive to these troubled times and to the many troubled minds living in them to return more frequently to the study of a man whose philosophy was himself, and who discovered how to make himself whole by rejecting no part of the life about him, and sane by keeping it in control. On such a foundation we may build according to our various temperaments and needs.

EDITOR'S NOTE

Spiller emphasizes Franklin's pragmatic attitude. Since 1943 other intellectual historians have noted that Franklin's attitude toward life was a pragmatic one. Max Savelle attributed to Franklin and other eighteenth-century American thinkers an "embryonic pragmatism" which could be traced to Francis Bacon but which was more suited to American conditions than to Europe's.[1] Joseph L. Blau has found intimations of a pragmatic attitude in Franklin's "schemes for the improvement of himself and his community," Jonathan Edwards's "criteria for the graciousness of affections," and Ralph Waldo Emerson's "argument for an ideal philosophy."[2]

---

[1]Max Savelle, *Seeds of Liberty: The Genesis of the American Mind* (New York: A.A. Knopf, 1948), pp. 176-178.

[2]Joseph L. Blau, *Men and Movements in American Philosophy* (New York: Prentice-Hall, 1955), p. 230.

Benjamin Franklin: Philosophical Revolutionist

BERNHARD KNOLLENBERG

Bernhard Knollenberg (1892-1973) practiced law from 1916 to 1938. In 1938 he became the Librarian of the Yale University Library, and served in that position until 1944. An authority in the history of Revolutionary America, he is the author of *Origin of the American Revolution* (1960), *Growth of the American Revolution, 1766-1775* (1975), and several studies of George Washington. His essay in this volume should be compared with Robert E. Spiller's. Franklin's critical evaluation of canons of thought and proposed solutions to life's problems, implied in such questions as "Is this logical? Does it hold water? Does it work?", suggested to Spiller the pragmatic attitude and to Knollenberg the philosophical revolutionist.

A Paper delivered at the "Meet Dr. Franklin" Conference in 1940.

I am so much interested in Franklin that I accepted your invitation to speak in this series of Franklin Memorial lectures without first inquiring as to my topic. I was later pleasantly surprised to learn that it was to be "Franklin as a Philosophical Revolutionist." This is a side of his character which is especially interesting to me and which has never been fully developed, though there are many sidelights on it in Mr. Van Doren's fine book.

Until the latter work appeared, the most careful study of Franklin's life was William Cabell Bruce's "Benjamin Franklin Self Revealed." Yet even Bruce profoundly misread Franklin's character in declaring that "By nature and training Franklin was profoundly conservative at the core." This means, I take it, that Bruce considered Franklin a person who tended to accept and adhere to the existing order of things, whereas, Franklin was in fact the very opposite of this. For from the beginning to the end of his life, we find him approaching every canon of thought or conduct with the question, "Is this logical? Does it hold water? Shall I be bound by it?"—no matter how old and generally accepted the idea, tradition or rule might be. True, he was cautious; he was shrewd; he was temperate. This, however, shows, I think, not that he was conservative but that he was wise; that he challenged the

163

status quo with the approach of the philosopher; that, in short, he was a *philosophical* revolutionist.

My grounds for this view are numerous and diverse. To begin with, one of the relatively few things we know about Franklin's youth is that he early challenged the established religious teachings of his day. His first serious difficulty, when a boy of only fifteen in Boston, arose out of his articles in his brother's newspaper and some challenging remarks in conversation about religious matters. True, his brother's harshness to the young printing apprentice may have been a factor, but, to judge from the "Autobiography," the decisive reason for Franklin's taking French leave from his apprenticeship was that things were getting a little hot for him among those resentful of his rebellious, revolutionary attitude toward the religious tenets of the community.

Again, when we get to Pennsylvania, we find evidence not only of the industry, economy, shrewdness in business we read and hear so much about, but also of his challenge to the established system of government in Pennsylvania. The wealthy and powerful Penn family, the proprietors of the province, their governor and satellites, were in a position to be most helpful to the ambitious Franklin by throwing printing business his way. But they were insisting that their relation to the colony was the same as that of the King of the royal colonies; that it would be as logically and legally indefensible for the legislature in Pennsylvania to tax the lands owned by the proprietors as for the legislatures in the royal colonies to tax the lands owned by the Crown. Franklin, approaching this question with his challenging mind, said: Why should these proprietors be exempt from taxation? As the community is developed, as peasants and yeomen come here from abroad and improve their lands, they are going to increase the value of these proprietors' lands. Whey should the proprietors receive that increase in value, while paying nothing in the meantime towards maintaining the community that is enriching them? The revolutionist, Henry George, you will recall, stressed that idea many years later.

I do not contend that Franklin was unique in holding this view. It is one of those ideas that might strike any intelligent mind at any time. But I think it was original in the sense that it was Franklin's own insight and reasoning that led him to take this, at that time, revolutionary stand.

Franklin's approach to science was another illustration of his revolutionist tendencies. The outstanding scientists have, of course, all had challenging minds—have all, in a sense, been revolutionists in their respective fields. But many able and useful scientists are not revolutionists. They may be teachers or conductors of research along previously well-defined lines. Most of them would not, if they had lived in Franklin's time and place, have risked playing with the sacrilegious idea that lightning—that threat of divine punishment for the wicked, more immediately visible than hell fire—was really but a manifestation of the "electric fluid" which the experimentally-minded were having so much fun collecting in Leyden jars. But Franklin, with the boldness, the openness of mind, the determination to try to find and act on the truth, irrespective of tradition, that marks the revolutionist, made his great discovery that lightning was but a large-scale electrical discharge.

Though I am later going to give further grounds for my thesis that Franklin was a thorough-going revolutionist, I shall stop for a moment to contrast Franklin with some others who were of a somewhat different calibre, and point out the essential difference between their revolutionism and Franklin's.

As you think back over the famous revolutionists who have cropped up in history, you will recall that most of them were highly pugnacious persons. This is, I think, one reason that so many of them have been, or started out to be, lawyers; the same instinct for the argumentative that made the lawyers' profession attractive led them to challenge certain of the established tenets held by those around them. Such men are likely to be revolutionists in but a single chosen field, while remaining otherwise conservative. Furthermore, even within the special field in which they became celebrated they are likely to revert to conservatism. Luther, perhaps the most noted of these in the field of religion, is an example of this familiar type. Highly pugnacious and, in most respects a hide-bound conservative, he eventually became extremely dogmatic and inflexible even in the field of religion. Incidentally, Luther, as you probably recall, started out to be a lawyer. Another of the same kind was Patrick Henry. Having had his day as a political revolutionist, he eventually became one of the conservative leaders of Virginia.

Another group of revolutionists are those who, having suffered injury at the hands of the existing political or economic order, strike out against it in the frenzy of their anguish or in the desire for revenge. Thomas Paine, and most of the Russian revolutionists seem to have been of this type. This fact may account for the iron-bound rule into which after Lenin's death, the Russian Revolution appears to have developed.

Franklin does not belong in either of these categories. He had no bitter scores to pay off, and, far from his revolutionism being but a passing phase, we find him a consistent challenger throughout life. The question: Is the existing way the sound way, never ceased to ring in his ears.

Take the part in which he made his most enduring contribution: his part in the American Revolution. Franklin was not like Washington, a tobacco planter, exploited and knowing that he was exploited by the British law requiring his tobacco to be sent exclusively to Britain, thereby restricting his market and reducing his profits. He was not a large owner of slaves, one of whose essential elements of food—salt—and most of whose clothing—the rough Osnaburg cloth—coming from the continent of Europe, must be imported through Great Britain so that the British merchant could take his toll. (I do not mean to imply by this comparison that economic motives alone swayed Washington, but his letters show how how important a part they played in forming his views.) Franklin was a clear gainer from his connection with the British Empire.

He held a lucrative job in the British Colonial Post Office Department. His newspapers flourished in part as a result of his connections with the British Government. His son, William, was appointed by the King to the governorship of New Jersey. When Franklin looked at the British government from the standpoint of gain or loss to himself, he must have realized that he was a beneficiary, not a victim, of the connection. Yet when the question of British taxation began acutely to present itself, we find his revolutionary character, his inevitable challenge to the existing, but logically indefensible order, slowly but surely unfolding.

In his first published statement on the matter in 1766, at the time the repeal of the Stamp Act was under consideration, Franklin said in his famous hearing before the House of Commons:

> I never heard any objection to the right of laying duties to regulate commerce; but a right to lay internal taxes was never supposed to be in Parliament, as we are not represented there.

Although he may conceivably have been concealing his feelings, I think it fair to assume that this was Franklin's honest approach to the question.

Later, after thinking the matter over more carefully, we find him writing on March 13, 1768, to his son William,

> The more I have thought and read on the subject the more I find myself confirmed in the opinion that no middle doctrine can be well maintained, I mean not clearly with intelligible arguments. Something might be made of either of the extremes; that Parliament has a power to make *all laws* for us or that it has a power to make *no laws* for us; and I think the argument for the latter more numerous and weighty, than those for the former.

Two years later we find a further development. At that time, in writing to an old friend—Samuel Cooper—Franklin is no longer balancing things this way and that. He says flatly

> I could wish that such Expressions as the Supreme Authority of Parliament...were no longer seen in our publick Pieces. They...tend to confirm a Claim of subjects in one Part of the King's dominions to be Sovereign over their Fellow Subjects in another Part of his Dominions, when in truth they have no such Right, and their Claim is founded only in Usurpation.

He concedes that the King has certain rights as the source of the colonial charters, but maintains that Parliament as a law-making body had no power whatsoever over the Colonies.

From this it was an easy transition to the view, expressed in a letter to Thomas Cushing, Speaker of the House of Representatives in Massachusetts, July 1773, in which, for the first time, Franklin puts himself squarely on record in favor of a program smacking strongly of treason. He writes Cushing that the Colonies

> should engage firmly with each other that they will never grant Aids to the Crown in any General War, till those rights are recognized by the King and both Houses of Parliament; communicating at the same time to the Crown this their Resolution.

The next step was, of course, the final one of open rebellion, when in 1776, as might be expected, we find Franklin among the five members of Congress who drafted the Declaration of Independence.

Unlike some of the other prominent signers, however, there was, in Franklin's case, no relapse into conservatism.

Death alone put an end to his challenging mind and the readiness to follow wherever the challenge might lead him. In November 1789, when Pennsylvania was going through the throes of a great constitutional crisis, the question arose whether a second house should be added to the Pennsylvania Legislature, to represent, not the people as a whole, but the wealth of the State. The wealthy—and Franklin was at the time one of the wealthy men of the State—were thus in effect to have a veto power over the legislation passed by the "mobility." But Franklin strongly opposed the bill, and replying to an article in the Federal Gazette of November 3, 1789, wrote in a memorandum headed "Queries and Remarks":

And why is property to be represented at all? The accumulation of property and its security to individuals in every society must be in effect the protection afforded it by the joint strength of the society in the executive of its law. Private property, therefore, is a creature of society and is subject to the call of that society whenever its necessities shall require, even to its last farthing.

This is a doctrine not far from Karl Marx's "from each according to his abilities, to each according to his needs" of a half century later; a doctrine which Lenin and some other well-known revolutionists have put into action in our present century.

To come back then to the statement of Bruce, I think that he must have been making the common error of using the term "conservative" as the equivalent of cautious, temperate, philosophic, wise. Franklin was all of these, but, far from being "at the core," a conservative, he was a revolutionist of extraordinary consistency. I will take a few moments more of your time to say a word, as I was asked to do, about our Mason-Franklin Collection at the Yale University Library. Most of you know something about this collection. But it is not generally known that of the unpublished Franklin letters in the collection, two of the finest were written to distinguished Pennsylvania colonials. The first is to Joseph Galloway, Franklin's closest American friend in middle life, who, unable to follow him in his career of political revolution, went to England as one of the loyalists. The second is to the Quaker, Isaac Norris, for many years Speaker of the Assembly in colonial Pennsylvania.

I hope Philadelphians will some day give a little more recognition to these two men, especially Galloway. Perhaps a visit to the Mason-Franklin Collection at Yale will move one of you to write a life of this man, so far more worthy of a biography than most of the people about whom books are written these days. I should enjoy showing you this Collection, for your presence and close attention indicate that you share my deep interest in your greatest citizen, the philosophical revolutionist, Benjamin Franklin.

EDITOR' NOTE

Two studies of Joseph Galloway have been published in recent years: Benjamin H. Newcomb, *Franklin and Galloway: A Political Partnership* (New Haven: Yale University Press, 1972) and John E. Ferling, *The Loyalist Mind: Joseph Galloway and the American Revolution* (University Park: Pennsylvania State University Press, c1977).

Looking Westward

GILBERT CHINARD

Gilbert Chinard (1881-1972) was the Pyne Professor of French Literature at Princeton University from 1937 to 1950. He wrote numerous books on eighteenth-century Americans, especially Thomas Jefferson.

Long before the Declaration of Independence, two entirely different and opposite views of the future of America manifested themselves in the British colonies. They corresponded in fact to two different philosophies of life: one reflecting what might be called an old world or European point of view; the other one already embodying some of the most essential features of what was to become the doctrine of Americanism.

It has been often observed that men modify very slowly their intellectual habits even in new surroundings. Despite new conditions and new ways of life, for a long time, many colonists failed to realize the limitless potentialities of the country in which they had established "plantations." Their thoughts continued to run in accustomed channels, even when they began to think of the new settlements as a sort of unit having an entity and rights of its own. One of the common sense conclusions, which had been reached before Montesquieu had given to it a final and almost axiomatic form, was that great danger lay in territorial expansion and in mere size. Between the ideal of a perfectly ordained society, which prevailed chiefly in New England, and the vast expanse of land extending beyond the horizon, existed a sort of antinomy. For various reasons, colonists had left the mother country, but they turned their eyes towards Europe; one of their chief preoccupations was to implant in the howling wilderness a form of life as closely resembling English life as they could. For generations they had watched the wars waged on the continent and had participated in them. The lessons of history and experience were clear: a small population occupying a large territory was at the mercy of powerful and envious neighbors. They had learned that frontiers have to be protected and defended and, in the North, already they were

171

hard pushed by the ambitious and "turbulent Gallicks" who, aided by their Indian allies, raided the isolated farmhouses and small settlements. To expand towards the West, at least before a strong civilization had developed along the Atlantic coast line, was to multiply the existing dangers.

An entirely different conception appeared in what has been called the pioneer or the frontier spirit. A yearning for adventure, a temperamental restlessness, an inability to adapt oneself to the give and take of a strongly knit society, much more than a thirst for riches, impelled many other colonists to look beyond the mountains, to dream of new territories to explore and settle, of fertile land to till, of unlimited spaces and unlimited possibilities. Thus was established the psychological foundation of the theory of "Manifest Destiny" which appeared very early in the history of the country. It was a dynamic conception of America, clashing with the static conception of fixed boundaries. To use a modern illustration, the first one corresponded to a horizontal development such as can be observed in the expansion of Western cities; the other to a vertical growth typified by the skyline of New York City.

Already during the colonial period, the issue was clearly defined; the problem became more pressing after the colonies had decided to sever the bonds which made them part of the British Empire. Was America to develop along the same lines as the European nations, concentrating a large population on a relatively small territory? More precisely, were the people who called themselves Americans to accept the natural boundaries which seemed to have been pre-established for them: on the North, Canada; on the West, the mountains. Were they justified, on the contrary, in entertaining the dream and the vision of an ever increasing population expanding westward, at least to the Mississippi and ultimately to the Pacific coast? To the first group belonged such men as John Adams and those of the New Englanders whose eyes were turned towards the West Indies and Europe. To the second, Thomas Jefferson who, from his very childhood had been in close contact with the frontier, and, curiously enough, Benjamin Franklin.

We have been so accustomed to thinking of Franklin in terms of Poor Richard's Almanac, as a world wise philosopher, slow and sure-footed, that we are apt to forget the adventurous lad who left Boston to explore the world, a restless, versatile, not easily curbed young man with a fervid imagination. As a point of fact, one should never speak of Franklin without keeping in mind at least the title of an old article of Paul Leicester Ford: "The Many-sided Franklin." It cannot be denied that he was a benign philosopher, the most European of all the Americans of his generation, the first American "bourgeois," a practical scientist and a theorist. But the grandfatherly "Papa Franklin" of the rue de Passy, the astute diplomat and the clear-minded patriot had worn in his youth the leather jacket of the hunter. In every American, even in our day, there is a "Westerner,"and the most sedate ones have not been untouched by the pioneering spirit.

With the West, this Boston-born printer and newspaperman had a first hand acquaintance, which he would never have obtained if he had remained in New England. Philadelphia has gained a reputation for level-headedness, frugality and wisdom largely because the whole trend of life in the city seems to be colored by the traditional and not wholly legendary Quaker and Franklinian characteristics. In the eighteenth century, however, it offered to the observer a curious mixture of advanced culture and pioneering ambitions. Very early and of necessity, the Philadelphians had to look westward, towards the mountains, and beyond the mountains, where began the rich region of the Ohio, the primeval wilderness and the limitless plains. There extended, at the back door of the colony, an enormous territory where the Indians roamed, and in which the French had established outposts. To limit oneself voluntarily and deliberately is one thing; to feel that one's future development may be determined and hampered by the presence and threats of a none too friendly nation is quite another matter, which cannot be easily dismissed.

As early as 1751, Benjamin Franklin became keenly aware of that situation and took position as an advocate of a greater America. Putting down his "Observations concerning the increase of mankind, peopling of countries, etc." he sketched out a grandiose picture of the development of the British colonies in North America:

There is, in short, no Bound to the prolific Nature of Plants or Animals, but what is made by their crowding and interfering with each other's means of Subsistence. Was the Face of the Earth vacant of other Plants, it might be gradually sowed and over-spread with one Kind only; as, for Instance, with Fennel; and were it empty of other Inhabitants, it might in a few Ages be replenish'd from one Nation only; as, for Instance, with *Englishmen*. Thus there are suppos'd to be now upwards of One Million *English* Souls in *North America*, (tho' 'tis thought scarce 80,000 have been brought over Sea,) and yet perhaps there is not one the fewer in *Britain*, but rather many more, on Account of the Employment the Colonies afford to Manufacturers at Home. This Million doubling, suppose but once in 25 years, will, in another Century, be more than the People of *England*, and the greatest Number of *Englishmen* will be on this Side of the Water. What an Accession of Power to the *British* Empire by Sea as well as by Land! What Increase of Trade and Navigation! What Numbers of Ships and Seamen! We have been here but little more than 100 years, and yet the Force of our Privateers in the late War, united, was greater, both in Men and Guns, than that of the whole *British* Navy in Queen *Elizabeth's* Time. How important an Affair then to *Britain* is the present Treaty for settling the Bounds between her Colonies and the *French*, and how careful should she be to secure Room enough, since on the room depends on much the Increase of her People. (Smyth ed. III, 71.)

There spake the seer and the prophet, but who could fail to recognize the pioneer in the concluding boast that "we are, as I may call it, *Scouring* our Planet, by *clearing America* of Woods, and so making this Side of our Globe reflect a brighter Light to the Eyes of the Inhabitants in *Mars* or *Venus?*" Almost exactly a century later, in 1856, another American reviewing the work done by the pioneers and their epic battle against the forest, was to sing of the "lands of the make of the axe". The "many-sided" Franklin thus happens to be one of the unexpected but authentic predecessors of Walt Whitman.

In 1751, Franklin could only speak of the West by hearsay; in 1753, after travelling the rough trail to the newly settled village of Carlisle, as a member of the Commission which was to meet with representatives of the Six Nations, he came into direct contact with the backwood country and the American wilderness. It is well known that the famous plan adopted a year later by "the Commissioners assembled at Albany in July, 1754," was a direct result of the conclusions drawn by Franklin from his Western experience. The objects of the plan were twofold. The necessity of uniting the colonies for their mutual defense and security was emphasized and constituted the strongest appeal for a union; but, tucked away among the considerations, was an article recognizing that "The establishing of new colonies Westward on the Ohio and the Lakes, a matter of considerable importance to the increase of the British trade and power, to the breaking that of the French...would be best carried on by a joint union."

The chapter entitled "Indian Purchases" made it even plainer that the plan did not contemplate "freezing" the territorial possessions of the colonies as they were, and admitted that "several of the colony charters in America extend their bounds to the South Seas, which may be perhaps three or four thousand miles in length to one hundred or two hundred miles in breadth..." Another chapter was frankly headed "New Settlements." It was proposed that 'the Grand Council' "make new settlements on such purchases, by granting lands in the King's name." To prevent the monopolization of the land by big purchasers, the grants were to be divided in small tracts. "Strong forts on the Lakes, the Ohio, etc., may at the same time they secure our present frontiers, serve to defend new colonies settled under their protection." Finally the whole scheme was revealed in the paragraph which read: "A particular colony has scarce strength enough to extend itself by new settlements, at so great a distance from the old; but the joint force of the Union might suddenly establish a new colony or two in those parts or extend an old colony to particular passes, greatly to the security of our present frontiers, increase of trade and people, breaking off the French communication between Canada and Louisiana, and speedy settlement of the intermediate lands." The plan adopted by the Albany Convention was premature and came to naught, but Franklin found time to put down on paper very definite proposals "For settling two Western colonies in North America, with reasons for the plan." (Smyth, III, 358.) The "Plan" started with an almost lyrical description of the country to be settled:

> The great country back of the Appalachian Mountains, on both sides of the Ohio, and between that river and the Lakes is now well known, both to the English and French, to be one of the finest in North America, for the extreme richness and fertility of the land; the healthy temperature of the air, and mildness of the climate; the plenty of hunting, fishing and fowling; the facility of trade with the Indians; and the vast convenience of inland navigation or water-carriage by the Lakes and great rivers, many hundreds of miles around.

Then came the claim that this rich country which "must undoubtedly (perhaps in less than another century) become a populous and powerful dominion" was indispensable for the natural development of the British colonies: "Our people, being confined to the country between the sea and the mountains, cannot much more increase in number; people increasing in proportion to their room and means of subsistence.''

Franklin's thesis was now complete. It had become a matter of life or death to prevent the junction between the French colonies of Louisiana and Canada, for such a junction would have "cut off" the British colonies from all commerce and alliance with the Western Indians and, at the same time, caused untold "inconveniences and mischiefs.''

What he had proposed as a political philosopher, he even tried to put into effect as a soldier, in that curious episode of his career when he organized the militia and, without any military commission whatsoever, led them to the defense of Western Pennsylvania. But the main object remained the settlement of the country west of the mountains. As he wrote to Peter Collinson, on June 20, 1755: "It is certain that People enough may be had, to make a strong English settlement or two in those parts. I wish to see it done, and I am almost indifferent how or by whom it is done. . . . ''

So urgent was the need and so imperious the necessity, so magnificent the opportunity that he even contemplated the possibility of giving up the pleasant life of Philadelphia, his philosophical friends of the Junto and his books, to take up the life of the pioneer and establish a model colony. Whether or not it was more than a play of his fancy, one cannot doubt that in the letter he wrote to Rev. George Whitefield, on July 2, 1756, he expressed the secret desire of his heart:

You mention your frequent wish that you were a Chaplain to an American Army. I sometimes wish that you and I were jointly employ'd by the Crown, to settle a Colony on the Ohio. I imagine we could do it effectually, and without putting the Nation to much expence. But I fear we shall never be called upon for such Service. What a glorious Thing it would be, to settle in that fine Country a large strong Body of Religious and Industrious People. What a Security to the other Colonies; and Advantage to Britain, by Increasing her People, Territory, Strength, and Commerce. Might it not greatly facilitate the Introduction of pure Religion among the Heathen, if we could, by such a Colony show them a better Sample of Christians than they commonly see in our Indian Traders, the most vicious and abandoned Wretches of our Nation?. . . Life, like a dramatic Piece should not only be conducted with Regularity, but methinks it should finish handsomely. Being now in the last Act, I begin to cast about for something fit to end with. Or if mine be more properly compar'd to an Epigram, as some of its few Lines are but barely tolerable, I am very desirous of concluding with a bright Point. In such an Enterprise I could spend the Remainder of Life with Pleasure; and I firmly believe God would bless us with Success, if we undertook it with a Sincere Regard to his Honour, the Service of our gracious King, and (which is the same thing) the Publick Good. (Smyth, III, 339.)

Little did he foresee at the time that, far from being "in the last act," the real play had not begun yet and that he would be called to be one of the main actors in a much greater drama, providing him with more "bright points" and a more "handsome finish" than he could have anticipated even in his wildest dreams. As a first unexpected turn, instead of establishing his philosophico-religious Utopia on the banks of the Ohio, at the beginning of the following years, he was sent to London, to present the case of Pennsylvania, and urge the adoption of measures to settle the frontier difficulties with the troublesome neighbors of the colonists.

While we cannot here dwell in detail on the many activities of Franklin in Europe, it may at least be recalled that, more than ever, he insisted on two main points, by him considered as absolutely essential if the colonies were to survive: security for the present, and possibilities of development for the future. He was still thinking of the American colonies as part of the British Empire, but in his imperialistic vision they were to play such a part as to decidedly eclipse the mother country. In his official communications, he observed a comparative reserve; in his private correspondence he threw all restraint to the winds and indulged in dreams of imperialistic grandeur. This appears in a most striking manner in the letter he wrote to Lord Kames to accompany a copy of his "Observations on the Peopling of Countries":

No one can rejoice more than I do, on the reduction of Canada; and this is not merely as I am a colonist, but as I am a Briton. I have long been of the opinion, that the *foundations of the future grandeur and stability of the British empire lie in America*: and though, like other foundations, they are low and little seen, they are, nevertheless, broad and strong enough to support the greatest political structure human wisdom ever yet erected. I am therefore by no means for restoring Canada. If we keep it, all the country from the St. Lawrence to the Mississippi will in another century be filled with British people. Britain itself will become vastly more populous, by the immense increase of its commerce; the Atlantic will be covered with your trading ships; and your naval power, thence continually increasing, will extend your influence round the whole globe, and awe the world. If the French remain in Canada, they will continually harass our colonies by the Indians, and impede if not prevent their growth; your progress to greatness will at best be slow, and give room for many accidents that may for ever prevent it. But I refrain, for I see you begin to think my notions extravagant, and look upon them as the ravings of a mad prophet. (Smyth, IV, 4.)

The booklet itself contained the most complete exposition of the Franklinian doctrine of expansionism ever given by the author. The philosopher proved himself a very realistic politician when it came to justifying in advance the annexation of Canada to the British Empire. The full title is sufficiently revealing: *The Interest of Great Britain Considered with regard to her Colonies and the acquisition of Canada and Guadaloupe to which are added Observations concerning the increase of Mankind, Peopling of Countries, &c.* It is more than the skillful plea of a very resourceful lawyer: throughout the whole argument is felt the deep conviction that the acquisition of Canada is a matter of life or death for the British colonies of America. It was of such importance that Franklin would not have hesitated a moment to give up all claims to the French possessions in the West Indies in order to obtain full "security" on the continent.

Nor did Franklin rest on his oars after the French had abandoned the main land and given up Canada and Louisiana. The problems of the "peopling" of the West remained opened, and to this task he gave his best efforts. It was at the same time to him a moral as well as a political problem. On the one hand, the Indians had to be persuaded to give up, for a consideration, a large part of their lands; but on the other hand, they had to be protected against the unscrupulous speculators and the brutal traders, adventurers and outlaws who lived on the fringe of the frontier. A complete expression of Franklin's views on the subject may be found in his *Remarks on the Plan for regulating the Indian Affairs*, written around 1766 at the request of Lord Shelburne. On September 12, of the same year, he wrote in the same vein to Sir William Johnson:

I have long been of the Opinion that a well-conducted Western Colony, if it could be settled with the Approbation of the Indians, would be of great national Advantage with respect to the Trade and particularly useful to the old Colonies as a Security to their Frontiers. I am glad to find that you, whose knowledge of Indian affairs and the Temper of those People far exceeds mine, entertain the same sentiments, and think such an establishment in the Illinois Country practicable. I shall not fail to use my best Endeavours here in promoting it, and obtaining for the purpose the necessary Grants.

But, immediately following that strictly realistic view of the situation comes a paragraph which shows that the humane philosopher had not yielded an inch:

It grieves me to hear that our Frontier people are yet greater Barbarians than the Indians, and continue to murder them in time of Peace. I hope your Negotiations will prevent a new war, which those Murders give great Reason to apprehend; and that the several governments will find some Method of preventing such horrid Outrages for the future.

Although not a specialist in Indian affairs and Indian psychology, he still remembered the negotiations conducted in 1753, in the village of Carlisle. He felt that it would not be fair to ask the Indians to change their customs to adopt ours. The moralist did not even attempt to conceal his sympathy and almost his admiration for these people who had not any prison system, no compulsion, knew no written contracts, and of whom it could be said that: "The Indian Trade, so far as Credit is concerned, has hitherto been carried on wholly upon Honour" (Smyth, IV, 470).

Neglecting no opportunity to advance what had now become with him a real mission, he has told us himself how, after a dinner with Lord Shelburne and Conway, he insisted again upon the desirability of establishing an outpost or rather settlement in the Illinois country. Apparently this was a very modest project, but the conclusion of the discussion indicated that he always kept in mind the possibility of a much more considerable expansion, for among the various advantages would be: "Furnishing provisions cheaper to the garrisons, securing the country, retaining the trade, raising the strength there which on occasion of a future war, might easily be poured down the Mississippi upon the lower country, and into the Bay of Mexico, to be used against Cuba or Mexico itself..." (Smyth, V, 46). This time the vision of a greater America extended not only beyond the Appalachian mountains but well into the Southwest.

Such dreams and such ambitions were not regarded with favor in London and were particularly objectionable to the Board of Trade. This became quite manifest in the controversy arising around the well-known "Walpole grant" which was the object of an adverse report written by Lord Hillsborough. Leaving aside the details of the controversy, the proposition made by the noble Lord amounted to restricting the settlements to a region where they could be kept under control and would profitably conduct their commerce with England. This could not be done with settlements too far in the interior, and it was further declared that "the laying open of new tracts of fertile territory in moderate climates might lessen her America's present produce; for is the passion of every man to be a landholder, and the people have a natural disposition to rove in search of good lands, however distant." (Smyth, V, 474.)

Franklin's answer to this argumentation should naturally be taken with a grain of salt. It is the plea of a very skillful advocate and not the dissertation of a political philosopher. Whether he believed it or not, he maintained that the new settlers would not have any tendency to become "a kind of separate and independent people." But his main point was, that nothing could prevent the colonies from expanding westward:

> To conclude: As it has been demonstrated, that neither royal nor provincial proclamations, nor the dread and horrors of a savage war, were sufficient, even *before* the country was purchased from the Indians, to prevent the settlement of the lands *over* the mountains, can it be conceived, that, *now* the country is purchased, and the people have seen the proprietors of Pennsylvania, who are the hereditary supporters of *British policy* in their own province, give every degree of encouragement to *settle* the lands *westward* of the mountains, the legislature of the province, at the same time, effectually corroborate the measure and several thousand families, in consequence thereof, settle in the *new county* of Bedford, that the inhabitants of the middle colonies will be *restrained* from cultivating the luxuriant country of the Ohio, joining to the *southern* line of Pennsylvania.

The note of defiance is sounded much more loudly, and the pioneer spirit taking pride in already conspicuous achievements manifests itself without any restraint in a piece printed in the *Gentleman's Magazine* for September 1773, under the title of "Rules by which a great empire may be reduced to a small one." "Those remote provinces have perhaps been acquired, purchased, or conquered, at the sole expence of the settlers, or their ancestors, without the aid of the mother country," declared Franklin. Then came the enumeration of the results already obtained by this new and practically self-made people:

> In laying these taxes, never regard the heavy burdens, those remote people already undergo, in defending their own frontiers, supporting their own provincial governments, making new roads, building bridges, churches, and

other public edifices, which in old countries have been done to your hands by your ancestors, but which occasion constant calls and demands on the course of a new people. (Smyth, VI, 131.)

Dr. Franklin still could proclaim himself a loyal Briton and remain attached to England intellectually and sentimentally; without perhaps fully realizing it, he had already become the spokesman of a new people and a greater America.

As we have seen, Franklin did not rely at any time on the support of Great Britain for the territorial development of the Colonies. Their expansion towards the West was a sort of natural force that no political power could stop or even control. The Independence did not change his views on the subject. In the draft of the Treaty of Alliance with France had been clearly expressed the firm purpose to exclude forever France from the American continent, and the clause had been accepted by the government of Louis XVI. In a brief outline, which he took along with him to France, Franklin had sketched tentative peace propositions in case an opportunity for negotiation should offer. One of the articles was quite in line with his previous expansionist views:

To prevent those occasions of misunderstanding, which are apt to arise where the territories of different powers border on each other, through the bad conduct of the frontier inhabitants on both sides, Britain shall cede to the United States the provinces or colonies of Quebec, St. John's Nova Scotia, Bermuda, East and West Florida, and the Bahama Islands, with all their adjoining and intermediate territories now claimed by her. (Smyth, VI 432.)

In the "motives," he even claimed that it was "absolutely necessary" for the United States to have these countries, "for our own security."

Through all the diplomatic negotiations which he conducted as American plenipotentiary in Europe, Franklin never departed from this view, even if finally he had to accept modifications when the final terms of the peace treaty were discussed.

Writing to d'Aranda, in April 1777, he maintains that in case Spain should conquer Pensacola, "the inhabitants of the United States shall have the free navigation of the Mississippi, and the use of the harbour of Pensacola." He is much more emphatic in a letter to John Jay, October 2, 1780: "Poor as we are, yet, as I know we shall be rich, I would rather agree with them to buy at a great price the whole of their right on the Mississippi, than sell a drop of its waters. A neighbour might as well ask me to sell my street door'' (Smyth, VIII, 144). And again, writing to Robert Livingston, on April 12, 1782: ''I see by the Newspapers that the Spaniards, having taken a little Post called St. Joseph, pretend to have made a Conquest of the Illinois Country. In what Light does this Proceeding appear to Congress? While they decline our offer'd Friendship, are they to be suffered to encroach on our Bounds, and shut us up within the Appalachian mountains?'' (Smyth, VIII, 425). On August 12, of the same year, the same idea is again expressed almost in the same terms: ''I will only mention that my conjecture of that court's design to coop us up within the Allegany Mountains is now manifested. I hope Congress will insist on the Mississippi as the boundary, and the free navigation of the river, from which they could entirely exclude us.'' (Smyth, VIII, 380). If he feared Spanish encroachments, he was equally fearful of the British: ''They wanted to bring their boundary down to the Ohio, and to settle their loyalists in the Illinois country. We did not choose such neighbours.'' (To Robert Livingston, Dec. 5, 1782. Smyth, VIII, 634).

On all these points, the peace treaty was to give entire satisfaction to Franklin. Navigation on the Mississippi was to be free from its source to its mouth, and the river became the western boundary of the United States, at least for the time being.

Meanwhile Franklin was thinking not only of the immediate issues to be settled, but of the future of the country. The territorial expansion of the United States was now secure; it remained to determine what kind of people were going to develop it. Here again the American philosopher had reached early very definite conclusions. The bulk of the population was to come from the natural increase of the people already established in the United States. Given room enough, the population would expand in close correspondence with the natural resources of the country. Immigrants would come, but immigration should be very carefully supervised, so as not to introduce undesirable elements. Newcomers from Europe would be welcome on two conditions only: if they were people of good character, and if they did not oppose an almost unsuperable resistance to the natural process of assimilation or, more exactly, Americanization. Such unfortunately was the case of the Germans already settled in Pennsylvania and for this reason, if for no other, German immigration was to be discouraged. The French would be acceptable, if they came only in small numbers, and such was the case of the colonists of Gallipolis who settled in the wilderness with the blessing of the old philosopher. But the most desirable element would remain in the future, as it had been in the past, the immigrants from the British Isles who could be assimilated with a minimum of difficulty. Quite striking in this respect is the letter written to William Strahan from Passy, on August 19, 1784:

> The subject, however, leads me to another Thought, which is, that you do wrong to discourage the Emigration of Englishmen to America. In my piece on Population, I have proved, I think, that Emigration does not diminish, but Multiplies a Nation. You will not have fewer at home for those that go Abroad and as every Man who comes among us, and takes up a piece of Land, becomes a Citizen, and by our Constitution has a voice in Elections, and a share in the Government of the Country, why should you be against acquiring by this fair Means a Repossession of it, and leave it to be taken by Foreigners of all Nations and Languages, who by their Numbers may drown and stifle the English, which otherwise would probably become in the course of two centuries the most extensive Language in the World, the Spanish only excepted. It is a fact, that the Irish emigrants and their children are now in Possession of the Government of Pennsylvania, by their Majority in the Assembly, as well as of a great Part of the Territory: and I remember well the first ship that brought any of them over. (Smyth, IX, 264.)

Two years earlier, in order to give of America "clearer and truer Notions of that part of the World than appear to have hitherto prevailed," he had written his "Information to those who would remove to America." In it, he had not failed to warn the prospective immigrants against exaggerated expectations. The famous passage in which he warned them, in his familiar humorous manner, has often been quoted:

> In short, America is the land of Labour, and by no means what the English call *Lubberland*, and the French *Pays de Cocagne*, where the streets are said to be pav'd with half-peck Loaves, the Houses til'd with Pancakes, and where the Fowls fly about ready roasted, crying, *Come eat me*.

But the rest of the picture must have been singularly attractive to ambitious people who, for generations, had lived in countries where every acre had been long pre-empted. To them, in spite of all warnings, America must have looked like a real Pays de Cocagne:

> Land being cheap in that Country, from the vast Forests still void of Inhabitants, and not likely to be occupied in an Age to come, insomuch that the

Propriety of an hundred Acres of fertile Soil full of Wood may be obtained near the Frontiers, in many Places, for Eight or Ten Guineas, hearty young Labouring Men, who understand the Husbandry of Corn and Cattle, which is nearly the same in that Country as in Europe, may easily establish themselves there. A little Money sav'd of the good wages they receive there, while they work for others, enables them to buy the Land and begin their Plantation, in which they are assisted by the Good-Will of their Neighbours, and some Credit. Multitudes of poor People from England, Ireland, Scotland, and Germany, have by this means in a few years become wealthy Farmers, who, in their own Countries where all the Lands are fully occupied, and the Wages of Labour low, could never have emerged from the poor Condition in which they were born.

Now was it to be feared that this condition might pass rapidly, and that America would ever experience the same crowding as the old world. There was place for everybody in the new world and particularly for persons "having a number of Children to provide for, and desirous of bringing them up to Industry and to secure Estates for their Posterity." To make it more conclusive and more striking, instead of vague promises particular instances and figures were quoted:

> There small Capitals laid out in Lands, which daily become more valuable by the Increase of People, afford a solid Prospect of ample Fortunes thereafter for those Children. The Writer of this has known several Instances of large Tracts of Land, bought, on what was then the Frontier of Pensilvania, for Ten Pounds per hundred Acres, which after them, sold readily, without any Improvement made upon them, for three Pounds per Acre.

Already the word "frontier," as used here by Franklin, had taken a special American meaning. It did not express anymore anything fixed, or a line to be modified only after hard-won battles or prolonged negotiations. The settlements of today were yesterday's frontiers and the frontiers of today would extend and expand almost indefinitely as America became more populous and as the American people advanced in their Westward march.

With this picture of the American frontier we may well bring our study to a close. From his early "Observations concerning the Increase of Mankind" of 1751 to the signing of the Peace Treaty with the British Commissioners, in 1782, Franklin had worked steadily and unswervingly to make his dream come true. No danger now remained of ever seeing the American people "cooped up within the Alleganys," or "cut off" from the rest of the continent.

There are many statues of Benjamin Franklin, but there is one yet to be erected that would fittingly call attention to one of the most outstanding achievements of a great American who was such a persistent and clearsighted prophet of a greater America. Somewhere, on the top of a ridge in the Alleghenys, on one of these mountain passes through which rode and tramped the pathetic line of the early settlers, we might well build a statue of Benjamin Franklin, not the arm-chair philosopher, but the young Postmaster General, the man whom the Moravians dubbed "General" Franklin, pointing towards the West, and looking over the rich land of Canaan whose gateways he had made accessible to his people.

Benjamin Franklin: The Printer at Work

LAWRENCE C. WROTH

Lawrence Counselman Wroth (1884-1970) was the Librarian of the John Carter Brown Library from 1923 to 1957 and Research Professor of American History at Brown University from 1932. He is the author of *The Colonial Printer* (1931 and 2nd rev. ed. 1938).

All of us who have given thought to Benjamin Franklin the printer, who have visualized him at case and press in Boston, Philadelphia, London, and Paris, have pondered that passage in the Autobiography in which he tells that in his boyhood his father so directed their walks together that in the course of them they might watch craftsmen of many sorts at their work. One may think with pleasure of that picture of father and son observing in the varied life of their town "the different ways that different things are done," the father improving the shining hour with observation and precept, the son—a happy and unusual circumstance—eager to know the whys and wherefores of preliminary operations, the names of tools, the ends of curious processes, the validity of short cuts, and the convenience of rules of thumb. What an education that proved to be! "It has ever since been a pleasure to me," wrote the son long afterwards, "to see good workmen handle their tools." A few lines below in his great and simple record of success occur the words: "From a child I was fond of reading." These two interests are the key to the life of Franklin the printer. Interest in the trades and handicrafts alone might have kept him in his father's soap-boiling establishment or sent him to Newport to join his brother John in candlemaking; love of reading, untempered by his interest in practical mechanics, might have sent him into a learned profession or taken the edge off his zeal in the routine of a handicraft or in trade. But neither of these destinies was to be his. The return of Brother James from London with a printing-house, just at the right time, made it possible for Benjamin to engage in the practice of a craft in which his particular combination of interests might have its exercise. He was articled to James in his twelfth year, and soon had become a useful hand to his brother in all the varied employment of an eighteenth century print shop.

With that discovery of aptitude a new life was foreshadowed for him and for the printing trade in America.

Though he had been trained to his craft, it is believed, in a London establishment, James Franklin's printing was never anything more than adequate, and frequently it was less. James was a journalist and a politician, without interest in the craft of printing beyond its utilitarian employment. Lacking any notable degree of taste, lacking curiosity, he was representative of the majority of contemporary printers in that he used his tools without distinction. Nevertheless, having learned their employment in England, he was able to pass on to his apprentice a thorough knowledge of the mechanics of printing. When Benjamin ran away after concluding that he had endured about as much as he could stand of brotherly correction, it is probable that he had assimilated all the typographical knowledge James had to give. He had learned not only how to print a newspaper, but how to edit and manage one. He had learned, moreover, the full round of his craft. When he went to work for Keimer in Philadelphia he was able to put in working order an old, shattered press, and go at once about the task of composition and the printing of the forms. The sense of superiority that comes from a comprehensive training appears in those words in which, after telling of his services to Keimer, he declares that his new employer was "a mere compositor, knowing nothing of presswork."

But if Benjamin had continued without interruption in his Philadelphia employment, there is no reason to believe that his workmanship would ever have advanced greatly beyond the normal degree of skill which had prevailed in his time in Boston, where, in the hands of Samuel Kneeland, Bartholomew Green, Thomas Fleet, and Brother James, the craft was still at the ebb at which it had stood esthetically for the eighty years of its existence in British America. Throughout that period in England, new type had been expensive and, even for the well-to-do printer, hard to procure in quantity and variety. Not too good to begin with, the common English press was used, and abused, by most printers until it became a ramshackle instrument, leaking force at every joint, and incapable of rendering accurate results. English ink, too, was carelessly made, and paper was an article of import and correspondingly dear. Because of their distance from European centers all these deterrents to good performance were intensified in the

American colonies. There, especially, paper economy demanded pages of the lesser formats, close set in letters of the smaller sizes. All too frequently, these were printed with muddy ink in a fashion that betrayed evidence of deterioration of the presses and of thoughtlessness in their operation.

The printers of Philadelphia were even less to be admired as technicians than those of Boston. Samuel Keimer, with whom Franklin first had employment, owned little skill in printing. The work of Keimer's rival, Andrew Bradford, was poor by any standards of the time. It may be that, sooner or later, Franklin's natural sense of decency and order, his intellectual clarity, his feeling for balanced form would have lifted him out of the class of these teachers and associates of Boston and Philadelphia. Nonetheless, those of us who are interested in the progress of the craft of printing in America are grateful to the chance which in 1724 took this young journeyman to England and set him down, a serious and apt student of his craft, in the busy London printing establishment of Samuel Palmer.

There was a new spirit showing in the printing houses of England in those early years of the century. There as everywhere appreciation of good workmanship and the ability to produce it upon occasion had never completely died out. But the successive Press Restriction Acts of the seventeenth century had kept the craft at a standstill for generations. Improvement in type design had been rendered unlikely by regulations which removed the spirit of competition from the industry of letter-founding. These acts had also confined the business of printing virtually to the city of London, and had allowed the Stationers' Company to encourage a monopoly among its members in certain fields of publication. All forces combined to make the English printing trade non-competitive and, in consequence, indifferent to improvement in materials and processes. It is true that in 1683 Joseph Moxon, printer and typefounder, had created in his "Mechanick Exercises" a manual of printing and typemaking in which he urged his contemporaries to take thought of what they were doing so as to do it better. He had shown them how they might improve their presses, their type, and their ink, and how they might more effectively execute their composition and presswork, but because he himself knew little of the esthetics of printing, he had said little in his treatise about the designing of books and the niceties of the arrangement of type. He improved the technique and tools of type casting in his foundry but the design of his own letter was hardly better than that of his contemporaries and rivals. It seems certain that his splendid book, the pioneer of printing manuals, had little influence upon his immediate contemporaries. But other forces besides Moxon's pleas and prescriptions were at work. The last of the Press Restriction Acts expired in 1695, and the control of the publishing trade by the Stationers' Company began at about the same time to decline in its rigor. With the limitations of locality removed, presses were set up throughout the English counties in the first quarter of the eighteenth century and competition arose between London and the provinces. Furthermore, intelligent printers had taken up the study of the mechanics of their craft. In his "History of the Art of Printing," published in Edinburgh in 1713, James Watson showed that he was thoroughly familiar with Moxon's book of thirty years before, and did his master honor by reaffirming his recommendations in the matter of presses, type, and ink. In 1723 appeared at Saint-Omer, across the Channel, Dominique Fertel's "Science de l'Imprimerie," in which, among other original and valuable features, the details of type arrangement were discussed on the basis of a tradition that had suffered less degradation in France than in any other country of Europe. About 1729, Samuel Palmer of London announced the publication of a history of printing of which the second part (never published) was to be, if I have read the prospectus correctly, a revision and modernization of Moxon, enriched by elements drawn from the book of Fertel.[1] But these literary events were not so important in the history of English typography as the fact that in 1720 John Watts, William Bowyer, and James Bettenham, three London printers, had lent £500 to William Caslon, a young engraver upon metals, for the purpose of establishing a type foundry. Five or six years later began to appear, in works printed by Bowyer, the clean, well-modelled, uniformly cast roman letter of William Caslon. That letter is not nearly so beautiful nor so imaginative in design as certain others of earlier and later date, but it is, as Mr. Updike says, "friendly to the eye," and it has the invaluable quality of being as nearly fool-proof as printing type may be. The appearance of the Caslon letter in 1726 was an event, wrote T.B. Reed, the

---

[1]Bigmore & Wyman, "A Bibliography of Printing," II, 109-110.

historian of English typefounding, "marking a distinct turning-point in...English typography, which from that time forward entered on a course of brilliant regeneration."[2]

It was this world of a freshening interest in typographical execution that Franklin entered when he reached London in December, 1724. His first employer, Samuel Palmer, was probably then at work upon his history and manual of printing; his second, John Watts, had recently helped young William Caslon set up his type foundry, and in the time that Franklin was with him, must have been watching Caslon's progress, talking about his achievements, and waiting with excited expectation for the appearance of the books in which the qualities of the new letter were to be manifested to the world.

Samuel Palmer was a printer of genuine ability. He, too, had encouraged Caslon, but with him book design, that is, the layout of pages, spacing, leading, color of letterpress, and evenness of impression, was a matter of equal interest with the design of the type face employed in the volume. One of Palmer's productions, well known to students of Franklin's life for more than one reason, was the third edition of Wollaston's "Religion of Nature Delineated," issued in the year 1725.[3] Set in one of the pre-Caslon faces, this book is a successful production for its generation. Palmer laid out his quarto volume in a style reminiscent of the better French printing of the day, though in saying this one need not suggest that the printer had a French model in view when designing his book. There

---

[2] I have always supposed, in common with most writers on typography, that the earliest appearance in print of Caslon roman was in the form of the English, or fourteen point, letters in the "Opera" of John Selden, London, 1725 and 1726, but Alfred F. Johnson of the British Museum, in "A Note on William Caslon" (*Monotype Recorder*, Vol. 35, No. 4) has disturbed our certainty in this article of faith. Mr. Johnson assures us that the Selden letter was cut by Christoffel van Dyck, and through reproductions of a page of the "Opera" and specimens of the Van Dyck and Caslon letters, gives opportunity for comparisons and conclusions. But though he has taken away from us the noble volumes of Selden as the first showing of Caslon roman, Mr. Johnson does not leave us without comfort; he gives us in place of them the notes in pica size in Bowyer's edition of Anacreon, 1724, and the pica in which is printed that same publisher's "Reliquae Baxterianae" of 1726.

[3] Franklin says in the Autobiography that it was the second edition of Wollaston he was employed upon in Palmer's shop, but Paul Leicester Ford's, "Franklin Bibliography," No. 5, asserts that the second edition was published before Franklin's arrival in England on December 24, 1724, and suggests that it must have been the third edition of 1725 for which our young journeyman set type.

were other English works of the period in which this influence was perceptible, and nothing is more dangerous than specific claims of typographic influence. But whatever its origin, the Wollaston book, not a notable production, was yet a decently produced volume in which a printer then at work on the compilation of a typographic manual was putting into effect in his own practice the concept of openly spaced lines, well-leaded but substantial pages, balanced headings, a dignified use of ornament, and an open but strong title-page display. In the text pages of the resulting book the type is too small for the page area, and the color of the ink is not so positive as it should be, though the impression upon the page is even and uniform in tone throughout the volume. This was a skillfully made book for an English press of 1725, and a better production by far than Franklin had seen from an American press. And from its printing in Palmer's shop he must have learned much because he had been himself one of the compositors who set the book in type. From it and other books he worked upon for Palmer, he may have acquired that touch of conscious artistry which, imposed upon his natural mechanical ability, gave grace and dignity and the quality of thoughtfulness to the work which he later produced under his own name in Philadelphia. The Autobiography tells us none of this except the actual fact of its author's employment upon the composition of Wollaston's "Religion of Nature Delineated,"and it would not have told us that much but for a precocious concern with the subject matter of that treatise which led the young compositor to write and publish a metaphysical reply to its argument. Franklin does not say unequivocally that he himself set in type that "erratum" of his youth, the "Dissertation on Liberty and Necessity, Pleasure and Pain," which came from the press in reply to Wollaston in 1725, but it is a fair assumption that the "Dissertation," in all probability the product of Palmer's establishment,[4] was composed in both senses of the word by our young printer. It is a superior bit of typography, composed in the new style of open setting and leaded pages, imposed in the relatively narrow octavo format that became almost universal in the later years of the century. Franklin's association

---

[4]Typographical details, especially the employment in the "Dissertation" on page 32 of the engraved printing house interior which ornaments the title-page of the Wollaston, bear out the assumption one makes from the text of the Autobiography that the Franklin book was produced at Palmer's.

with it whether as printer or as the individual who commissioned its printing, marks another stage in his typographic education.

The traveller does not necessarily bring home either things or ideas from his travels. Dr. Johnson said of a celebrated traveller of his day: "I never but once heard him talk of what he had seen, and that was of a large serpent in one of the Pyramids of Egypt." In this chemistry of the mind in contact with experience the result is not predictable but it happened that to the particular combination of men and events he encountered in London, Franklin's reaction was positive. A new compound was produced in consequence.

The lucky breaks fall to the good players. How often in reflecting upon Franklin's life are we reminded of that homely aphorism! What affinity for excellence was it that drew this unknown lad, ignorant of London, successively to the two printing houses in which he might learn most of future usefulness, might find himself lifted immediately upon the first wave of the new spirit in English printing? Who told him to go to the James typefoundry and watch closely the steps employed in the making of type? How could he have known that at Palmer's, probably, and at Watts's, certainly, he would hear talk of the new roman letter being made by William Caslon, a letter he was afterwards to use extensively himself and to purchase for the use of his American partners and associates? These are questions that we cannot answer until we understand better the nature of genius. A simplified statement of Franklin's success in life, which, however, does not explain that success, is that he had the knack of doing the right thing at the right time. In further development of this familiar characterization of him, we must add that what seems to have been chance or accident invariably took him to the *right place* at the right time.

We must now review briefly the activities of this young journeyman printer after his return to Philadelphia and his reemployment by Samuel Keimer in 1727. The increased value of his services to Keimer would be clear to us who read the record even if he had not impressed upon us with unction his importance to the business of his despised master. But it speaks for itself that a journeyman who could both work and teach others to work was important in that city in which the art of printing was at the moment characterless and slovenly. This journeyman possessed, he tells us, "uncommon quickness at composing," and his earlier experience as pressman had recently been supplemented by what we might call a graduate course in the London establishment of John Watts. His visit or visits to the James foundry in London enabled him, when Keimer ran low on sorts, to contrive a mould, make use of what letters were left as puncheons, strike matrices in lead, and thus supply "in a pretty tolerable way all deficiencies." This "factotum" of Keimer's establishment could also engrave upon copper well enough to justify his employer in taking on the job of printing paper money for the Province of New Jersey. He was able also, in connection with this job, to construct "a copperplate press for it, the first that had been seen in the country." Some of these statements require amendment. The types he cast for Keimer without precision instruments were doubtless pretty bad; his engravings have never been singled out for the praise of critics; and when he wrote that the copperplate press he "contrived" was "the first that had been seen in the country," he doubtless meant "in the vicinity." As a printer's apprentice in Boston he must have known that one Francis Dewing, from about 1716 onwards, was printing copperplate maps in that city and advertising his ability to do other copperplate printing.[5] But despite this ungenerous examination of his story (his complacency sometimes moves one to pick flaws in his assertions), it is clear enough why Keimer cherished him, and why his fellow-workman Meredith proposed a partnership with him.

One reads with mixed feelings the story of Franklin's associations with Keimer and with Meredith and his early severance of them. The eccentric Keimer was a poor printer, and a poor man of business, but he was undoubtedly a man of ideas, undeserving, I am convinced, of the contemptuous treatment he receives in the Autobiography. Meredith was one of the weaker brethren, whose subsequent history as related by Franklin and as recorded in Franklin's Account Books, was anything but edifying. Nevertheless I wish that one of those two, or, better, Andrew Bradford,

---

[5] Wroth, "Colonial Printer," 2d ed. 1938, page 285, records, from information supplied by Miss Clara Egli of the Division of Maps, Library of Congress, "A Chart of the English Plantations...by Captain Cyprian Southack...Engraved and printed by Fra. Dewing, Boston...1717." At that time (1938) the only known copy of this map was in the Public Record Office, London, but since then a second copy has been discovered and is now owned by the John Carter Brown Library, Providence. Dewing was still in Boston in 1722 when there was published in that city John Bonner's *Town of Boston in New England*, "Engraven and Printed by Fra. Dewing..."

had left us an account of young Ben Franklin in these years of their association. It would show us, I believe, the picture of a thruster, a go-getter, a superior youth unable to conceal his superiority, a calculating young tradesman very much unlike the benevolent philosopher of later years. The possession in later life of ten thousand a year or its equivalent did for Franklin what Becky Sharp was sure that comfortable sum would have done for her. Andrew Bradford must have loved him greatly from that day in 1729 when the young business builder got the public printing away from him by reprinting one of the slovenly Bradford jobs and distributing his own neater production to the members of Assembly for comparison. Pennsylvania deserved better printing than Bradford was executing in its behalf, so that one can heartily approve this action in the public service. But at the time of it Franklin had experienced, so far as the record shows, nothing but kindness from William and Andrew Bradford, and when, sometime later, Andrew as postmaster forbade his riders to take Franklin's newspaper for distribution, both men, Bradford the opportunistic official and Franklin the injured innocent, must have recalled with varying emotions that preliminary skirmish in the marketplace.

It was in October, 1729, that Franklin took over Keimer's newspaper, thus adding to his growing business that form of publication which every colonial printer needed to complete his happiness. Too often the result was bankruptcy, but it was anything but that in the case of Franklin's venture into newspaper production. In the same year he wrote his "Modest Enquiry into the Nature and Necessity of a Paper-Currency," and when the argument there presented led to an act of Assembly for the issuance of bills of credit, he was given as a matter of course the profitable job of printing the money. Mr. J. Bennett Nolan has recently added to the gaiety of life by calling attention to a later transaction in which Franklin was paid by the Assembly for printing issue of paper money and, some years later, when the bills had become badly worn through use, was paid also for destroying them.[6] It is pleasant to get something going and coming. He made a special effort to please all those who needed blank forms, supplying lawyers, officials, merchants, and ship captains with, he says, "the

---

[6]Nolan, J. Bennett. *Printer Strahan's Book Account. A Colonial Controversy*, page 32.

correctest that ever appear'd among us.'' His appointment to the office of clerk of Assembly proved valuable to him, he informed one of his correspondents, as a means of securing the public business for his printing house. Mr. Nolan has calculated that in the twelve-year period 1739-1750 he received from the Assembly as clerk's fees and as a payment for printing statutes and paper money the sum of £2,762 in Pennsylvania money.[7] Translated by a rough rule into terms understandable today, that sum would have been in the neighborhood of $40,000.

Very soon after the dissolution of his agreement with Meredith in 1730, Franklin began the establishment of those silent partnerships in other colonies which were to contribute so greatly to the influence he established over the printing trade in British America as well as to the spread of his personal reputation throughout the country. It was a bold action, in harmony with the American spirit of business aggressiveness, or perhaps one of its keynotes, for a young man still in debt for his own plant, still fighting for place against older rivals, to broaden his base of operations by sending one of his journeymen on a partnership agreement to a distant city. When Thomas Whitemarsh, the individual in question, died soon after arrival in South Carolina, Franklin saved the situation by promptly sending to fill his place another of his journeymen, Lewis Timothy. In July, 1743, he wrote in the first of his many letters to William Strahan, his English correspondent, that he had already three printing houses in different colonies and was planning a fourth. This meant, I believe, his own establishment in Philadelphia, that of the Timothys in Charleston, South Carolina, and the New York office of James Parker, then little more than a year old. In later years he sent, first, Thomas Smith and, later, his own nephew, Benjamin Mecom, to Antigua, and another nephew, James Franklin, Jr., to join his mother, the Widow Ann Franklin, in carrying on Brother James's business in Newport. Still later, according to a letter of 1785, he established Holland and Miller at Lancaster, and Dunlap and Hall in Philadelphia. His relationship with Jonas Green of Annapolis, another of his journeymen, and with William Parks of Williamsburg does not seem to have been formally that of partner, but to these and to several others even more distant he was banker and source of supply for materials and equipment.

[7]Work cited in note 6, page 33.

It was not alone by the activities of his establishment in Philadelphia, therefore, that Franklin had come to be regarded as the leading individual in the American printing trade when he virtually gave up his active practice of it at the time of taking David Hall for partner in 1748. These associations through formal and informal partnership with printers in several colonies had been a prime means by which that situation was brought about. The business he built up in ink-making and the sale of paper, as we shall see later, also contributed importantly to the attainment of leadership which continued until the firm of Franklin & Hall was dissolved in 1766. At that time his active participation in the concerns of his Philadelphia shop was but a memory.

This is a bare outline of Franklin's active career as printer. Stated in these terms it might be regarded as the career of any vigorous, enterprising craftsman and man of business. To learn its distinctive features, we shall have to discuss separately certain of his special interests and activities.

THE PENNSYLVANIA GAZETTE

The Pennsylvania Gazette differed from the normal newspaper of its time only in having for its printer, publisher, and editor a publicist who had deliberately trained himself in polemics. The consequence was that the quality of the *Gazette* articles on local politics was such as to give it a special interest among colonial American journals. For the rest—general content, typographical style, exchange matter, and character of advertisements—it belongs in that group of admirable weeklies published by William Parks in Williamsburg, Jonas Green in Annapolis, and William Goddard in Providence, Philadelphia, and Baltimore. The *Gazette* was one of the best, and there is good reason to believe that few could equal it in circulation. We have no direct statement from Franklin as to the size of his subscription list, though there exists a letter from him to Strahan, written in 1785, in which he says, "I shall have an old account to settle then with the family of our friend Hall....It was the value of a copyright in an established newspaper, of each of which from eight to ten thousand were printed."[8]

[8]Franklin to Strahan, March 5, 1785 ("Life and Writings," Smyth edition, ix:290-291.)

This figure seems large for the time and the conditions of publication. Reflecting upon it, one begins to ask whether Franklin's statement really means that the weekly circulation of the *Gazette*, over a period of years, attained this average of 9,000 copies. If we assume that fact to be true and arbitrarily, and generously, perhaps, fix upon 2,000 copies as the number sent to subscribers outside the city,[9] we shall still have a weekly Philadelphia circulation of 7,000 copies. That circulation seems incredibly large for a city of which the population in the decade 1750-1760 ran from seventeen to twenty-four thousand persons,[10] or, roughly, a city of 4,000 families. The normal family contents itself with a single copy of a newspaper, but if we take Franklin's statement as meaning what it seems to say, each Philadelphia family of that decade took in 1¾ copies of the *Gazette*. We may, indeed, say that each family took in two papers, because some of the 4,000 were illiterate and a good number of them spoke no language but German. Furthermore, one asks, if each family was supplied with two *Gazettes*, what market remained for the *Pennsylvania Journal*, the newspaper which, under William Bradford the younger, continued to thrive throughout this period?

When we examine the statement of accounts of the Franklin and Hall partnership[11] for the whole eighteen-year period of its existence, we are able to segregate the sum of £13,500, or £750 a year, received from subscriptions to the *Gazette*. At ten shillings each this means an average for the period of 1,500 paid subscriptions a year. Adding to these the copies sent out as exchanges and to advertisers, it seems probable that the actual number printed each week would have been from 1,600 to 1,700 copies. In view of the circumstances outlined in the foregoing paragraph this seems a more likely figure than the eight to ten thousand of which Franklin spoke in his letter of 1785. If Franklin's figure were correct we

---

[9]Twenty-five per cent of the edition or thereabouts seems a reasonable proportion of out-of-town subscriptions.

[10]The population figures here given were compiled by Professor Carl Bridenbaugh of Brown University from the Proud Manuscripts in the Historical Society of Pennsylvania, the Du Simitiere Scraps in the Library Company of Philadelphia, and the *Pennsylvania Journal* for January 18, 1770.

[11]Original manuscript of James Parker's statement of the Franklin & Hall accounts, at the time of the dissolution of the partnership, is in the Historical Society of Pennsylvania. A photostat copy is in the John Carter Brown Library.

should expect to find that the *Gazette* subscriptions for eighteen years amounted to something like £80,000. Actually that sum is nearly three times the gross cash receipts of the firm from all elements of its business for the whole of that period.

The newspaper subscription lists of those days of small populations and large proportions of illiteracy were normally small. Writing to Franklin in 1747, Jonas Green, of Annapolis, mentioned that he had about 540 paid subscriptions for his *Maryland Gazette*. It was thought auspicious that in 1767 William Goddard could begin his *Pennsylvania Chronicle* with 700 subscribers. In 1774 James Rivington announced a weekly impression of 3,600 copies of his *New-York Gazetteer*, adding that this was "a number far beyond the most sanguine expectations of the Printer's warmest friends; as the presses of very few, if any of his brethren, including those in Great Britain, exceed it."[12] These reflections upon Franklin's statement seem to suggest the probability that another interpretation exists for it than the obvious one that his *Gazette* circulated to the pleasant tune of eight to ten thousand copies weekly. That was certainly not the case if, as I believe, the Franklin & Hall Partnership Account included the whole business of the firm in that period 1748-1765. Isaiah Thomas asserted that according to information he had received, Franklin customarily drew £1,000 currency a year from the firm.[13] Actually the accounts show that his income from the firm was £800 currency a year, but the hearsay figure and the actual figure are close enough to suggest that the Partnership Account was a statement in full of the firm's affairs. If the *Gazette* had circulated 9,000 copies a week for any considerable part of the period 1748-1765, that Account would have told a very different story in such items as paper consumption and subscriptions to the *Gazette*, and in the figures which make up its totals.

INK MAKING

It must be remembered, however, that neither Franklin's income nor his influence upon the printing trade of the country were

[12]Jonas Green to Franklin, July 5, 1747, "Calendar of the Franklin Papers in the American Philosophical Society," I:3; Thomas Wharton to Franklin, February 7, 1767, "Calender..." I:69, gives the Goddard figure here cited; the Rivington statement is found in Stokes, "Iconography of Manhattan Island," IV:836. My attention was called to the Rivington figure by Professor Carl Bridgenbaugh of Brown University.

[13]Thomas, "History of Printing," 2d ed. 1874, I:235.

based wholly upon the *Gazette* and the other business of the printing house. Realizing from experience the difficulties that faced the
American printer in maintaining a supply of ink and paper, the
essential articles of his commerce, he lost little time in entering the
business of ink making and in becoming an agent of the Pennsylvania paper mills, thereby planning to ensure his own peace of
mind and to give comfort to other printers throughout the colonies. On March 21, 1733, as his first step in this direction, he purchased a lampblack manufactory from Nathaniel
Jenkins.[14] Lampblack mixed with varnish, that is, linseed oil
thickened by boiling, forms the black, viscid substance we know as
printers' ink. About six weeks after his purchase of the lampblack
house from Jenkins, Franklin advertised in the *Gazette* his ability
to supply very good lampblack. One of the earliest reports of the
industrial possibilities of Pennsylvania informs us that linen, made
from flax, was being manufactured at Germantown in 1692, and
from a later source we learn that in 1729 Pennsylvania exported
1,800 bushels of flaxseed, or linseed, to Scotland and Ireland. An
oil mill was erected in the colony as early as 1691. There was,
therefore, no lack of the raw materials that went into the making
of printer's ink when Franklin took up the business of selling it and
of manufacturing one of its constituents. In 1735 he is found selling printers' ink to the celebrated firm of Kneeland & Green of
Boston, and thereafter, for years, he sold to printers north and
south of Pennsylvania, quantities of lampblack and varnish, or
ready-mixed printers' ink in keg or canister. Nowhere do we learn
the source of his supply of varnish. The boiling of the oil was a
disagreeable job, attended with some danger of setting fire to the
house in which it was done. He does not tell us that this unpleasant
task was among his personal activities, but his accounts make it
clear that he was in the business of selling the product of it.

But a little bit of printers' ink goes a long way, and one doubts
that with his limited market, he expected to make much money
from the sale of ink to his brother printers. But one does not doubt

---

[14]Eddy, "Account Books Kept by Benjamin Franklin, 1728-1739," 1928, page 45.
Andrew Bradford also had been interested in lampblack. As early as 1721 he asked the
Pennsylvania Assembly to give him a monopoly of its production and sale. Mr. Nelson
B. Gaskill has called my attention to the fact that even earlier than this, in 1712, a five-
year monopoly in lampblack had been granted John Parmyter by the Assembly of New
York.

that his ability to supply this essential of their business was among the factors that made him indispensable to them, kept them upon his books, and encouraged them to buy from him the paper which he was soon in a position to supply.

RAG MAN AND PAPER MERCHANT

In his participation in the paper business, Franklin once more approached the problem of money making from a sound point of vantage, that of supplying the manufacturers with their essential raw material. About 1734 he began that business of exchanging old linen rags for new paper which became one of his most profitable and most useful activities. His consignments of rags to Pennsylvania papermakers, at the rate of a shilling half-penny a pound for the better quality, ran in the period 1735-1741 to nearly 75,000 pounds, or thirty-seven tons in weight. In the period 1741-1747, he sold 11,000 pounds of rags to William Parks of Williamsburg alone, and in that period and the next ten years he sold to the Pennsylvania mills more than 166,000 pounds.[15] This service was of the utmost value to the papermakers, especially as our rag merchant seems to have been willing to accept from them payment in kind, taking paper of all sorts which he used either in his own printing house or sold for cash to the printers with whom he was in correspndence in several colonies. The purchasing of the rags was one of the duties of Mrs. Franklin. It was probably her job also to pick and sort them.

After analyzing Franklin's accounts with papermakers, Mr. George Simpson Eddy wrote that in his belief "no one else in the Colonies, between 1739 and 1757, dealt so largely in paper" as did the industrious rag collector of Philadelphia.

It is not merely as a source of wealth to Franklin that we contemplate his long years of bartering with the Pennsylvania papermakers. In a letter of 1771 to Humphrey Marshall, he wrote: "I was the more pleased to see in your letter the improvement of our paper, having had a principal share in establishing that manufacture among us many years ago, by the encouragement I gave it." Years later Brissot de Warville wrote, "Dr. Franklin told me that

---

[15]Work cited in note 14, page 30. Also Eddy, "Account Books Kept by Benjamin Franklin," 1739-1747, pages 16-35, 98-99.

he had established about 18 paper mills,''[16] One of these statements, at least, requires clarification. Papermaking was established in Pennsylvania in 1690, a good many years before Franklin was born, and a mill was being set up in New England in 1729 at a time when his chief concern was to get the newly established printing firm of Franklin & Meredith on its feet. Papermaking, therefore, was an established industry in Pennsylvania and New England before Franklin engaged in it, and his use of the word "establishing" in the letter to Humphrey Marshall was intended in the sense of "expanding." There is no question that his activities as a collector of rags for the papermakers provided a stimulus to their business and that through them he splendidly served himself, his craft, and his nation. Regarding the extent of his service to himself one wonders whether his papermaking trade was not as great a factor in the financial ease of his later life as the *Gazette* and the printing house.

THE AMATEUR OF TYPE

We have seen that Franklin observed the processes of typefounding so closely in London that upon his return to Philadelphia he was able to make up deficiencies in Keimer's fonts by a crude casting of sorts. This interest in type and the making of type stayed with him until the end, though we hear no more of it for some years. But in the year 1744, or earlier, his interest in typefounding seems to have revived. In that year we find him ordering from Caslon, through Strahan, a font of English.[17] This was a normal procedure. Because there were no type foundries in the colonies, all American printers of the time must secure their type from Europe. But it was not to be expected that Franklin would sit quietly under this necessity if he could devise a way to remove the burden of importation from himself and his countrymen. Earlier in the same month, he had thanked Strahan for his "care and pains in procuring me the founding tools; though I think, with you, that the workmen have not been at all bashful in making their bills."

---

[16]Work last cited, page 16.

[17]In this letter Franklin does not specify by name the founder for the 300 lbs. weight of "good new English letter," which he ordered, but in a letter dated February 12, 1744, which internal evidence suggests should be 1744-45, he writes "I hope Caslon will not delay casting the English Fount I wrote to you for..."

These in all probability, were the first typefounding tools to come to any part of America north of Mexico. They enter history on the fourth of July, 1744, and so far as any direct information about them is concerned, they leave it on the same day. Franklin never mentions them again, and it is certain that he continued to order from British founders whenever he needed new type for himself or for any of the journeymen he set up in business. Though he sold a certain amount of type to his associates, there are no entries in his account books which indicate that he was selling them type of his own casting. It is clear that whatever his fortune with this experiment may have been it was not so notably successful as to lead him to mention it in the Autobiography, or to recall it, so far as I have discovered, in any one of his many letters on typographical subjects. But from another source than Franklin's own words there comes a suggestion that these founding tools were not cast aside as soon as received as an unwise purchase. Gustav Mori, writing in the *Gutenberg-Jahrbuch* for 1934, declares on the authority of the elder Christopher Sauer that about the year 1747 Franklin offered the printers of the Ephrata Monastery certain articles of typefounding equipment, without matrices, for a specified sum, and demanded a similar sum to teach them to make matrices of lead and to cast type therefrom. Mr. Mori goes on to say that the good brothers declared in the colophon of one of the books from the monastery press that the volume had been printed from type of their own casting, and from this assertion he assumed that, as proposed, the Ephrata brothers had been instructed in typefounding by Franklin. Unfortunately these statements are not documented by their author, and in the absence of record of any Ephrata book bearing a colophon of the character described, I have concluded that when he wrote of such a work Mr. Mori was thinking of the younger Sauer's *Ein Geistliches Magazien*, one number of which (of 1771 or 1772) a colophon declares, and declares incorrectly, was printed with the first type cast in America. It stands, therefore, at this: Franklin acquired founding tools from England in 1744, and about 1747 is reported to have been negotiating the sale of certain typefounding tools to the brothers at Ephrata, and further to have offered to teach them, for a price, the art of making matrices. We can go no further than this in the absence of documents. I should not, perhaps, have brought up a matter which I am compelled to leave with you in this state, but I have always wanted to share with someone my uncertainty regarding this early venture of Franklin's into typefounding. Furthermore, the story is important in the consideration of his enduring interest in type.

It is not easy to know when Franklin first began the use of that type of William Caslon's which was so greatly to improve the general run of printing in England and America. The first mention of a purchase of Caslon type in the correspondence is in a letter to Strahan of July 31, 1744. But Caslon had begun selling to printers ten years before that date, and one would look for an earlier use of his type by a printer of Franklin's enterprise. Though I cannot boast an accurate eye for type differences, it seems to me that new type was put into the Franklin cases while the "Collection of all the Laws of Pennsylvania" of 1742 was going through the press, that, to be more specific, its pages are set in the Caslon letter from signature 5 P to the end of the volume. Furthermore the "Cato Major" of 1744 is in what I think is Caslon, and that book was printed before Franklin sent in his order of July 31 of that year. For these reasons I fix the year 1741, or thereabouts, as that of Franklin's first patronage of the Caslon foundry. If someone more expert in the identification of type faces takes issue with me on this opinion, he will not find me making a stubborn defense of it. At any rate, Franklin's association with Caslon continued, to the advantage of American printing, for many years, though at one time an error in one of the founder's bills seemed likely to bring it to an abrupt ending. The matter was adjusted, and through Franklin the admirably clear letters of Caslon continued to effect improvement in the appearance of American printing.

It is not always easy to understand just where Franklin drew the line between business and sentiment. We do not find, for example, that he ordered for Franklin & Hall or for others of his American associates any of the type of John Baskerville, yet his admiration for Baskerville's product was of the highest. That distinguished printer and type designer brought out his earliest book, the Vergil, in 1757, the year in which Franklin went to England as colonial agent for the Province of Pennsylvania. One of his first actions upon arrival in England was to subscribe for six copies of the Vergil, and when in 1758 Baskerville was bringing out his Milton, Franklin subscribed for that work also and wrote to Isaac Norris in Philadelphia, "I have inserted your name in his List of Subscribers, as you mention your Inclination to encourage so deserving an Artist." In 1760 he wrote the Birmingham founder of the trick he had played upon one of the detractors of the new type-face, mischievously, he says, showing him as Baskerville letters the upper part of a Caslon specimen and listening with glee while the amateur critic of types (there were many of us even in those days) inveighed against the blinding qualities of the new design. The association with this distinguished printer and founder evidently continued, for, years later, in 1773, Baskerville wrote Franklin that he was enlarging his foundry in order to sell types abroad, especial-ly to the colonies. He begged Franklin's good offices in helping him sell his fonts to printers in North America. But Baskerville's hopes proved abortive. Even with Franklin's good will to help him, he did not sell much type to American printers. The American printer in general was a conservative; it had taken him a long time to realize that Caslon was better than James and he had no inten-tion of changing again in favor of the upstart who now sought his custom.

Though he had retired from active printing as early as 1748, Franklin's interest in the problems of typography continued to the end of his life. For a long period we read in his correspondence lit-tle of printing matters, but events in a world which included the Fourniers, the Didots, and the Anissons led him in his French so-journ to a revival of interest in printing and to an actual resump-tion of its practice. My belief is that he set up a private press and type foundry in his house at Passy as a relief from the vexations of his daily life. He knew exciting moments in plenty in the course of that mission to France, but there was a great deal of routine in it of a tiresome nature. Replying to cadets of good family who had no money but wished to enter the American army at ranks con-siderably in advance of those they held in the French establishment was enough in itself to compel a search for relaxation. It is in-teresting, I think, that in this need the old man fell back upon the craft he had learned in boyhood. There at Passy, with a French press and types, and probably with a French journeyman to help, he printed for his friends a group of frivolous little pieces, a few serious ones, and many blank forms for the use of his office. One can be sure of the interest and delight with which he learned and accustomed himself to the French style of setting and page design.

The press which Franklin established at Passy was, however, more than a toy and a diversion. Through its operation he en-

countered again, this time as an experimenter, the problems of
type design and press construction, and once more circumstances
lead us to remark upon his knack of being at the right place at the
right time. The tendency towards "modern face" in type design
had begun in France as long ago as 1702 with the letters of Grand-
jean. Further developed by Pierre Simon Fournier, the new style,
in Franklin's time in France, was claiming much of the thought of
Firmin Didot. Some years before, Fournier had devised the point
system for the measurement of type and had written his "Manuel
Typographique." At this very time, Anisson and Didot were making presses with platens large enought to permit an entire type form
to be impressed with one pull of the bar, thus cutting down ap-
preciably the time and effort of presswork. Into all this activity,
preliminary to the great changes in typographical practice that occurred in the generation after his death, Franklin entered with zest,
corresponding with different members of the Fournier and Didot
families and with others interested in typecasting; reading a work
on logographic casting, the "Nouveau Systeme typographique" of
Madame de Saint Paul; experimenting himself with the making of
logotypes; and corresponding with Anisson *fils* on that subject
and on improvements in the press.

But he was not satisfied in this instance with talk. He bought
typefounding equipment, and in his house at Passy cast quantities
of type, some of which he afterwards sold in America.[18] In this
time also he caused his grandson, Benjamin Franklin Bache, to be
taught the mysteries of printing and typefounding by the Didots
and the Fourniers. In 1785 he brought young Bache back to
Philadelphia, equipped with a foundry and prepared to cast type
for all who would buy. These were wonderful years for Franklin,
the typographer, but for a greater effect upon the history of printing, they should have come earlier in his life.

A BRIEF ANALYSIS OF THE PRINTING BUSINESS

It is of interest to consider for a moment the character of the
printed matter which issued from the Franklin establishment in
Philadelphia. Neither with Franklin alone as proprietor nor as the

---

[18]Livingston, "Franklin and his Press at Passy." Chapter VI. "The Passy Types in
America."

firm of Franklin & Hall was its accomplishment such as to justify us in claiming for it a great degree of influence upon the cultural life of its community. Franklin was an assiduous reader of books, a self-educated man enthusiastic in the cause of practical culture, and the founder of a library and a learned society, but even with this predilection he was not a publisher of books on anything like the scale one might expect. It would not occur to the historian to apply to him the epithet "Nurse of Literature," which seems to belong to his contemporary William Parks of Annapolis and Williamsburg. His bookshop, Mr. Van Doren has pointed out, served the literary interests of Philadelphia, and, in the other ways just specified, his activities made him a leader in the intellectual progress of his community. It seems clear, however, that he regarded his printing house as solely for utilitarian service, and that he had no intention of jeopardizing its prosperity by going into the business of publishing on his own account. It is something of a disappointment to learn that, with all his interest in the subject, he published no works of science except the Pennsylvanian Fireplace book and a few books of household medicine. It is difficult to understand why he never printed in his own establishment some record of those fundamental experiments in electricity which he and his group of Philadelphia associates carried out from 1746 onwards. He was not alone among American printers in his indifference to the honor of publishing books of science and letters. He and they realized, probably, that, except within certain narrow categories, there was little sale for the book published with an American imprint. The imported book was the thing. Inventories of colonial libraries, north and south, are heavy with titles of British production; rarely does an American-printed work appear upon them. Locally printed books either were not given place on the library shelves beside the London production, or were regarded by owners and estate appraisers as ephemeral material of a value too small to justify their inclusion in the inventories. Franklin was not quixotic enough to tilt at this particular windmill of custom and fashion.

This is not to say that Franklin failed to engage in publishing ventures of any sort. The *Gazette* was one of those he fostered; the *Poor Richard's Almanac* was another. I have found no figures for the early years of *Poor Richard,* but in the period of the Franklin & Hall partnership measured by the years 1752-1765, the average annual impression of that homely production was something over 10,000 copies, sold at 4d. each. But we may not pause for too close an analysis of the firm's accounts.[19] Turning to the statement of cash receipts for 1748-1765, we find the total to be £28,266 Pennsylvania currency, or about $416,000 in today's money. The proceeds from the *Gazette* account for more than half this sum. Then in order come the job work, *Poor Richard,* and the public work. The amount received from the sale of primers, catechisms, spelling books, Votes, Laws, and Indian treaties, respectable in the aggregate, was relatively small under the head of each category. One item "Books & Pamphlets, printed and sold in the shop" ran to £1,118 Pennsylvania currency. Analyzing the account in a different way, we find that the public work and the job printing brought in £6,314 Pennsylvania currency, the *Gazette* subscriptions and advertising £17,000, *Poor Richard* and the lesser categories some £5,000. A summarized statement of the partnership account informs us that about 61 percent of the firm's income was from the *Gazette*, 21 per cent from the public work and job printing, and 18 per cent from miscellaneous publishing projects at its own risk. If figures were available for the period in which Franklin was alone, I believe the proportions would not be greatly different.

FRANKLIN AS TYPOGRAPHER

Comparing the printing done by Franklin in his early years as a master printer with contemporary work executed in Boston, New York and Philadelphia, it is obvious that the revival of interest in the esthetics of printing which he had encountered in England in 1725 and 1726 had affected permanently his own attitude towards his craft. There is no doubt that thenceforth he attempted consciously to produce work that would be pleasing in typographical form, kind to the reader's eyesight, and a correct presentation of the author's text. It must always be remembered that this revival was not based upon new type designs or new implements, but upon a new thoughtfulness in the use of the available types and equipment. An appreciation of correct spacing and leading of letterpress, of evenness of presswork, symmetry and balance of page

---

[19]The figures quoted here are drawn from the important document cited in note 11, above.

design, the reduction and symmetrical distribution of the wording of title-pages were all factors that the English printers were giving renewed attention to before Caslon produced his mechanically uniform type faces. All these were characteristics of an age that sought clarity, balance, and ease in the forms of its art as well as in its intellectual processes.

Franklin was not an innovator in typographical design. One of his few excursions from the well-beaten path was his "Cato Major" of 1744, but I have never felt that this book was as successful as the general run of his government publications, and the style of these was an inheritance from the seventeenth century. Until he began printing at Passy under the French influence he never for long got away from that form of title-page in which a rather narrow rectangle of display matter was enclosed within ruled borders. But working within this limitation dictated by his conservatism he created a variant upon the earlier style which became the norm for American printers. Instead of attempting in the old manner to crowd his title-page with a complete synopsis of the text, he stripped its wording to the barest statement of the matter of the book and, by taking thought, displayed this concise statement in such fashion that each word had its own place and its own weight in the design. His pages of letterpress were set upon the paper page with proper regard for margins, and composed with a spacing and leading consciously intended to make easy reading without the sacrifice of solidity and color. Economical of paper, he and his successors for generations employed in the text setting a type size somewhat small for the page size. The need for paper economy prevented in these American printers the ease and generosity, the lavishness which demand admiration when one examines the work of the great printers at the end of the century—Baskerville, Bodoni, and Didot. There is, in consequence, always a feeling of frustration when one finds the monumental title-page of Franklin, and those contemporaries who learned from him, followed by pages of text correctly designed but executed in a type too small for the area covered. But within that limitation imposed by the need for paper economy Franklin at his best, as in the Indian Treaties (I like especially his first, the Treaty of 1737), and in his books of Pennsylvania statutes (I like the "Collection of all the Laws" of 1742), gave his patrons a book that pleased their critical sense and was easy to read. At the same time, and through the agency of such books as these, he provided contemporary printers with models which they might follow, not by a large expenditure for new equipment, but merely by taking thought of what they were doing.

It is my belief that Franklin allowed himself to be satisfied when he had achieved this standard of excellence. He was interested in printing as a means of earning a living, not as a means of artistic expression. He believed that to earn his living honestly he must give a good job to his customers, give them printing they could read with ease and look at with pleasure. He never went beyond the necessary in practical matters, and his typographical style, once set in a good mould, made no further progress. But his competency had results that reached beyond the doors of his own shop. He was a better teacher of printers than printer. His apprentice and journeyman James Parker learned from him the fundamental principles of the art and carried them on to a finer eventuation. The "Charter of the College of New York" which Parker printed in 1754 is strictly in the style I have described as characteristic of Franklin, but the matter of the ruled title-pages is so admirably placed and the composition and presswork have such a degree of brilliancy, convey so impressively the sense of having uttered the last word in that particular form, that any work of Franklin's I have seen is of an inferior order to them. Jonas Green worked for Franklin, learned from him the integrity of type, and went on to produce his "Laws of Maryland" of 1765, a book which has the honesty, symmetry, and balance of Franklin's work rendered distinguished by a sort of freedom and boldness, a generosity, not found in the work of the master. One thing we are prone to forget is that Franklin's interest in printing as a practice was dormant from the day of his partnership with David Hall in 1748 until he took it up again as an experimental hobby conducted in his own house at Passy in the period 1779-1785. Hall carried on the Franklin style without change, except a change for the worse in presswork, until 1766. The imprint Franklin & Hall, therefore, means Franklin's style of 1730 and Hall's inferior workmanship. We shall never know what Franklin's skill would have become if he had continued at work after 1748, if he had been active in the practice of typography when Baskerville was giving a new quality to the printed word, and when throughout Europe the ferment of experiment was working in the printing shops and the type foundries. But long before that day he had become so absorbed by philosophic, scientific, and political ideas that his trade became a matter of secondary interest in his life. Comparing Bradford's "Laws of Pennsylvania" or B. Green's "Acts and Laws" of Massachusetts, both of 1714, or B. Green's Indian Treaties of 1726, 1732, and 1735, or Kneeland & Green's "Acts and Laws" of Massachusetts of 1742 with Franklin's Treaty of 1737 or his "Collection of all the Laws" of 1742, we think of him as having established in his country an admirable standard of printing. Having achieved that standard, he passed on his taste, good sense, and skill to others more interested than he in carrying their art to higher levels.

There must always remain a feeling of disappointment among those who love the craft of printing that the most distinguished figure in the history of American typography has no place among the inventors responsible for the technical progress of the art. When in 1743 Cadwallader Colden described to Franklin his ideas about a process which must have been a form of stereotyping, one wonders why with all his mechanical ingenuity, his industry, his passion for new ideas, he did not make Colden's proposed method effective. He probably knew of Ged's previous invention, and he certainly realized that the printing trade in America was in no need of a process visualized at that time chiefly as a means in the production of large editions for which type was to be kept standing. But even so, why didn't he get excited about it just as an idea? Probably the answer lies in his natural pragmatism; the American printing trade had little need in that day for the stereotype process. In later years, when that need arose, he or another would find time to satisfy it. Sufficient to the day are the implements thereof, is a concept that might be regarded as a tenet of Franklin's philosophy.

And so with other aspects of his interest in press and type. As early as 1753, he made an admirable suggestion for the increase of ease in running the carriage of the press back and forth,[20] and there is reason to believe that he built a press or presses embodying this improvement for his printing-house at Passy.[21] Neither at one time nor the other, however, did he force that idea upon the world by constructing presses which printers would have been compelled to buy because of the improved mechanism of their carriages. It re-

---

[20]Franklin to Strahan, October 27, 1753 ("Life and Writings," Smyth edition, III: 165-167).

[21]Livingston, "Franklin and his Press at Passy," page 124.

mained for another man of science, William Nicholson, to make in
the year of Franklin's death the fundamental change from the vertical principle of impression to the horizontal, and thereby to give
the world the cylinder press. Franklin bought typefounding tools,
he was an early patron of Caslon, a staunch supporter of Baskerville, and a patron of the Fourniers and Didots, but so far as we
know he designed no type and made no improvements in the
mechanism of its production. He had more to do with the paper
trade than any man in America, but it was after his death that the
Fourdrinier papermaking machine came into being.

It was greatly to our advantage, of course, that he should have
given up reflection upon the printing processes to talk and write
and cogitate upon problems that had to do with the happiness of
man. It was essential that printing should be carried beyond the
primitive stage in which he found and left it, but it was not
necessary that this advance be brought about by him. His interests
were fundamental, universal. The world just then needed Franklin
the scientist and practical political philosopher, and his country
needed the man who could stand before the House of Commons
and by sheer sense and good temper encourage it to reconsider the
Stamp Act. When we complain that his name is absent from the
role of those who have changed the aspect of his beloved craft, his
silence replies in terms that seem to mean: "It is more fitting at this
time to discourse of men and states, to build better chimneys, and
to fly kites."

EDITOR'S NOTE

Aside from Wroth's essay, little has been done on Franklin exclusively as a printer, although he made his fortune in the printing
business and related entrepreneurial activities. Even after his
retirement from active printing in 1748, his interest in printing
never flagged. At the peak of his diplomatic career and in the last
years of his life he considered himself a printer first. He began his
last will and testament: "I, Benjamin Franklin, of Philadelphia,
Printer, late Minister Plenipotentiary from the United States of
America to the Court of France...."

Wroth observes that Franklin published very few works on the
sciences. It is not that he was unwilling to print such works,
although there was some financial risk involved. In 1745 Franklin

offered to publish Cadwallader Colden's essay on the cause of gravitation at his "own Expence and Risque." He asserted: "If I can be a Means of Communicating anything valuable to the World, I do not always think of Gaining, nor even of Saving by my Business; But a Piece of that kind, as it must excite the Curiosity of all the Learned, can hardly fail of bearing its own Expence."[1] Colden, however, had a limited edition of his essay published by James Parker in New York with the title *An Expliction of the First Causes of Action in Matter, and, of Cause of Gravitation*. The *Explication* was introductory to the larger work, *The Principles of Action in Matter*, published by Robert Dodsley in London in 1752. Franklin's electrical papers were published in London. As a rule, a colonial intellectual who believed that he could make a contribution to scientific progress in Europe preferred to have his work published in Great Britain or on the Continent.

Wroth wonders why Franklin did not get excited about Colden's description of a new method of printing "just as an idea." No written observation on the subject by Franklin is extant. London printers, among them William Straham, a friend of Franklin, considered the new method (stereotype printing) too costly and impracticable.[2] Franklin may have shared that opinion. About 1775 Benjamin Mecom, printer and nephew of Franklin, attempted stereotype printing of the New Testament, but never completed the task. In the early nineteenth century stereotype printing was commonly used in the United States in the publication of periodicals.[3]

Wroth shares with the reader his uncertainty regarding Franklin's early venture into typefounding. Because of the high cost of importing type from England, the establishment of a typefoundry in the colonies would have been a saving to the printers, not to mention a profitable enterprise for an ambitious colonial craftsman. The question Wroth raises remains unanswered; it is

---

[1]Franklin to Colden, Philadelphia, Nov. 28, 1745, *The Papers of Benjamin Franklin*, ed. by Leonard W. Labaree *et al.*, III, 46.

[2]Peter Collinson to Colden, London March 2, 1742/3, *Collections* of the New York Historical Society for the Year 1919, p. 11; Will Strahan to Colden, May 9, 1744, *ibid.*, p. 58.

[3]Isaiah Thomas, *The History of Printing in America with a Biography of Printers & an Account of Newspapers*, ed. by Marcus A. McCorison from the 2nd ed. of 1874 (Barre, Mass.: Imprint Society, 1970), p.34.

not clear what Franklin was doing with typefounding tools between 1744 and 1747. So far as is known, the earliest American typefoundries were operated by Abe Buell in Connecticut, David Mitchelson in Boston, and Christopher Sauer, the younger, in Germantown after 1768.[4] Franklin became seriously interested in typefounding while in Passy in the 1780s. There he purchased foundry equipment, and had his grandson, Benjamin Franklin Bache, study typefounding with leading French authorities.[5] Young Bache, however, evinced little interest in the typefoundry his grandfather established in Philadelphia in 1786. In 1806 the Franklin Foundry equipment became the property of Binney and Ronaldson, printers, and in 1892 the equipment was inherited by American Type Founders, Inc. Some years later the equipment was deposited in the Columbia University Library for preservation.[6]

---

[4]Richard F. Hixson, *Isaac Collins, A Quaker Printer in 18th Century America* (New Brunswick, N.J.: Rutgers University Press, c1968), p. 27.

[5]Douglas C. McMurtrie, *A History of Printing in the United States*, 2 vols. (New York: R.R. Bowker Co., 1936), II, 53.

[6]Thomas Roy Jones, *Printing in America — and American Type Founders* (New York: The Newcomen Society of England, American Branch, 1948), pp. 10-11.

Benjamin Franklin: Adventures in Agriculture

CARL R. WOODWARD

Carl Raymond Woodward (1890-1974) served as President of the University of Rhode Island from 1941. He followed up on this essay, presented at The Franklin Institute on March 15, 1940, with the publication of *Ploughs and Politicks: Charles Read of New Jersey and His Notes on Agriculture, 1715-1774* in 1941. He is also the author of *The Development of Agriculture in New Jersey, 1640-1880, a Monographic Study in Agricultural History*, published in 1927.

Although Benjamin Franklin was essentially a big-town man, city-born and city-bred, and although his tastes were urban rather than rural, the manifold activities of his amazingly varied career frequently led him into the field of agriculture. This was but natural in a land which was still predominantly rural; it was inevitable for one of such universal interests and boundless talents.

In dealing with Benjamin Franklin's adventures in agriculture we must think of him in two separate roles: first "Franklin the Farmer"; and second, "Franklin the Agricultural Leader." The latter term, I admit, is commonplace, but I have not succeeded in finding a better one. I started out with "Franklin the agricultural scientist," but he was more than this. "Franklin the agricultural philosopher" seemed better, but not altogether satisfactory, suggesting, as it does, the scientist and the thinker. He was more than this; he was above all a man of action, who translated philosophy into works. Presently we shall see how substantially his leadership contributed to agricultural progress. There is much to be said about this phase of his career—more than we can treat exhaustively in the time at our disposal.

FRANKLIN THE FARMER

The record of Franklin the Farmer has long been shrouded in mystery. Biographers and students of Franklin have been puzzled by the absence of specific evidence and by seemingly conflicting

215

data dealing with his practical farm operations. The mystery was projected just one hundred years ago, when Dr. Jared Sparks issued his 10-volume edition of "The Works of Benjamin Franklin."[1] Here for the first time was published a collection of letters from Franklin to Jared Eliot, clergyman-physician of Guilford, Connecticut, Yale graduate and trustee, who had experimented with agriculture on the side, and whose "Essays on Field Husbandry in New England" constituted the first major American work on agriculture. Included with the letters, which are now in the Sterling Library at Yale, was one bearing no date, in which the author informed Mr. Eliot, "I have perused your two Essays on Field Husbandry, and think the Publick may be much benefited by them; But if the Farmers in your neighbourhood are as unwilling to leave the beaten path of their Ancestors as they are near me, it will be difficult to persuade them to attempt any improvement. About 18 months ago I made a Purchase of about three hundred Acres of Land near Burlington, and resolved to Improve it in the best and Speediest Manner, that I might be Enabled to Indulge my Self in that kind of life which was most agreeable."[2] Then the author proceded to describe the place, and give a detailed account of his farm operations. There were about eighty acres of deep meadow land. The soil was very fine and black, three feet deep, then it came to "a fatt bluish clay." He scoured out the ditches, plowed it, sowed oats, mowed them, plowed again, and seeded with red clover and herd grass. He made a minute examination of the clover as it sprouted and grew. On the upland he had a 12-acre depression which formed a round pond because there was no outlet. He drained the pond and found black soil about a foot deep, underlain with a light-colored sandy subsoil. This he seeded to grass and rye.

Ever since this letter was published, it has been accepted tradition that Franklin operated an experimental farm in New Jersey. The letter suggests a desire to retire to a rural life, and although it is undated, the time of the purchase of the farm seems to have been near the time Franklin turned the operation of the printshop over to his partner David Hall. But curiously enough, in his "Autobiography," he made no mention of the farm and gave no

[1] Boston, 1840.
[2] Smyth, Albert Henry, "The Life and Writings of Benjamin Franklin," New York, 1905-07, v. 2, p.383.

indication that he removed his residence from Philadelphia to Burlington for such a period as would be required for the farm operations described. In other letters, he frequently discussed agricultural matters but gave not the slightest hint that he had a farm in New Jersey. Hence upon this letter alone was based the story of the Burlington farm. The letter has been included in all later collections of Franklin's works, e.g., John Bigelow's "The Complete Works of Benjamin Franklin" (10 vols., New York, 1887-89) and Albert Henry Smyth's "The Life and Writings of Benjamin Franklin" (10 vols., New York, 1905-07). And it has been accepted freely and without reservation by Franklin's numerous biographers.

The Quest of the Farm

From time to time it has been asked, "Where was the farm located?" and "What became of it?" For many years, it was thought to have been the same as Governor William Franklin's estate near Burlington on the Rancocas Creek, commonly known as Franklin Park. It seemed plausible that Benjamin should have conveyed the place to his son for a country seat when the latter became Governor of New Jersey, especially since he could have no personal use for it while he was on his official missions in London. Subsequent events indicate that Benjamin must have been familiar with this place. In 1769, the Governor wrote his father, that he had "entered far into the spirit of farming."[3] and asked the elder Franklin to send him a drain plow, and a patent plow from England. Then came the Revolution which interrupted William Franklin's career as a country gentleman and the farm was left without a master. But in 1785, when Benjamin was returning from France accompanied by his grandson William Temple Franklin, he visited the exiled William in England. During that historic reconciliation, papers were drawn conveying the Rancocas farm to William Temple, and upon reaching home the grandson took possession. To infer that this was Benjamin's New Jersey farm was, after all, a natural conclusion.

An examination of the recorded deeds in the State House at Trenton, however, revealed that the estate comprised approx-

---

[3]Duane, Wm., "Letters to Benjamin Franklin from his Family and Friends," 1750-1790. New York, 1859, p. 42.

imately six hundred (not three hundred) acres, that William had purchased it in the three separate tracts, and that Benjamin had never owned any portion of it. So it was necessary to seek elsewhere for an answer.

Then began a determined hunt, in which a number of Franklin followers collaborated. Mr. George DeCou of Moorestown, N.J., Mr. William Mason of Evanston, Ill., Mr. George Simpson Eddy of New York City, and Mr. Franklin Bache, of West Chester, Pa., were especially active. No deed or record of transfer or of ownership was to be found in State archives at Trenton, at the County record office in Mt. Holly, or at the West Jersey Proprietors' office in Burlington. It was suggested that the farm may have been across the river in Pennsylvania, and still be "near Burlington," but in a search of the Bucks County records was likewise fruitless. So the riddle continued unsolved.

The scheduling of this lecture furnished the incentive for one more effort. To some of you I remarked facetiously three months ago that I proposed to find the farm and to announce its location here this afternoon. I have been making a further study, and I have something to announce, but it is not what I had hoped it would be. On the basis of new evidence, unearthed these recent weeks, we have come reluctantly to the conclusion that Franklin was not the author of the letter to Eliot in which the Burlington farm was described, and furthermore, that he neither owned nor operated a farm in New Jersey.

How, you ask, did we arrive at this conclusion? Let me outline briefly the course of our investigation. First of all, we are indebted to Mr. George DeCou for putting us on the right track. In January, 1940, he visited the Yale Library and examined the Eliot letters. He found that the letter relating to the farm was incomplete—the last page was gone and the signature missing; furthermore he detected a difference in the handwriting as compared with the other letters clearly written in Franklin's hand and signed by him. He wrote me of his suspicions and I went to New Haven for a further examination. Mr. Bernard Knollenberg, the librarian, himself, as you know, a keen student of Franklin, aided me in my efforts. We found not only that the handwriting was not Franklin's, but further evidence in the context, when related to statements in other letters, which pointed strongly toward another author.

For example, in a signed letter written December 24, 1751, Franklin suggested to Eliot that he could get certain agricultural information from John Bartram, the Quaker botanist of Philadelphia, and from Peter Collinson of London. Then followed this significant comment: "And since for want of skill in agriculture I cannot converse with you pertinently on that valuable subject, I am pleased that I have procured you two correspondents who can."[4] Which naturally gives rise to the question: Why would Franklin say this if two years earlier he had written at length about his farm experiments?

Another point of evidence is the absence of local tradition about a Franklin-owned farm. Franklin's temporary printshop at Burlington where in 1727 he printed currency for the province of New Jersey, has long been marked a point of historic interest. If he had really owned a farm near the same place it would certainly have been known in the community at the time, and for a person of his prominence, word would have been passed down from generation to generation. However, there seems to have been no tradition of Benjamin Franklin in the role of farmer in the neighborhood of Burlington.

If not Franklin, then who was the author of the letter? During the search for the so-called Franklin farm, evidence was unearthed which led to the irrefutable conclusion that the letter was written by Charles Read, cousin of Deborah Franklin, who was also related to the Logans, the Pembertons and other prominent Philadelphia families. In 1739 Read moved to Burlington and became a dominant figure in the affairs of New Jersey. Between 1740 and 1770, he served as provincial secretary, as justice of the Supreme Court, as member of the Royal Council, and in other offices. In 1747 he purchased a farm of 212 acres in Springfield Township, Burlington County, midway between the present villages of Jobstown and Juliustown, and subsequently acquired an adjacent tract. He named the place *Sharon*, and in 1750 sold it to his friend Daniel Doughty. Many years later it was acquired by Barclay White, father of the late Joseph J. White, New Jersey's premier cranberry grower. The present owner is Mr. Hilary Tilghman.

About twelve years ago there came to light in Burlington County an old farm record book, with miscellaneous entries made

---

[4]Smyth, v.3, p. 61.

between 1746 and 1777. It contained descriptions of numerous farm experiments by the owner, together with the observations and experiences of more than a hundred other persons, and extracts from various books on agriculture. (Among the items, incidentally was a recipe for making glue from sturgeon which Benjamin Franklin had got from a correspondent in London, and sent to the owner of the book.) The cover and flyleaf were gone, and the owner's name did not appear, but the content, the handwriting and other factors all pointed conclusively to Charles Read.

On studying the text, we found a record of the same experiment with red clover that is described in the letter supposedly from Franklin to Eliot. There can be no mistake about it. They coincide to the very day of the month, the length and number of roots, and the same peculiar terminology, e.g. "deep meadow," planted "23rd of August," "came up in four days," measured "the last of October," "the tap-roots penetrated five inches"—and threw out from the sides "near 30 horizontal roots some of which were six inches long and branched," and in freezing weather the plants "hove out much where thin sown." The identical words, and the identical statistics, in both documents—and in the first person, too. Mr. Knollenberg and his associates considered this sufficient evidence to change the record in the Yale Library catalogue, and the letter to Eliot was removed from the list of Franklin items.

But was the farm described in the letter, Charles Read's *Sharon?* Read was involved in many speculative enterprises, and had extensive land holdings. Regardless of whether it was owned by Frankin or by Read, we wanted, if possible, to locate the subject of the letter.

Early in March, 1940, accompanied by Dr. Linnwood Lee, head of the New Jersey Soil Conservation Service, I paid a visit to *Sharon*—curious, expectant, but prepared for disappointment. Imagine our mixed feelings when we found that the farm corresponded, to a remarkable degree, with the description in the letter—the 80-acre meadow, the deep black soil, the bluish-green clay, or marl; and the round depression that was the 12-acre pond—here they all were.

But what of the handwriting of the letter? Was it Charles Read's? Although it was similar to some portions of the Read notebook, to the eye of a layman it seemed not to correspond with the general run of Read's letters or his notes. So I enlisted the help of Dr. Samuel Tannenbaum, of New York, Shakesperian scholar and handwriting expert. After a week's study of the Read notebook and a collection of Read letters, and quite unaware of my findings on the Burlington County farm, he came to the conclusion that the letter alleged to be by Franklin is really in the handwriting of Charles Read.[5]

With this body of evidence, we cannot escape the conclusion that Charles Read was the author of the letter to Eliot, which for a century has been attributed to Franklin. So we shall have to revise our concept of Franklin the farmer, and this phase of Franklin's biography will have to be rewritten. Our former concept of Franklin's farm operations has been proved false. I have been guilty, with others, of perpetuating the pleasant myth that the great philosopher had one of America's first experimental farms within the boundaries of New Jersey. Now I am obliged to take back what I have previously written on the subject.

The Philadelphia Pasture Lot

Are we to conclude from this that Franklin never engaged in farm operations, or that he never owned any farm property? Happily the story of Franklin the Farmer is not wholly negative. He did plant seeds and grow crops, to a limited extent. In Deborah Franklin's letters to her husband while he was in England, there is mention of a pasture. In 1747 Franklin wrote to Jared Eliot that the grass seed he had sent him, supposed to be herd-grass, when planted proved to be timothy. Again in 1753 he wrote Eliot, "I wish the Barbary Barley may grow. I have some of it, and have sow'd it; but it seem'd to me to have been cut too green."[6] Perhaps he sowed it in the back yard of his home on High (Market) Street or perhaps in a neighbor's garden. It seems more probable, however, that he planted it on a lot which he rented in Philadelphia. In 1741 he leased from William Coates, a brickmaker, a 2½-acre lot in the Northern Liberties.[7] It was about a mile from Franklin's High Street residence, and lay across what

---

[5] Dr. Tannenbaum's comment, together with other evidence of Read's authorship of the letter and of the notebook, is given in the foreword of "Ploughs and Politicks," by C.R. Woodward, Rutgers University Press, 1941.

[6] Smyth, v.3., p. 128.

[7] Phila. County Deeds, Lib. H7, p. 423.

is now North Tenth Street, extending two blocks from the present Fairmount Avenue to Parrish Street. Franklin contracted to pay Coates an annual rental of 3 pounds, 4 shillings and in signing the lease, agreed not to dig clay for the manufacture of bricks, nor to sink any sand pits on the premises without the owner's consent.

It has been suggested that Franklin leased the lot as a suitable site for a glue factory, or for the boiling of linseed oil for the manufacture of varnish. More likely, it seems, he secured it as a pasture for a pony of his son, William, who was then eleven years old. The following spring the pony was lost, and in June, Benjamin advertised for him in the *Pennsylvania Gazette*: "Strayed, about two months ago from the Northern Liberties of this city, a small bay mare branded IW on the near shoulder and buttock. She, being but little and bare-footed, cannot be supposed to have gone far; therefore if any of the town boys find her and bring her to the subscriber, they shall for their trouble have the liberty to ride her when they please." Likely enough the pony had strayed from the pasture lot. It has been suggested also that Franklin may have had a cow which he kept on the lot, or possibly a horse of his own, but there seems to be no authentic record of either.

Perhaps it was on this lot he planted the barley and other crops as well. Perhaps, too, it was here that he flew his electric kite. The precise site of this famous experiment will probably never be known, but it is reputed to have been in this vicinity.

Franklin's lease on the lot continued at least twenty-four years and probably longer. Entries in his receipt books, now in the Library of the American Philosophical Society, show that while he was in England pleading the cause of the American colonies, the rent was paid by his wife Deborah, who remained in Philadelphia. In one of the letters to her husband written in 1765, she reported that she had the rubbish of lime from their new house spread on the pasture, along with some ashes.[8] Presumably the pasture was on this lot.

Many changes have come to the pasture lot since the philosopher leased it two centuries ago. For years it was an area of tenement houses. Curiously enough, however, the vicinity in 1940, when the lot was identified, had reverted to its former status of an open field. It had recently been chosen for a slum clearance pro-

---

[8] Duane, p. 22.

ject; the buildings for several blocks were completely razed; and the open squares enclosed with board fences. Here and there some ancient trees suggested its former natural state. Among them were specimens of the rare varnish tree (*Koelreuteria paniculata*), a native of the Far East, possibly the offspring of trees which grew from seeds or young plants imported in Franklin's time.[9]

Although the pasture was only leased, the leasehold seems to have been regarded as equivalent to ownership, as indicated in Deborah Franklin's letters. Also, in an unpublished will dated April 28, 1757, Franklin bequeathed to his son William "my Pasture Ground in the Northern Liberties."

Somewhere the Franklins had apple trees, for in 1758 Benjamin wrote to Deborah, "You have dispos'd of the Apple-Trees very properly," and added, "I condole with you on the Loss of your Walnuts."[10] Sometime later Deborah wrote Benjamin that she had been advised to plant an orchard on the pasture, but she was not disposed to do so.

Besides the rented lot, there was another tract of land which Franklin might have utilized for agricultural purposes. We know now that he did own a farm which was located, not in New Jersey, but in Chester County, Pennsylvania. Information about this place, too, has only recently come to light, and likewise, the information is but fragmentary. Thanks to evidence unearthed by Mr. Charles Montgomery, of Philadelphia, and Mr. John M. Okie, of Lansdowne, Pennsylvania, it appears that the farm embraced two tracts lying close by the village of Kemblesville, in New London Township. No record of the deed has been found in the State or County Archives. However, certain tax records, mortgages[11] and letters together supply conclusive evidence of Franklin's ownership. The New London Township tax lists show that Franklin was assessed for 200 acres of land in 1766, and he appears also in the lists of 1767 and 1771.[12] The farm is mentioned also in two letters among the Franklin Papers of the American Philosophical Society, one of them to Deborah Franklin from

---

[9] An article about this pasture lot by the present author appears in *The Merck Review* (Rahway, N.J.), I, 1-2, Sept. 1940.

[10] Smyth, v.3. p. 441

[11] Chester Co., Pa., Deeds, Book M, p. 315; N, p. 14, 44; Sheriff's Deed Books, No. 1, p. 39, 68.

[12] *Pennsylvania Archives*, 3rd series, v. 11, p. 246, 352, 717.

George Read of New Castle, the youthful lawyer who became a signer of both the Declaration of Independence and the Constitution.[13] Also Deborah Franklin in an unpublished letter now in the collection of Mr. Franklin Bache, wrote to her husband in London in 1766 about her troubles in managing their land in Chester County.

The records do not show precisely when Franklin acquired the lands, or why. A plausible explanation would be that he took them in settlement of a debt. The transaction seems to have been handled by Deborah, in the absence of her husband, who after a two years' stay in Philadelphia returned to England in November, 1764. From her letter, we infer that the deed was delivered but she probably never took the trouble to have it recorded, hoping soon to dispose of the place.

From the available sources we gather that the place was acquired from George McCleave, a tavern keeper, that the land was poor and the dwelling in need of repair, that the tenants had destroyed the fences, that there was neither barn nor stable, that the neighbors were generally poor and worthless, and that the Franklins would be better off if they could get rid of it. Deborah wrote to Benjamin that she had one or two to "hire the place," but she was afraid they would spoil it, because, she said, "there is none but rogues all about." And she added that George Read, who seems to have been acting as her agent, thought it was "the worst place in all the country."[14]

So is our picture of Benjamin Franklin the Farmer deflated! The situation is not without a measure of humor. Instead of the country gentleman, proprietor of an experimental farm in the rich marl-belt of New Jersey, we find him the owner of a dilapidated, worn-out place in a then undesirable neighborhood!

It seems quite improbable that Franklin ever operated the Kemblesville farm, or carried on any experiments there. When he disposed of it we have not learned. After 1757 he spent only 8 of the remaining 33 years of his life in America—a 2-year interlude from 1762 to 1764; 17 months in 1775-76, and somewhat less than five years after his return from France in 1785 until his death in 1790. The Kemblesville farm seems to have been acquired after his

---

[13]Amer. Phil. Soc., *Franklin Papers*, v. 2, no. 6, p. 1.

[14]"Deborah Franklin to Benjamin Franklin," Jan. 12, 1766; in collection of Mr. Franklin Bache.

return to England in 1764. Between 1766 and 1771, the years he was on the tax lists, he was in England, and the responsibility for the place was carried by the faithful and reliable Deborah. During his brief Philadelphia sojourn in 1775-76, he was so completely engrossed with the political and military activities of the Revolution as to preclude adventures in agriculture, and in the meantime Deborah had died. After his final homecoming in 1785, he was so ill and feeble as to make travel a burden, and a trip to a run-down farm 40 miles from Philadelphia would seem to be out of the question.

In Franklin's later years, he acquired other lands—in Nova Scotia and on the Ohio. But obviously these were for speculative investment rather than for agricultural purposes.

Eighteenth Century Farm Demonstration

There remains to be mentioned one last incident of Franklin the Farmer—his well-known demonstration of the benefits of land plaster. It has become a well-established Franklin tradition, a worthy companion to the story of the electric kite. But its source is not to be found in any of Franklin's published works. For it, we are indebted to Jean Antoine Claude Chaptal, Compte De Chanteloup, author of the French work, "Chimie Appliquée a l'Agriculture," published in Paris in 1825. I quote from the English translation of 1835:

"The use of plaster, or gypsum, which has become common in Europe as a manure, is one of the most important improvements that has ever been made in agriculture. It has even been introduced into America, where it was made known by Franklin upon his return from Paris. As this celebrated philosopher wished that the effects of this manure should strike the gaze of all cultivators, he wrote in great letters, formed by the use of the ground plaster, in a field of clover lying upon the great road to Washington, 'This has been plastered.' The prodigious vegetation which was developed in the plastered portion led him to adopt this method. Volumes upon the excellences of plaster would not have produced so speedy a revolution. From that period the Americas have imported great quantities of plaster of Paris."[15]

Where was the field on which the demonstration was staged? What was the "great road to Washington"? According to Chaptal, the event must have occurred after 1785. William Temple

---

[15]Chaptal, J.A.C., "Chymistry Applied to Agriculture," 1835, p. 73.

Franklin had settled on the Rancocas farm, but there is no evidence that Benjamin ever visited his grandson there. Also, since Temple's country seat was not situated on a main highway, it can be eliminated as the site of the demonstration. And we have already observed the improbability that Franklin ever visited the Kemblesville farm. Might it have been done on the leased pasture in the Northern Liberties? This seems doubtful. We do not know that Franklin continued his lease of the pasture after the Revolution. Furthermore, so far as we know, no main highway ran beside it. Even if there were, a road lying north of the center of the city would scarcely be called "the main highway to Washington." Besides, the city of Washington was not founded until after Franklin's death.

The account does not say that Franklin spread plaster on a field of his own. If he actually conducted the demonstration as late in life as Chaptal indicates it seems more probable that he borrowed for the purpose the field of a friend along the Chester Road near the outskirts of Philadelphia.

We shall probably never know the precise answer. Presumably Chaptal got the story from some friend or correspondent of Franklin's in France. We cannot confirm it from Franklin's known works; nor can we dispute it. Let's hope it will never be disproved. It is too good a story for debunking. We should like to see it stand for all time.

You will agree, I think, that contrary to my natural inclination, I haven't been able to make a very strong case for Franklin the Farmer. But this need not subtract one jot or one title from Franklin's great service as an Agricultural Leader. It is to this phase of his career we shall now direct our attention.

FRANKLIN THE AGRICULTURAL LEADER

Benjamin Franklin exemplified to a remarkable degree the modern agencies of agricultural progress. As an individual he performed many of the major functions now sponsored by the Government in its national agricultural program. He anticipated something of the work of the agricultural experiment station, of the consular service and of the agricultural educator. Perhaps the most distinctive agency for the promotion of agriculture in America is our system of Land-Grant Colleges, which we popularly call the state agricultural colleges. These institutions, supported jointly by state and federal funds, perform a three-fold function; viz., research, resident instruction, and extension. They cooperate closely with the United States Department of Agriculture, which, in addition to its extensive policing powers, also conducts a great program of research, and is engaged in the introduction of new plants, and other measures for the improvement of agriculture. Let us see how Franklin touched these same fields of activity even before the birth of our government.

Long before the movement for farm organization took hold either in Europe or in America, Franklin recognized the possibilities of agricultural societies as a means of discovering and extending agricultural knowledge. In his plan for the American Philosophical Society, formulated in 1743, he listed among its chief objects, "all new-discovered plants, herbs, trees, roots, their virtues, uses &c.draining of meadows; nature of the soil and productions; new methods of improving the breed of useful animals; introducing other sorts from foreign countries; new improvements in planting, gardening, and clearing land; and all philosophical experiments that let light into the nature of things, tend to increase the power of man over matter, and multiply the conveniences or pleasures of life."[16] When the society got under way, one section was devoted to "husbandry and American improvements."[17]

Here was the germ of the American agricultural experiment station, and the agricultural extension service. As if an outgrowth of the Philosophical Society, in 1785 a group of prominent citizens in and about Philadelphia formed the Philadelphia Society for Promoting Agriculture. This was the first successful effort in America to establish a society devoted exclusively to agriculture. Happily, the society has had a long and notable history, and is still a vigorous and going concern. If Franklin had been in America at the time of its founding, he almost certainly would have been among the charter members. However, he did not return from Paris until seven months later. Shortly thereafter he joined the Society and two years later his grandson, William Temple, was elected to honorary membership. Because the Agricultural Society confined its activities to the one special field, it could deal more ef-

---

[16]Smyth, v. 2, p. 229-230.
[17] *Trans. Amer. Phil. Soc.*, 1 (Phila., 1771), p. 117-280.

fectively with the agricultural interests outlined by Franklin than the Philosophical Society was ever able to do.

Also Frankin was more than a century in advance of his time, in advocating instruction in the science and practice of agriculture. In his proposal for the Philadelphia Academy, forerunner of the University of Pennsylvania, made in 1749, he included the suggestion:

> While they are reading Natural History, might not a little *Gardening, Planting, Grafting, Inoculating*, etc. be taught and practiced; and now and then Excursions made to the neighbouring Plantations of the best Farmers, their methods observ'd and reason'd upon for the Information of Youth? The Improvement of Agriculture being useful to all, and Skill in it not Disparagement to any.[18]

This is believed to have been the first suggestion by an American that agriculture be studied in school. His advice in this matter was not followed by the directors of the academy, but subsequent developments show that he was proposing a sound scheme of vocational education. We have seen also that he was far ahead of his time in agricultural extension, for his object lesson with land plaster has been called the first instance of farm demonstration on record.

Agricultural Missionary

Quite independently of any formal organization, however, Franklin quietly went about his investigations, and the dissemination of useful information. His travels about the colonies as postmaster-general gave him an opportunity to note the farm practices of different regions, and he always had his eye open for new things. For example, while in Virginia he gathered some broomcorn seed and sent it to his sister in Rhode Island to be distributed among friends. He read Jared Eliot's "Essays upon Field Husbandry," he visited Eliot, exchanged seeds and plants with him and corresponded with him on agricultural subjects. Fencing was a problem the colonial farmer always had with him. On Long Island Franklin saw a new kind of hedge that caught his fancy. So he wrote to Eliot:

---

[18]Smyth, v. 2, p. 395.

"I would know every particular relating to this Matter, as the best Thickness, Height, and Slope of the Bank; the Manner of erecting it, the best Time for the Work, the Way of planting the Hedge, the Price of the Work to Labourers per Rod or Perch, and whatever may be of Use for our Information here, who begin in many Places to be at a Loss for Wood to make Fence with."[19]

There is the legend, seemingly well authenticated, that the introduction of the yellow willow into America was due to him. The story is told that a basket in which some foreign commodity had been imported, having been thrown into a creek, was observed by Franklin to be putting forth green sprouts. He caused the sprouts to be planted on the ground later occupied by the Philadelphia Customs House. They took root and grew, and proved to be the yellow-willow.[20]

During his residence in England, and subsequently in France, he came in touch with European practices, and passed along his observations for the benefit of his American compatriots. His membership in the Royal Society of London and the London Society of Arts put him in touch with many Englishmen who were interested in agriculture and botany—men like Peter Collinson and Dr. John Fothergill. These Englishmen wanted American plants and seeds, and Franklin wrote to John Bartram and Humphry Marshall for them. Likewise he cooperated with the English doctors who were anxious to get herbs for medicinal purposes. He secured for John Bartram his appointment as American botanist to George III. He studied books and pamphlets by English writers on agriculture, ordered them for the American Philosophical Society, and distributed them among his former friends. On excursions about the countryside to seek relaxation from the formalities of court and tension of diplomatic circles, he was quick to perceive new varieties of plants, along with new ideas of culture, to pass on to his American friends. On one occasion he sent John Bartram from England seeds of new varieties of turnips, cabbage and peas; again he forwarded to his wife some naked oats, recommended for oatmeal, and some Swiss barley, "six rows to an ear," with the request that she divide it among his friends Hugh Roberts, Samuel Rhoades, John Bartram and others. At another time it was some upland rice from China that he wanted tried out in America. Again

[19]Smyth, v. 3, p. 31.
[20]Smyth, v. 1, p. 84-85.

he procured some scions of the Newtown Pippin apple from Pennsylvania, and some hickory nuts, walnuts and chestnuts, for friends in France. Then it was Penshurst peas, and again a new sort of beans that he sent home across the water.

Of the many new varieties of plants that he introduced into the New World, two are of special economic value today. In 1772 he got some seeds of rhubarb from Scotland, and sent them to Bartram. This, we are told, was the first rhubarb on record in America. Concerning it he wrote:

"I hope the Rhubarb you have sown and distributed will be taken care of. There seems to be no doubt of its doing well with us as in Scotland. Remember that for Use the Root does not come to Perfection of Power and Virtue in less than Seven Years. The Physicians here who have try'd the Scotch, approve it very much, and say it is fully equal to the best imported."[21]

The other crop was Scotch kale, one of the two varieties of kale now grown commercially in the United States.

Alfalfa, then called "lucerne," also commanded his interest and he was a champion of Indian corn as the most profitable grain for the colonies. He wrote at length during his stay in England on the merits of this crop, urging prospective settlers to try corn in preference to the more familiar wheat.

In the ancient controversy on the relative merits of the horse and the ox as a farm work animal he sided with the latter, for did it not provide both labor and meat? "I have observed in America," he wrote Lord Kames, "that the farmers are more thriving in those parts of the country where cattle are used, than in those where the labour is done by horses."[22]

While in France his advice was sought on various matters agricultural. He secured American seeds for the Comte de Buffon, for the *Jardin des Plantes*. The Royal physician from the court of Vienna wrote him about the diseases of wheat. He gave information on the construction of a drill plow, and on machines for the pulling of tree stumps. He was asked how to protect fruit trees from frost. He discoursed on the value of practical methods for controlling insects, befriending birds as the destroyers of the pests.

Franklin was interested in the culture of hemp, flax and silk,

---

[21]Smyth, v. 5, p. 443.
[22]Smyth, v. 5, p. 194.

and believed that these crops had great possibilities in America. Time and again he used his efforts to encourage the growing of silk. The British Government offered a bounty on silk produced in the colonies, and similar bounties were voted by the Pennsylvania and New Jersey assemblies, doubtless in some measure due to his influence.

While in England he gathered information on silk culture and sent it to America. In 1772 the "Filature of Philadelphia," a company organized for the manufacture of silk, sent Franklin several trunks full of their product, mostly for sale, but some of it intended for a gift to the Queen. The presentation was made by Franklin through his friend Sir John Pringle, physician of the Royal family. Subsequently his records show that in 1773 he received at auction 19 shillings sixpence per pound for American silk.

Franklin advanced many reasons why Americans should grow silk. Writing to Mrs. Franklin, he said, "I shall honour very much every young Lady that I find on my Return dress'd in Silk of their own raising."[23] But the Revolutionary War for the time put an end to the commercial production of silk, which otherwise might have become of considerable importance.

The thoroughness and diligence which marked Franklin's endeavors as an agricultural missionary are revealed in an interesting anecdote which John Adams recorded in his diary in 1760. Adams got the story from Edmund Quincy, of Boston, the recipient of favors at Franklin's hand. It is as follows, in Adams' words:

"Mr. Quincy told a remarkable instance of Mr. Benjamin Franklin's activity and resolution to improve the productions of his own country; for from that source it must have sprung, or else from an unheard of stretch of benevolence to a stranger. Mr. Franklin happening, upon a visit to friends, was asked to drink tea at Mr. Quincy's. The conversation turned upon the qualities of American soil, and the different commodities raised in these provinces. Among the rest, Mr. Franklin mentioned that the Rhenish grape vines had been introduced into Pennsylvania, and that some had been lately planted in Philadelphia, and succeeded very well. Mr. Quincy said, upon it, 'I wish I could get some into my garden; I doubt not they would do very well in this province.' Mr. Franklin

[23] Smyth, v. 5, p. 373.

replied, 'sir, if I can supply you with some of the cuttings, I shall be glad to.' Ouincy thanked him and said, 'I don't know but some time or other I shall presume to trouble you.' And so the conversation passed off. Within a few weeks, Mr. Quincy was surprised with a letter from some of Franklin's friends in Boston, that a bundle of these Rhenish slips were ready for him; these came by water. Well, soon afterwards he had another message that another parcel of slips were left for him by the post. The next time Mr. Franklin was in Boston, Mr. Quincy waited on him to thank him for his slips; 'but I am sorry, sir, to give you so much trouble.' 'O, sir,' says Franklin, 'the trouble is nothing to me, if the vines do but succeed in your province. However, I was obliged to take more pains than I expected, when I saw you. I had been told that the vines were in the city, but I found none, and was obliged to send up to a village, seventy miles from the city, for them.' Thus, he took the trouble to hunt over the city, and not finding vines there, he sends seventy miles into the country, and then sends one bundle by water, and, lest they should miscarry, another by land, to a gentleman whom he owed nothing and was but little acquainted with, purely for the sake of doing good in the world by propagating the Rhenish vines through these provinces. And Mr. Quincy has some of them now growing in his garden.''[24]

Agricultural Economist

Even more important than his plant introductions, at least from the point of view of the economist and the sociologist, were his contributions to agriculture as a manner of life. He seemed constantly alert to ways and means of advancing the economic and social status of the agricultural population. For example, to protect the farmer against the destructive forces of nature he proposed a scheme of crop insurance. Following a disastrous storm in France in 1788 he wrote: "I have sometimes thought that it might be well to establish an office of insurance for farms against the damage that may occur to them from storms, blights, insects, etc. A small sum paid by a number would repair such losses and prevent much poverty and distress.''[25] This sounds more like the

---

[24]Adams, C.F., "The Works of John Adams," Boston, 1850, v. 2, p. 81-82.
[25]Smyth, v. 9, p. 674.

agricultural economics of the present day than of the eighteenth Century.

Franklin, the economist, placed agriculture first among the industries. He believed with the Physiocrats of France, that agriculture is the chief source of wealth; that it is from the soil we derive our real riches. Thus in 1768 he wrote to a friend in true physiocratic vein: "Agriculture is truly *productive of new wealth;* manufacturers only change forms, and whatever value they give to the materials they work upon, they in the meantime consume an equal value in provisions, &c. So that riches are not *increased* by manufacturing."[26] As late as 1784 he was still of the opinion that the "first Elements of Wealth are obtained by Labour, from the Earth and Waters" and drew the striking figure, "He that puts a Seed into the Earth is recompens'd, perhaps, by receiving twenty out of it; and he who draws a Fish out of our waters, draws up a Piece of Silver."[27]

A bushel of wheat, or the labor required to produce it, rather than an ounce of silver, he claimed, might well be the standard of economic values.

"There seem to be but three ways for a nation to acquire wealth," he wrote in a passage quoted by Dr. Spiller in the last lecture in this series. "The first is by *war,* as the Romans did, in plundering their conquered neighbours. This is *robbery.* The second by *commerce,* which is generally *cheating.* The third by *agriculture,* the only *honest way,* wherein man receives a real increase of the seed thrown into the ground, in a kind of continual miracle, wrought by the hand of God in his favour, as a reward for his innocent life and his virtuous industry."[28]

Like Jefferson, he was a great admirer of the New England system of land settlement as opposed to the Proprietary system in Pennsylvania and New Jersey. The small independent farmers, he believed, formed the social and political backbone of the new nation. He lauded "the country habits of temperance, frugality, and industry, which give the most pleasing prospect of future national felicity."[29]

---

[26]Smyth, v. 5, p. 102.
[27]Smyth, v. 9, p. 246; v. 10, p. 122.
[28]Smyth, v. 1, p. 148-149.
[29]Smyth, v. 10, p. 61.

Still he did not go to extremes in championing the common man. Although of the anti-proprietary party, he sought after the Revolution for an equitable adjustment of the proprietors' rights. Mid conflicting forces he clung persistently to the middle road of "constructive liberalism." Had he lived another generation he probably would have been found among the leaders in the camp of "Jeffersonian agrarian democracy." He foresaw the great promise of American expansion westward, and recognized that one of the pressing needs of the future would be adequate market outlets for the produce of western farms.[30]

Agricultural Philosopher

The picture would not be complete without a word about Franklin's agricultural philosophy. His insight into rural life is reflected in the homely sayings of Poor Richard. The almanac no doubt exercised an important influence upon agricultural practices. Next to the Bible, probably, it was the most commonly read publication in colonial farm homes. Poor Richard could speak the language of the farmer. Some of the best known of his sayings are drawn from farm experience. For example:

> Plough deep while sluggards sleep,
> And you shall have corn to sell and to keep.

> He that by the plough would thrive,
> Himself must either hold or drive.

> The rotten apple spoils his companions.

> A sleeping fox catches no poultry.

> The worst wheel of the cart makes the most noise.

From the days when Poor Richard composed his epigrams to the time of the constitutional convention was a long and epic period, yet in the elder statesman who returned from his last European mission, we find a rural philosophy that had become mellowed and deepened through the years.

---

[30]Ross, Earle D., "Benjamin Franklin as an Eighteenth Century Agricultural Leader." In *Jour. Pol. Econ.*, **37**, 52-72 (1929).

Near the close of life, looking back over one of the most extraordinary of careers, which had embraced the several roles of printer, publisher, merchant, scientist, soldier, statesman and diplomat, and had touched all manner of activities, both rural and urban, on both sides of the Atlantic, he concluded that agriculture was "the most useful, the most independent, and therefore the noblest of Employments."[31] He took delight in seeing William Temple, the apple of his eye, established on the ex-governor's estate in Burlington County. Giving rein to his sentiments in a letter to General Lafayette, he wrote in 1787 "My grandson is at his estate in the Jerseys, and amuses himself with cultivating his lands. I wish he would seriously make a business of it, and renounce all thoughts of public employment, for I think agriculture the most honourable, because the most independent, of all professions."[32]

American agriculture was enriched by Benjamin Franklin's contributions, and through his leadership the march of agricultural progress was advanced both at home and abroad. It seems appropriate to close with a tribute to Frankin from a work on agriculture by a native of France residing in America. We have observed Franklin's active interest in the growing of Rhenish grapes in this country and his efforts to promote wine culture. In 1827 Alphonse Loubat published a handbook entitled "The American Vine Dressers' Guide," which he dedicated to the memory of Benjamin Franklin. Although the text appears in both French and English, the dedicatory address is in French alone. I give you the translation of one paragrpah:

"O Franklin, you who taught us the way to keep grapes in all their freshness; you who were one of the fathers of domestic economy, you will stand by my vineyard; your shadow will come to wander beneath its branches, weighted down with fruit; your kind spirit will gaze with delight upon the hills of your dear fatherland, adorned with gifts from Bacchus; and in the dwelling-place of the righteous you will rejoice in hearing the echoes from the dales which saw your birth, to repeat the songs of joy of the happy grape-gatherer."[33]

---

[31]Smyth, v. 9, p. 491.
[32]Smyth, v. 9, p. 571.
[33]Op. cit., p. iv.

Dr. Franklin: Friend of the Indians

JULIAN P. BOYD

Julian Parks Boyd (1903-1980) was the Librarian at Princeton University from 1940 to 1952, a Professor of History at Princeton from 1952 to 1972, and President of the American Philosophical Society from 1973 to 1976. He was the Editor of *The Papers of Thomas Jefferson* , and was co-editor of *Indian Treaties by Benjamin Franklin*, published in 1938. He is also the author of *Anglo-American Union: Joseph Galloway's Plans to Preserve the British Empire* (1941).

Shortly after Franklin's death in 1790 the Abbé Morellet published in the *Gazette Nationale* a series of Franklin anecdotes which the great diplomat had used to charm his circle of admirers in France. One of them concerned the mental processes of the American Indians. According to Franklin, the savages never traced or desired to trace the connection between cause and effect. An Indian came to see Franklin in Philadelphia to witness the experiment of lighting brandy with an electric spark. When he had seen it, he neither exhibited surprise nor gave any evidence of reflection on the cause, but merely remarked: "These white men are clever rascals."

This anecdote, if Morellet has reported Franklin correctly, may be interpreted in two ways and both ways have significance. It may be taken to indicate that Franklin really did not understand the Indians. To accept this interpretation we must believe that one of the wisest of men, whose greatness was due largely to his understanding of the complex humanity of civilized society, failed completely to understand the simple and childlike nature of the forest inhabitants. The second interpretation is more important. The anecdote may be taken as an indication of the intellectual approach of Franklin as well as of that of the Indian. The Indian, schooled by habit not to betray emotion or surprise, probably went back to his village and pondered for days over what to him was a supernatural phenomenon. Franklin, busy with cause and effect viewed in a natural light, was concerned with the immediate and practical application of his laboratory experiment. If the primitive brain of the Indian was limited to ponderings over a supernatural phenomenon, the powerful mind of Franklin was limited to the immediate use of a new instrument. He did not soar into metaphysics, whether contemplating electricity or society. He left no great legacy of systematic thought to the world, as did Rousseau. Rousseau contemplated the American Indian and created a great school of romantic political thought, a systematic ideology that turned a world upside down. Franklin regarded the Indian, as he did everything else, with profound interest. But he did not bother to draw out of the forest society any abstract philosophy for the government of civilized society. He used his knowledge of the Indian for more immediate objectives. This is the key to Franklin's attitude toward the Indian, as it is the key to the working of his mind in the realms of science, politics, diplomacy, and literature.

Two of the most famous productions of his little press at Passy concerned the Indians. The first, a famous hoax, was an alleged account of the barbarities of the Indians in the employ of the British army. This was war propaganda, pure and simple, and so effectively and brilliantly conceived that Horace Walpole immediately identified Franklin as the author. The second was Franklin's delightful bagatelle, *Remarques su la politesse des sauvages de l'Amerique Septentrionale*. It was less an analysis of the manners of the Indians than it was a subtle and gentle commentary on the civilized society that Franklin saw, understood, and loved, even though he recognized its artificialities and weaknesses. "Savages we call them," he began, "because their manners differ from ours, which we think the perfection of civility: they think the same of theirs. The Indian men, when young, are hunters and warriors; when old, counsellors; for all their government is by counsel of the sages; there is no force, there are no prisons, no officers to compel obedience or inflict punishment." This, as Frankin well knew, was the sort of thing the romanticists of the Rousseau tradition wanted to hear. His remarks on the manners of the savages must be interpreted in that light. As such, the *Remarques* is superbly suited to its purpose; as a treatise on the Indians, it cannot bear comparison with such serious works as Cadwallader Colden's *History of the Five Nations* or James Adair's *History of the American Indians*. Franklin knew the Indians and they interested him, but he would not write a systematic treatise about them. He would not write about them at all, any more than he would about anything else, unless an immediate result was apparent: a result that might be a political end, a diplomatic strategy, or an amusing narrative, useful only for politeness' sake.

He proposed a plan for the union of the colonies and he found his materials in the great confederacy of the Iroquois. He championed the cause of the drunken Teedyuscung and the Delawares, not primarily because he thought they had been imposed upon, but because any instrument was good if it helped in the fight against Thomas Penn and the proprietors of Pennsylvania. In the realm of gallantry as in the political world he found the Indians useful: he told Madam Helvetius of the Indian custom of adoption to take the place of departed relatives and argued for his own adoption.

Yet, if Franklin used his knowledge of the Indians, as he used his knowledge of other things, to achieve immediate ends, it is not apparent that he misused the Indians. If we call him a friend of the Indians, we do so because he was a friend of all humanity. When we call the roll of great names associated with the American aborigines, we do not, at first, think of including his. He was no burning zealot, striving to convert the savage to the white man's way of life. He had no illusions about the red man any more than he had about his white brother. We do not think of him as we think of Eliot, Zinzindorf, Brainerd, Kirkland, Hawley, and the other great Indian missionaries. Franklin's first diplomatic effort was in the realm of forest diplomacy, yet we do not rank him with such a diplomatist as Conrad Weiser. He was an agent and emissary to the Indians, yet he does not compare in that respect with Sir William Johnson. He wrote much about the Indians and he printed their treaties and the writings of others about the Indians. Yet we do not consider Franklin himself as a great source of Indian lore in the same manner that we consider Colden, Adair, or Weiser.

It will help to define Franklin's interest in the Indian if we consider also his interest in the Negro. These two races of non-Caucasian stock were about evenly matched in numbers in Pennsylvania in the eighteenth century. But the problems that they evoked and the attitudes toward these problems that they induced in the minds of the white race were enormously different. The Indian affected almost every phase of colonial life. He held the balance of power between the French and English and thus was the key to the whole question of international rivalry in America. He was not domesticated, but lived in his own villages beyond the frontier and thus impeded the natural flow of population westward. Every new immigrant who landed at Philadelphia was affected by this fact and in turn aggravated it, whether he knew it or not. The Indian supplied furs and peltry to traders, who exchanged them for London goods at such points as Philadelphia and Albany. Thus a whole commercial structure was erected with the Indian at the base—an Indian who, as Franklin told Lord Shelburne, knew nothing about credit and knew only how to respect an honorable obligation without the need for or an understanding of debtors' prisons. The Indian could wreck this commercial structure by the simple expedient of refusing to hunt. Thus he was an economic factor of the first importance, influencing and often determining the course of events from the wages of the counting-house clerk in Philadelphia to the decisions of the ministry in Whitehall. In the political realm the Indian was an ever-present problem, and one has only to read the journals of assemblies, the voluminous archives of governors and their councils, or the files of Indian treaties to see how potent a force he was in the politics of the colonies. More than one governor was ruined because he could not cope with the problem; more than one was made because he was astute enough to handle it. In the realm of political thought the Indian probably had a greater influence over civilized society than any other savage race. Marc Lescarbot, Gabriel Sagard, and the authors of the great Jesuit Relations began in the 16th and 17th centuries by describing Indian society and ended by praising it with a praise which carried an implied criticism of the European political system. From this it was an easy step for Baron Lahontan to put in the mouth of an American savage a blunt criticism of civilized political organization. From these materials Montesquieu drew in part the inspiration for his *Spirit of Laws* and from the same sources emerged Rousseau's *Social Contract*. From Montesquieu and Rousseau to the French Revolution was but another link in the chain of influence that stretched from the western frontiers to the capitals of Europe, thus paralleling in political theory the links binding the American Indian to Europe in the economic world. The Indian, therefore, was a factor of immense importance in the 18th century, far out of proportion to his actual numbers.

The Negro on the other hand, while sharing similar racial handicaps, presented no baffling problems of power to the colonials.

He was domesticated, serving in homes and on farms, and was not congregated in mass anywhere; indeed, there were laws to forbid it. His claims to social and civil rights were answered by simple denial. The one problem presented by the Negro was the problem of slavery, which was attacked, when it became urgent, on moral and economic grounds. It did not become an urgent problem until the 19th century.

Here, then, were the two minority elements in the population which presented actual and potential problems. The first was so complex and of such magnitude that it can be fully understood only when we compare it with some great social problem of our own day, such as the problem of capital and labor. The Indian was such a question in the eighteenth century, demanding of the merchant, the politician, the scholar, the clergyman, the frontiersman, and the soldier constant search for an adequate answer. The Negro made no such insistent demands by his presence even when he outnumbered the Indian. His appeal was only to the humanitarian instincts of the Age of Enlightenment.

Such as appeal was met, in the case of Franklin, by active intercession. Franklin was among the first to point out the economic disadvantages of slavery. He suggested the first school for Negroes in Philadelphia. He was president of the first abolition society in America. Among his last public acts, three concerned slavery. One was an *Address to the Public* issued in November, 1789; another was a memorial to the first Congress on the subject; and the third, published in the *Federal Gazette* within a month of his death, was a hoax and a parody ridiculing the debate in Congress on this memorial. With respect to the Negro, Franklin leaned in the direction of the social reformer, lending his name and his influence to such ardent leaders of the movement as Clarkson, Benezet, and Brissot de Warville. The Society of Friends were mobilized then, and have been ever since, to aid the Indian and to improve his status. But Franklin's name, so conspicuous in the history of abolition of Negro slavery in eighteenth-century Pennsylvania, is not to be found among those who promoted the Friendly Association and other ventures designed to help the Indian.

We would make a mistake to assume that because of this Franklin was less interested in the Indian than he was in the Negro. He was fully aware of the tremendous importance of the Indian. He knew that the answer of the frontiersman to the Indian problem, that of extermination, was dangerous, unwise, and unjust. He knew that the merchant and the Indian trader too often exploited the Indian for the sake of profit and played upon his weakness for strong drink. He knew that the demands of the missionaries that the Indian give up his traditional ideas of government, morality, and religion were essentially futile. He knew that the answer of the scholar—the answer of thinkers like Lahontan and Rousseau looking at Indian society from a distance of three thousand miles—had little of reality in it. Franklin realized the need for practical political adjustments to solve the multiform problems raised by the Indian. His humanitarian instincts carried him only so far as to stand against injustice to him. In the final analysis, the difference between Franklin's attitude toward the Negro and his attitude toward the Indian was not humanitarian in origin but intellectual. The Negro was transplanted and needed support and encouragement. The Indian was on his native soil and had developed his own civilization. Franklin had a wholesome respect for any civilization that could produce noble specimens of intellect and sagacity. Hence his solution of the problem was simple: the American forest was ample and apparently inexhaustible—let the Indian inhabit it, continue in his own way of life, and be protected against injustice by means of established boundaries and protective legislation. In his own day, this may have been an adequate solution; certainly it was realistic. The fallacy in it was that the forest was not inexhaustible.

If respect for the Indian was the measure of Franklin's attitude, it was also the surest basis for a friendly and just treatment. Franklin, who understood people so well, knew a statesman when he saw one, whether he lived in Versailles or belonged to the Iroquois Long House. In 1747 he received the first copy of Colden's *History of the Five Nations* in the London edition of that year. He must have read with approval Colden's appraisal of the Iroquois. "The Five Nations," Colden wrote, "are a poor Barbarous People, under the darkest Ignorance, and yet a bright and noble genius shines through these black clouds. None of the greatest Roman Heroes have discovered a greater love to their Country, or a greater Contempt of Death than these Barbarians have done, when Life and Liberty came in Competition: Indeed, I think our Indians have outdone the Romans in this particular; for some of the greatest Romans have Murder'd themselves to avoid shame or

Torments, Whereas our Indians have refused to Die meanly with the least pain when they thought their country's Honour would be at stake by it, but gave their Bodies willingly up to the most cruel Torments of their Enemies, to show, that the Five Nations consisted of Men whose Courage and Resolution could not be shaken.'' Colden may also have told Franklin the story of Consora, the famous sachem of the Senecas, who spoke for them at all treaties. In 1721 Consora, described by Colden as "a very cunning suttle Fellow," told the five Nations that they should join neither the French nor the English "but to keep the balance betwixt the two, for if the English should prevail over the French the Five Nations would enslave themselves [to the English].But if [they] would now observe an exact Neutrality they would be courted and feared by both sides." Consora, like other Iroquois statesmen before and after him, followed this policy invariably and exacted concessions for his neutrality time after time. But when he was unable to restrain the warlike habits of his followers he put himself at their head and called out: "I did not dissuade you out of fear, but for your own good and since you will go to war, I shall be the first to lead you to slavery and destruction."

It is unthinkable that Franklin would establish schools or attempt to reform a way of life that produced such astute manipulators of statecraft as Consora. It is not certain that Franklin ever met the great Onondaga leader who was one of the successors of Consora, but I should like to imagine that he did. Canasatego, one of the most intelligent of all the Iroquois leaders, and perhaps the most eloquent, witnessed his greatest triumph of diplomacy at the Lancaster treaty of 1744, attended by representatives of Virginia, Maryland, and Pennsylvania. Whether Franklin ever met Canasatego or not, he has immortalized him in one of his famous Passy bagatelles. But the story that Franklin told in his *Remarks Concerning the Savages* is not comparable to the Onondaga orator's own arguments and negotiations as set forth in the account of the treaty of Lancaster which Franklin printed in 1744.

Perhaps in the printing of this treaty, and the thirteen other stately folios like it, Franklin performed his greatest act of friendship for the Indians. For in them are to be found the eloquent words, often wise and profound, of the best of their leaders. In them are to be found the exact rituals of the forest people in their formal conferences and contracts with their conquerors. In them are to be found metaphors and images of the forest, poetic clothing for the harsh realities of land deals and trade in the ephemeral trinkets for which a proud and imperious people sold their birthright because the sale was forced. In them are to be found the evidences of genuine statecraft on the part of such intelligent leaders as Shikellamy, astute and aloof, Canasatego, logical and crafty as well as eloquent, Teedyuscung, drunken and bombastic, but courageous and daring enough to lead his people to a temporary independence. Franklin did not attend the conference at Lancaster in 1744, but if he read the minutes of the negotiations, in which Canasatego proved more than a match for the embassies from Maryland and Virginia combined, he must have agreed with Richard Peters, who wrote of that picturesque conclave: "I make no doubt that the Indian treaty will give everyone pleasure that reads it and as the Indians really appear superior to the Commissioners in point of sense and argument, it will raise peoples opinions of the wisdom of the Six Nations and give the government at home higher notions of their consequence than they could have before." When Peters, who was present at the treaty, spoke of the superior sense and argument of the Indians, he really was speaking of Canasatego, who made all of the speeches for the Iroquois and who was the dominant figure at Lancaster.

In our effort to see the Indians as Franklin and his contemporaries saw them, let us picture Canasatego and his counsellors at Lancaster. It was a colorful assembly. Hundreds of Indians in full panoply, men, women and children—grave leaders, savage-looking warriors; Conrad Weiser, the skilful diplomat; Governor George Thomas of Pennsylvania, presiding over the sessions with a warm friendship and full respect for the powers of Canasatego; the Virginia and Maryland Commissioners, described by Richard Peters as "seven fine flaming gentlemen"; members of the Society of Friends come to see justice done to the Indians; finally the great Onondaga, Canasatego, "a tall well-made man" with "a very full chest and brawny limbs, a manly countenance, with a good natired smile. He was about sixty years of age, very active, strong, and had a surprising liveliness in his speech." Day after day the ritual of replenishing the Council Fire, of smoothing the road between the two peoples, of brightening the chain of friendship occupied the attention of all those present. Then Canasatego made his demands,

demands in the form of ultimata. Maryland cited deeds a century old to the lands claimed by Canasatego. Canasatego replied that a hundred years meant nothing to a people as ancient as the Iroquois. In the end he won, single-handed, and, laden with goods and gold, clothed in a scarlet camblet coat and a fine gold-laced hat, he marched his people off to Canada to sell his pledge of neutrality to the Governor of Canada for the highest price his astute diplomacy could achieve.

To think of Franklin trying to domesticate a leader such as Canastego, to establish schools to mold him and his followers in the white man's image, to teach him the arts and sciences of civilized society, to make him conform to its government, its laws, and its political theories, is impossible. It would have been like attempting to make a domestic fowl out of a proud and imperious eagle. Franklin understood humanity better than to make the attempt. He would assist in doing it for the Negro, because the Negro was differently situated; but, in Franklin's day at least, the Indian was untameable.

The Canasatego episode that Franklin recounts in his Passy bagatelle emphasises this. It was said to have occurred at the Lancaster Treaty, though there is no account of it in the official minutes of that conference. It seems that the Virginia commissioners offered to take six Indian boys and educate them at the College of William and Mary. Canasatego, deferring his answer of politeness until the next day, declined the proposal. Some of their young men, he said, had gone to college in the northern provinces and had come back "bad runners, ignorant of every means of living in the woods unable to bear either cold or hunger, knew neither how to build a cabin, take a deer, or kill an enemy, spoke our language imperfectly, were therefore neither fit for warriors, hunters, nor counsellors; they were totally good for nothing." But, subtle and cunning as well as polite, betraying also the proud belief he held in the validity of his own way of life, Canasatego turned to the commissioners with a counter-proposal that was two-edged. To show the Indians' grateful sense of the Virginians' offer, he said, he and his counsellors desired to make this offer: "If the Gentlemen of Virginia will send us a Dozen of their Sons, we will take great care of their Education, instruct them in all we know, and make *Men* of them."

The story, as Franklin knew, would delight the romanticists of the Rousseau tradition. It was the sort of anecdote that made him appear to all France as the apotheosis of the natural man, the forerunner of the Golden Age of simplicity and of institutions grounded on nature's law. But for us it is also a story that illuminates Franklin's attitude toward the Indians. If Franklin never met Canasatego, he would have liked him and he would have respected a diplomat who could parry a stroke in such a fashion. It was, in fact, a Franklinian feat.

Franklin, then, respected the Indians and was content to let them live their own life. But he was also wise enough to profit from the things that he learned of them. One of America's great contributions to the history of political thought has been its working out the problem of federation. Franklin, as all the world knows, erected one of the mileposts in the development of the theory of federation in America when he met the commissioners of the various colonies at the famous Albany Congress of 1754. What he proposed there came in part from the Iroquois. Again we must go back to the wise Canasatego. At Lancaster in 1744 and at Albany in 1745, he admonished the jealous, bickering colonists to be united, and pointed again to the Indian example as a wise precedent to follow. "Our Wise forefathers," he said "established Union and Amity between the Five Nations. This has made us formidable. This has given us great weight and authority with our neighboring Nations. We are a powerful confederacy, and by your observing the same methods our Wise Forefathers have taken, you will acquire such strength and power. Therefore whatever befals you, never fall out with one another." Though he did not realize it, Canasatego was advising one of the first steps in the long story of the American Revolution.

Franklin plainly had the Confederation in mind when he drew up his Plan of Union to be presented at the Albany Congress. He well knew that strength came through union, that the Iroquois confederation of 15,000 persons wielded an influence all out of proportion to their numbers; that its empire held sway from the St. Lawrence to the James, and from the Hudson nearly to the Mississippi; that conquered tribes paid tribute to the Iroquois, who alone could say who should make war and who should dictate the terms of peace. Here indeed was an example worthy of copying. "It would be a strange thing," wrote Franklin, "if Six Nations of ignorant savages should be capable of forming a scheme for such an union and be able to execute it in such a manner that it has subsisted ages and appears indissoluble, and yet that a like union should be impracticable for ten or a dozen English colonies, to whom it is more necessary and must be more advantageous, and who cannot be supposed to want an equal understanding of their interest." I do not mean to imply, as some students would have it, that the principle of federation, indeed that the roots of the federal constitution, go back to the Iroquois Confederacy. The idea is much older than that. Franklin merely pointed to an obvious American precedent, already in existence and working effectively.

Franklin's first argument for Union was not thrown off, as his *Autobiography* has it, on his way to Albany. It appeared in the form of a letter to James Parker, the printer of a pamphlet by Archibald Kennedy on *The Importance of Gaining and Preserving the Friendship of the Indians to the British Interest, Considered.* This pamphlet was published in 1751, at a period when Thomas Penn, Richard Peters, and others were advocating a union of the colonies to solve the common problem of the Indian. Indeed, less than a month before Franklin wrote his observations on Kennedy's pamphlet in the form of a letter to Parker, Thomas Penn wrote Peters: "I think it would be of the greatest advantage to the English interest for several colonies to join in the management of Indian Affairs and appoint, as you suggest, deputies from each of them to manage the whole, agreeing upon a proportion that each colony will bear of the expense." This was the germ of the idea contained in Franklin's *Concise Hints on a Plan of Union* of 1754. *Concise Hints* contained, among its most important proposals, provision for a governor general and a grand council to be made up of representatives of colonies. The very first power that Franklin would have granted to this central government was the authority to negotiate all Indian treaties in which the general interest or welfare of the colonies was concerned; to make peace or war with the Indians: to make laws regulating Indian trade; and to have exclusive control over all purchases of Indian lands. This was a logical outcome of the sentiments expressed in his letter to Parker in 1751, commenting on Kennedy's manuscript. "I have read the Manuscript you sent me," he wrote Parker, "and am of Opinion with the Public Spirited Author, that securing the Friendship of the Indians is of the greatest Consequence to these Colonies; and that the surest means of doing it are to regulate the Indian Trade, so as to convince them by experience, that they may have the best

and cheapest Goods, and the fairest Dealings from the English;
and to unite the several Governments so as to form a strength that
the Indians may depend upon for protection in case of a rupture
with the French; or apprehend great danger from, if they should
break with us.'' When Franklin thus approved Kennedy's proposal
for a union of the colonies and for a unified Indian policy based on
decent treatment of the Indian as a neighbor in peace and an ally in
war, he concluded with a modest note: ''I wish I could offer any
Thing for the Improvement of the Author's Piece, but I have little
Knowledge and less Experience in these Matters.'' Almost half a
century later he declared that if the colonies or the ministry had accepted the Plan of 1754, which both rejected because each feared it
allowed too much power to the other, the American Revolution
would never have occurred when it did or perhaps not for another
century.

Too late—and too ineffectual when it came—was the
crystallization of the need felt by all for united counsels. Dissen-
sions between governors and assemblies, intercolonial jealousies,
and trade rivalries were too strong to be overcome by the efforts of
men like Franklin, Kennedy, Colden, Penn, Peters, and others to
secure some sort of colonial union. The Albany Plan of Union,
wrote Governor Thomas from Antigua, ''smells strong of Pennsylvania.'' Pennsylvania had indeed had a leading hand in the
events of the three years leading up to the Albany Congress, and
Franklin was its architect, but it was not accepted by the colonies
and was never submitted to Parliament. The treaty with the Indians at which the Plan was drawn up only served to drive another
wedge between Pennsylvania and the western Indians, to drive
deeper the wedge between Pennsylvania and the Iroquois. On his
way home from Albany, Franklin wrote his old friend Colden:
''After all nothing of much importance was transacted with [the
Indians]: At least nothing equal to the extent and trouble of so
many colonies.'' For once Franklin, so intent on the crying need
for the solution of the problem, seemed to be unaware of the fact
that the Albany Treaty constituted one of the most glaring examples in colonial history of the dangerous if not unfair manipulation of Indian affairs by colonies with conflicting interests. As one
of the commissioners from Pennsylvania, it was his official duty to
do what his Plan of Union forbade: to hold private councils with
the Indians, over their protests, and to purchase from the Iroquois

almost all of the lands of Northwestern Pennsylvania. A few days later the Commissioners of Connecticut, in an even more secretive manner, induced some of the same chiefs to sell some of the same lands to Connecticut. Thus as Franklin was pressing his *Concise Hints* for a unified and just plan of dealing with the great common problem of the Indian, he was officially a partner to the evils that he hoped to correct. The blow that united counsels might have warded off fell in full strength on the defenseless frontiers of Pennsylvania the next year.

When that blow fell, Franklin wasted no effort in useless argument over what might have been. His habitual approach in all fields of endeavour was to do the thing at hand that needed to be done. He had counselled for just and united dealings with the Indians. That had failed. The Indians were now murdering defenseless settlers, burning their houses and barns, slaughtering their animals, and carrying away their wives and daughters. The problem now was one of fighting. Franklin proved that, though a good friend to the Indians, he could also be a good enemy. In the early summer he secured almost single-handedly the wagons that were essential to the progress of Braddock's ill-fated army. In September, as Speaker of the Assembly, he was no doubt present at the State House to see and hear one of the most dramatic spectacles that ever took place in that historic building. Scarouady, the Oneida chieftain, who had served with Braddock and had lost a son, gave the Pennsylvania government a final opportunity to support the western Indians against the French. Demanding that he be heard by the principal men of the colony, he was granted the privilege of speaking in the State House before the governor, the Assembly, and a large audience of civilians. In a sense he was announcing the declaration of independence of the Delawares, and he came not as a supplicant but as a proud warrior. He demanded in the name of the Indians he represented that Pennsylvania declare whether she intended to be an ally or an enemy. To the Assembly he said: "We do, therefore, once more invite and request you to act like men, and be no longer women, pursuing weak measures, that render your names despicable." To the governor he said: "One word of yours will bring the Delawares to join you." That word was not given. For the governor and the Assembly were already at loggerheads over the taxation of the proprietary estates, a fight which Franklin had helped to precipitate and which would carry him to London a year and a half later. But when the angry frontiersmen threatened to march on Philadelphia and when they dumped a wagonload of scalped corpses on the steps of the State House to show the Assembly and governor what their idle bickering over prerogative had produced, an appropriation of £60,000 was promptly made for defense. A month later, in December, 1755, Colonel Benjamin Franklin, at the head of a military command, marched on the frontier and assumed charge of the erection of block-houses for defense. Franklin was as open an enemy as he was a friend of the Indians.

Whether he was planning measures to win the friendship of the Indians, as at Albany, or whether he was leading an expedition against them, he always had concise hints to throw out. This time it was to suggest a new method of fighting. Franklin had shown in his letter to James Parker in 1751 that he too knew something about Indian fighting. "Every Indian is a Hunter," he had said, "and as their manner of making War, *via.,* Skulking, Surprizing and Killing particular persons and families is just the same as their manner of Hunting, only changing the object. Every Indian is a Disciplin'd Soldier. Soldiers of this kind are always wanted in the colonies in an Indian War, for the European Military Discipline is of little Use in these Woods." Now, lacking enough soldiers of the Indian type, Franklin proposed that Indians be hunted down with dogs. "If dogs are carried out with any party," he wrote to James Reed and Conrad Weiser, "they should be large strong and fierce and every dog lead in a slip-string to prevent their tiring themselves by running and discovering the party by barking at squirrels, etc. Only when the party come near thick woods and suspicious places they should turn out a dog or two to search them. In case of meeting a party of the enemy the dogs are all then to be turned loose and set on. They will be fresher and finer for having been previously confined and will confound the enemy a good deal and be very serviceable. This was the Spanish method of guarding their marches." Apparently the suggestion was not acted upon at the time but it is interesting to note that no less a military authority than Colonel Bouquet proposed to Sir Jeffery Amherst the same expedient in fighting Indians. Franklin's keen interest in making things more effective was never-failing, whether it was a problem of ventilation, of correcting a smoking chimney, of navigating the Gulf Stream, or of making better friends with or better war against the Indians.

In 1756 Franklin had his second experience of forest diplomacy. He had been one of the principal commissioners at the Carlisle Treaty of 1753 and in 1775 he would again be called upon to negotiate for the united colonies with the western tribes. But his service as a commissioner at the Easton Treaty of 1756 had more important consequences than any of his other experiences as an Indian diplomat. For there he saw Teedyuscung, the leader of the Delawares against whom he had led his expedition in 1755, and he heard the fiery chieftain demand compensation from the Penns for the lands that he claimed his people had been defrauded of in the famous Indian Walking Purchase twenty years before. He witnessed also the dramatic ritual by which the Six Nations conceded the independence of the Delawares and acknowledged openly that Teedyuscung had thrown off the mantle of womanhood that the Iroquois had placed on his people and had achieved, if not the full stature of manhood, at least the right to make war and peace as men. Of all the vexations that Thomas Penn had endured as proprietor of the province, none stung him so deeply as this charge that he had made use of fraud in the purchase of lands. He had bought the same lands over and over from the Indians and he had made a sincere effort to continue the wise and humane policies of his father in this respect. Franklin knew this and had said so in the *Pennsylvania Gazette* as long ago as 1736. He knew also that there were many forces back of Teedyuscung's charge that would make it appear less as an original thought on the part of the Indian leader than as an insinuation on the part of those desiring to embarrass the proprietors politically. Eventually even Teedyuscung admitted that this was true. But now Franklin was engaged in a struggle with the proprietary system, and any grievance, real or imaginary was ammunition for his armory. When he went to London to represent the Assembly, he personally presented the grievances of the Delawares to the ministry. His friendship for the Indians was now bound up with the popular movement against the Penns—a movement which Richard Peters, not without cause, described as "Mr. Franklin's Declaration of War against the Proprietaries." "The [Indians'] complaints are now in the hands of the Ministry," Franklin wrote Galloway in 1758, "but when they will have leisure to consider them, God only knows. For tho' securing the affections of the Indians by doing them justice, be a matter of great consequency, they have other affairs at present on their hands that seem to them of more immediate importance."

About this time the manuscript of Charles Thomson's "Enquiry into the Causes of the Alienation of the Delawares and Shawanese" came into Franklin's possession. This was a strongly partisan statement, growing out of the activities of the Quaker Friendly Association. But its indictment of the Penns, in a strange mixture of humanitarianism and political expediency, immediately appealed to Franklin as a means of arraying public and official opinion against the proprietors. Accordingly he assumed charge of the manuscript, edited it, and procured its publication. He informed Galloway in 1758 that "It is more read that I expected. It will, I think, have a good effect." The almost apoplectic rage that filled Thomas Penn when he read it is revealed in the many marginal notes that he scribbled in the copy that now reposes in the John Carter Brown Library. The effect on the ministry is apparent from the peremptory order issued to Sir William Johnson to hear the complaints of the Delawares and to see that justice was done. This was bitter medicine for Thomas Penn, but he accepted it manfully and made full peace with the Delawares. Franklin, though moved perhaps more by political considerations than by altruistic motives, could be a friend of the Indians even when there was grave doubt of their deserving it. He had fought against Teedyuscung's people in the forests of America. He was now fighting for them at Whitehall, fighting all the more effectively because he and Teedyuscung had a common foe in Thomas Penn.

If Franklin's motive in this fight was identified with a popular movement with which he sympathized, he nevertheless showed that he could stand courageously for justice to the Indian even when such a stand called for opposition to popular clamor. In one of the few examples of Franklin's opposing the people, he acted as he did because he was outraged by the behavior of his fellow men. This stand he took in the year that the Indians really needed friendship, the year 1763 which brought to an end the ancient rivalry with France in the struggle for North America and also brought to an end the power that the Indians had long held and for which they had been courted and treated with respect. The so-called Conspiracy of Pontiac brought the horrors of Indian warfare again to the Province of Pennsylvania. The long-suffering frontiersmen, seeing no good in an Indian except in a dead one, threatened to march on Philadelphia to inflict punishment on the friendly Moravian Indians interned there, and the Paxton Boys fell on the peaceful Conestoga Indians at Lancaster, killing old men, women, and children with a brutality scarcely matched by anything the Indians had done. This famous massacre set off a tempest of political and religious controversy in the province, and while Franklin was fully aware of whatever extenuating circumstances there may have been, he boldly proclaimed the act of the Paxton Boys to be what it was—cold-blooded murder. This forthright comment made more enemies than friends for him, but he did not spare the murderers. Branding the Paxton Boys as "Christian White Savages," he said: "There are some (I am ashamed to hear it), who would extenuate the enormous wickedness of these actions by saying: 'The inhabitants of the frontiers are exasperated with the murder of their relations by the enemy Indians in the present war.' It is possible. But though this might justify their going out into the woods, to seek for those enemies and avenge upon them those murders, it can never justify their turning into the heart of the country to murder their friends. The only crime of these poor wretches seems to have been that they had a reddish-brown skin and black hair; and some people of that sort, it seems had murdered some of our relations. If it be right to kill men for such a reason, then, should any man with a freckled face and red hair kill a wife or child of mine, it would be right for me to revenge it by killing all the freckled face and red hair men, women and children I could afterwards anywhere meet with." Citing instances of hospitality among the ancient Greeks, Turks and Saracens, Franklin concluded that the peaceful Conestoga Indians "would have been safe in any part of the known world except in the neighborhood of the Christian White Savages of Peckstang and Donegall." When the frontier mobs finally moved on the city, determined to exterminate the Moravian Indians and to browbeat the Assembly into granting measures of defense against the Indians, it was to Frankin, the author of this philippic against brutal murder, that the governor turned for assistance. The insurgents halted at Germantown and Franklin with three other men went out to reason with the leaders in behalf of law and order. He was successful in dissuading the insurgents. "Within four-and-twenty hours," he wrote Dr. Fothergill, "your old friend was a common soldier, a councillor, a kind of dictator, an ambassador to a country mob, and, on his returning home, nobody again."

Two central facts emerge from an examination of Franklin's long experience with the American Indian: his natural respect for them and his desire to see no injustice come to them. At the end of his great career he wrote: "During the course of a long life in which I have made observations of public affairs, it has appeared to me that almost every war between the Indians and whites has been occasioned by some injustice of the latter towards the former. It is indeed extremely imprudent in us to quarrel with them for their lands, as they are generally willing to sell, and sell such good bargains: And a war with them is so mischievous to us, in unsettling frequently a great part of our Frontier, and reducing the Inhabitants to poverty and Distress, and is besides so expensive that it is much cheaper as well as honester, to buy their Lands than to take them by Force." In this homely advice to the governor of Georgia, as well as in his counsel to Lord Shelburne on the Indian problem, Frankin viewed the subject dispassionately and openmindedly, his clear intellect going at once to the heart of the issue and offering the simplest of solutions. His wise solutions were not always adopted. His genuine respect for the Indians and his stout advocacy of justice and fair-dealing were not always shared. Franklin must have realized, as he witnessed the Indians' decline to a pitiful remnant of their former power, that this was one of the inevitable results of the establishment of a nation to which his own genius had contributed so much.

EDITOR'S NOTE

Boyd suggests that Franklin, after receiving the first copy of Cadwallader Colden's *History of the Five Nations* in the London edition of 1747, "must have read with approval Colden's appraisal of the Iroquois." Franklin's written opinion of the book was "that 'tis a well wrote, entertaining and instructive Piece, and [must] be exceedingly useful to all those Colonies who have anything to [do] with Indian Affairs."[1]

---

[1]Frankin to Colden, Philadelphia, January 27, 1747 </48>, *The Papers of Benjamin Franklin*, ed. by Leonard W. Labaree *et al.*, III, 272.

Franklin and the Twentieth Century

I. BERNARD COHEN

I. Bernard Cohen (1914-   ) is Victor S. Thomas Professor of History at Harvard University, and a member of the editorial advisory committee of *The Papers of Benjamin Franklin*. In *Franklin and Newton,* (1956, 1966, 1981) his most important published work on Franklin, he has stressed the influence of speculative Newtonian experimental science on Franklin's electrical theories; in *Benjamin Franklin: Scientist and Statesman* (1975), he has portrayed for the general reader the whole scope and significance of Franklin's scientific career.

Professor Cohen delivered this address at the dinner honoring the 250th anniversary of Franklin's birth, held in conjunction with the Annual Meeting of the Franklin Institute, January 18, 1956. His evaluation of Franklin remains as valid today as it was twenty-five years ago.

A half century ago the philosopher Charles Sanders Peirce explored canons of greatness, wondering whether there might be some rule or set of rules to tell who were the century's great men. Definitions of greatness, he felt, were only like rules of grammar; these do not "render an expression bad English, but only generalize the fact that good writers do not use it." Hence, according to Peirce, "in order to establish a definition of greatness, it would be necessary to begin by ascertaining what men were and what men were not great, and that having been done the rule might as well be dispensed with." Peirce's own "opinion" of the matter seems a strange issue from a mind steeped in logical analysis, a mind which invented the term "pragmatism." It is the romantic "opinion," which more of us hold than are apt to be willing to admit the fact in public, and so we may understand why Peirce stated that his "opinion . . . has not been lightly formed nor without long years of experimentation." But he did fear that "some intellectual men" would consider only as "foolishness" the view "that the way to judge of whether a man was great or not is to put aside all analysis, to contemplate attentively his life and works, and then to look into one's heart and estimate the impression one finds to have been made. This is the way in which one would decide whether a mountain were sublime or not. The great man is the impressive personality, and the question whether he is great is a question of impression.''

We do not hold Franklin to be a great man, and gather to celebrate [this] anniversary of his birth, because of objective standards that set him apart from other men of his day — as that he belonged to more scientific societies, had more honorary degrees, signed more treaties, made more discoveries, or wrote more laws — but rather because our sentiments find in his person a symbolic image of our values and our aspirations. The impression of the heart, evoked by Peirce, is not purely subjective in the sense of being one man's reaction; it is bound in time to the qualities of the age — our age even more than Franklin's. At the founding of this republic Franklin was considered to be the ''father'' of his country, a title we now associate with Washington on whom it was only later conferred. The father image was a natural one to the men of the 1780's because they had only to look about them to see that he was their patriarch. Franklin had been the oldest member of the Second Continental Congress in 1776 and he was again the oldest delegate to the Constitutional Convention in 1787. He had been active in his country's affairs when most of the other great men had been only boys. In 1754, almost 50, he had advocated a united America, drafting the Albany Plan of Union, when Washington was barely out of his teens, Jefferson was eleven, John Adams nine, and Madison but three years old. Even in the 1760's his political opponents had begun to call him ''pappy,'' his wife's favorite nickname. If he was a contemporary of Jefferson, Washington, Hamilton and Madison, he had also been a contemporary of Increase and Cotton Mather and he had been born less than a century after the death of Shakespeare.

In the nineteenth century Franklin no longer was thought of in terms of this image. The ''founding fathers'' generally included only the men who were active in the early federal period. Franklin ceased to be conceived an architect of our liberties and a daring inventor of new scientific concepts, but became the mentor of material success — the original poor boy who made good. He was considered the teacher of the ''Way to Wealth,'' how to gain material success here and now — the smug, self-righteous and self-made man whose life set a pattern that others might do likewise. His autobiography became a moral tale other than he had intended because the editors removed his confessions of youthful imprudences. Those who published his writings cleansed him of coarse and indelicate phrases and suppressed certain pieces which they considered too "broad" for our delicate national sensibilities. Had the good man returned to earth he would scarcely have recognized his own image and would surely have made the same kind of joke that was evoked on his seeing a portrait made in France in which he had come to look like a Frenchman.

The nineteenth century knew Franklin not only as the author of a guide to success in this world, "The Way to Wealth," but as the inventor of practical devices like the lightning rod, the rocking chair, the Franklin stove, and bifocal glasses. His name immediately evoked Poor Richard's statement, that is inscribed on the walls of savings banks throughout the land. The worth of this precept in the middle of the twentieth century, in an age of plenty and inflation, may be questionable. The value of the penny, in any event, is so small that it would take an extraordinary number of them to make a worth-while savings account. Even the famous one-cent stamp bearing Franklin's likeness is now only a philatelist's curiosity and Franklin now adorns a tuppence card. If we do save pennies, it is probably only to have a supply on hand to feed the parking meters. Curiously enough, the phrase used by Poor Richard was not Franklin's, but an adaptation of William Penn's "A penny saved is a penny got."

For some reason, the nineteenth-century moralists forgot that Franklin's material success came not only from frugality, thrift, and hard work, but derived in even greater measure from heroic initiative. Poor Richard said other things that may attract us today more than the squibb about pennies. "A house without woman and firelight," he said, "is like a body without soul or sprite." "Where there's marriage without love there will be love without marriage." "Fish and visitors stink in three days." "There are no ugly loves nor handsome prisons." He also said, "There are more old drunkards than old doctors." In the almanac for 1739 Franklin warned: "Be not thou disturbed, O grave and sober reader, if among the many various sentences in my book thou findest me trifling now and then, and talking idly. In all the dishes I have hitherto cooked for thee, there is solid meat enough for thy money.

There are scraps from the table of wisdom that will, if well digested, yield strong nourishment to the mind. But squeamish stomachs cannot eat without pickles; which, 'tis true, are good for nothing else, but they provoke an appetite.'' Shall we thus comprehend Poor Richard's advice: "Let thy maid-servant be faithful, strong, and homely''? Or "Keep your eyes wide open before marriage, half shut afterwards.'' He also said: "An egg today is better than a hen tomorrow.'' Two of my favorites are: "A plowman on his legs is higher than a gentleman on his knees''; "Genius without education is like silver in the mine.''

As a student of Franklin I have always been struck most by his humane qualities. Never a mealy-mouthed moralizer, he was quite aware that assent given to precepts did not mean they would be adopted in actual conduct. In "The Way to Wealth,'' he observed that after the people had heard Father Abraham recite the best precepts of Poor Richard, "they approved the doctrine, and immediately practised the contrary, just as if it had been a common sermon.'' Franklin plainly never suffered from the evil of taking himself too seriously. He loved people and he loved conversation and he never lost his sense of humor, even about his own doings and his sayings. He wrote about himself once, in the *Pennsylvania Gazette*, as "a certain printer,'' it being "not customary to give names on these occasions,'' who had been walking "in clean clothes over some barrels of tar . . . ,'' when "the head of one of them unluckily gave way . . . 'Twas observed he sprang out again briskly, verifying the common saying, as nimble as a bee in a tarbarrel. You must know there are several sorts of bees: 'tis true he was no honey bee, nor yet a bumble bee; but a boo-bee he may be allowed to be, namely B.F.''

Even at serious moments, such as his famous address at the close of the Constitutional Convention, his expressions of high purpose were made palatable by the spice of humor; he could not help telling the delegates a story about a "certain French lady, who, in a dispute with her sister, said: 'But I meet with nobody but myself that is always in the right.' '' It is said that the writing of the Declaration of Independence could not be entrusted to Franklin for fear that a pun would be concealed in it. "You know every thing makes me recollect some story,'' he wrote his daughter and he related an anecdote against pride. A certain gentleman had "built a very fine house, and thereby much impaired his fortune.''

He took great pride in showing his house to all his acquaintances, one of whom, having seen it, was bothered by a motto carved over the door, "OIA VANITAS" it seemed to read. "What," says the friend, "is the meaning of this OIA? It is a word I don't understand." The gentleman replied: "I had a mind to have the motto cut on a piece of smooth marble, but there was not room for it between the ornaments, to be put in characters large enough to be read. I therefore made use of a contraction antiently very common in Latin manuscripts, by which the *m*'s and *n*'s in words are omitted, and the omission noted by a little dash above, which you may see there; so that the word is *omnia*, OMNIA VANITAS." "O," replied the friend, "I now comprehend the meaning of your motto; it relates to your edifice; and signifies that, if you have abridged your *omnia*, you have nevertheless left your VANITAS legible at full length."

Writing "Information to those who would remove to America," Benjamin Franklin expressed the aspirations of his age that a country where liberty flourishes and where the laws are just provides opportunity for all men according to their capacities, their initiative and industry, and integrity. In America, he said, any man with a useful art is welcome "and if he exercises it, and behaves well, he will be respected by all that know him; but a mere man of quality, who, on that account, wants to live upon the public, by some office or salary, will be despised and disregarded. The husbandman is in honor ..., and even the mechanic ..." Americans, said Franklin, "are pleased with the observations of a Negro, and frequently mention it, that *Bocarrora* (meaning the white men) *make de black man workee, make de horse workee, make de ox workee, make ebery ting workee; only de hog. He, de hog, no workee; he eat, he drink, he walk about, he go to sleep when he please, he libb like a gentleman.*"

The Franklin I have been describing was a warm-hearted gay man who liked people more than he liked things. He preached a way to wealth, but he did not practice avarice—and in his own life and in the counsels he gave to others he was aware of the dangers of too much money and too many things. Wealth was a means to an end and poor Richard warned that "Avarice and Happiness never saw each other," that "Wealth is not his that has it, but his that enjoys it." Characteristically, when he had accumulated enough wealth to live in modest comfort, he set out to enjoy it by retiring from business so that he could devote himself to research in pure science, to analyzing the mysteries of electrical attraction and repulsion, searching out the secrets of the operation of the condenser or Leyden jar, and studying atmospheric electricity. Because Franklin loved people more than he loved things, he exerted himself in bettering the lives of his fellow-men. His organization of hospitals, schools, fire companies, libraries, and his civic improvements are all instances of his concern for the welfare of his fellow-man. Active in the promotion of religious toleration, he signed his name in support of a synagogue in Philadelphia, aided in the appointment of the first Roman Catholic Bishop in the United States, and conceived of a free house of worship where even a Mahometan might preach.

If, in the nineteenth century, men could be complacent about the battles for freedom of action, thought, and expression, we in the mid-twentieth century see these issues in jeopardy as Franklin did. The impression of the heart, to which Peirce referred in his consideration of the meaning of greatness, finds nourishment in Franklin's straightforward defense of freedom and his continuous activities in behalf of our liberty. If Franklin has any meaning as a symbol for us in the year that marks the 250th anniversary of his birth, if we may find in his writings and his actions any inspiration to strengthen us as we face the problems ahead of us, then the one Franklinian aspect that most commands our attention is that blend of the highest idealism with the empirical temper that marked his life. Franklin's ideals of respect for human dignity and service to man are a part of the age in which he lived and, in some measure, were exemplified in both the Calvinistic Boston of his youth and the Quaker Philadelphia of his young manhood. The environment does not wholly account for any man and in Franklin's case we can see how his personality developed both by accepting and warring against certain features in his background. Clearly, and we have his own testimony in this regard, he was influenced in his career of service to man by his early reading of Cotton Mather's "Essays to do good." But his principles of liberty were formed by his abhorrence of the rigid theocratic domination of the Mathers and their circle and he never forgot his brother's imprisonment for having dared to assume that the press was free. Each individual reacts differently to his environment and so the development of the personality is still obscure, however illuminated by the genius of Sigmund Freud; we fall back on such poetic phrases as inspiration, well-springs of the heart, or mysteries of the human spirit.

Franklin's empirical temperament is easier to comprehend; after all, every master craftsman is an empiricist, struggling with the brute facts of experience at first hand—and so is the successful businessman. Franklin's "Autobiography" was intended to show, as he said, that he owed the "happiness of my past life" to God's "kind providence, which led me to the means I used and gave them success." But the reader cannot help observing that one of the singular features of Franklin's life as he recounted it is the willingness with which he was able to accept the lessons of experience and to profit from them. Thus he recounted his "faults" and the "sinister accidents" of his life, calling them also his "errata," and he told how he corrected each erratum to the best of his ability. In his reading during the 1740's, this empirical turn of mind led him to study the master-works of experimental science: Newton's *Opticks*, Hales' *Statical essays*, Desaguliers's *Experimental philosophy*, Boerhaave's *Chemistry*, and s'Gravesande's *Newtonian philosophy*. By self-education in the best textbooks of his day, Franklin prepared himself for his later role of experimental scientist. A myth has grown up that when Franklin heard about the new subject of electricity, he had no training in science and that merely by some untrained natural instinct he rapidly became one of the leading scientists of his age, called the "Newton" of electricity because his theory of electrical action and his experiments promised to bring order to that subject as the *Principia* had done for the mechanics of heaven and earth a generation earlier. This myth collapses without further ado when we see the quality of the scientific books Franklin was studying in the decade before he began his electrical experiments. And, at once, when we take cognizance of Franklin's scientific training, his career in science becomes meaningful in its true dimensions.

If I seem to be stressing this point unduly, the reason is that there is a parallel of misunderstanding between Franklin's scientific career and the rest of his life. When we say that Franklin was an experimental scientist we do not mean only that he sought to understand the secrets of nature's operations by direct experience in the laboratory, as opposed to the method of analysis which attempts to comprehend vast ranges of experience within the structure of mathematical equations. The distinction between these two major approaches to science does not lie primarily in the fact that one is based more directly on fruitful experiment, while the other is abstract and theoretical, but rather in that they are two different roads to inventing concepts and building theories to explain, correlate, and order the phenomena observed in the world about us and in the laboratory. The experimental scientist, just like the mathematical scientist, sets as his highest goal the understanding of nature. All observations and all experimental facts are not of equal interest, those that are most significant having the special quality of illuminating an important area of knowledge and suggesting new theories, providing ground for the invalidation of older theories, or opening up new areas in which theories are needed.

Franklin's friend, Joseph Priestley, a distinguished historian of scientific ideas and a man of incisive views about the philosophy of science, wrote in his history of electricity that every important experiment is conceived to test or explore some hypothesis. Two of Franklin's major scientific experiments well illustrate this point. He had conceived a theory of electrical action in which electrification is supposed to occur by the transfer of a subtle elastic fluid. When two bodies are rubbed together, according to this theory, one body gains electric fluid (and so, said Franklin, is charged "plus" or "positive"), while the other body loses electric fluid (and so, in Franklin's language, becomes charged "negative" or "minus"). Now an immediate consequence of this basic hypothesis is that electrifications always occur in such a fashion that the charge produced in one body must be exactly equal to that produced in some other body or bodies, although of the opposite sign, so that in general charges always appear in equal magnitudes of positive and negative electrification. Franklin's contemporaries considered that one of the most important applications of this hypothesis was in the experiments he performed which showed the basic principles of the Leyden jar, or condenser, or capacitor. This jar, made of glass, had two conductors in contact with the glass: an outer coating of metal foil, the inside filled with water or shot. Franklin showed that when one of these conductors is charged by contact, the other one (grounded) becomes charged by a process which we call today "electrostatic induction" or "influence." Franklin devised experiments to prove that the charges obtained by the two conductors on either side of the glass were always of the opposite sign but of equal magnitude. Thus, in a sense, what Franklin showed was that there was no more "electricity" in a charged jar than in an uncharged jar, because one of the two conductors had gained as much electric fluid as the other had lost. We call this principle today the principle of conservation of charge, and it is one of the corner stones of our whole system of physical thought. One of the most famous experiments ever performed by Franklin was to test the electrification of clouds. Here, again, Franklin had adopted an hypothesis—that the lightning discharge is similar to the kind of electric discharges which he was able to produce in the laboratory. The famous experiments performed in 1752 were designed to verify this hypothesis.

The reason for stressing this aspect of Franklin's scientific career is that it illustrates the thesis that the experimental scientist does not, so to speak, "try everything," that his method is not an uninformed search by "trial and error." He performs particular experiments and makes certain observations which are related to basic principles which he has conceived on the basis of studying other experiments and observations.

J. J. Thomson, one of the founders of the physics of the twentieth century, wrote, "From the point of view of the physicist, a theory of matter is a policy rather than a creed; its object is to connect or coordinate apparently diverse phenomena, and above all to suggest, stimulate and direct experiment." This description applies not only to Franklin's scientific work, but it also illuminates his political life and social thought. The student of political and social thought is sometimes disturbed, when studying Franklin, by the fact that there is not associated with his name a particular doctrine, a formal treatise, some set of rules, or the Franklinian theory of this or that. The name of Washington suggests at once the first president's warning to his countrymen to beware of foreign entanglements. Monroe's name is enshrined forever in his doctrine about Europe and the New World. Franklin stands only for such beliefs as the rights of man, human dignity, respect for liberty, tolerance, and a concern for the rights and needs of others.

As the scientist goes step by step, from one experiment to another, from concept to concept, and from better theory to better theory, so Franklin embodies his ideals in particular actions that would help to make a better world for his countrymen to live in.

He was concerned with the daily issues of experience, guided by his general principles. In these terms, we may understand one aspect of the secret of Franklin's success in the world of men.

Franklin was a confirmed abolitionist, and some of the last things he did in his life were to aid the cause of the Negro. For many of his contemporaries, freeing the slaves took the level of a theoretical creed, which they hoped to implement. Franklin, however, acting like the scientist who sees theories producing experiments, felt that to talk of freeing the slaves was not enough. Experience showed that Negroes were not the equal of whites, and anyone could observe that "Negroes, who are free [and] live among the white people . . . are generally improvident and poor." How could such an observation be reconciled with the doctrine that all men are equal? The answer again must lie in experience. Franklin tells us that free Negroes are not by nature "deficient in natural understanding," but suffer because they "have not the advantage of education." Hence Franklin advocated not only the freeing of Negro slaves, but the establishment of schools in which Negroes could learn trades and become useful members of society. What he said, in effect, was: Let us educate the Negroes and see whether they will not then be able to do the work of Whites. This attitude reminds us of the words he wrote when he conceived that lightning is an electrical discharge: "Let the experiment be made."

Many of Franklin's contemporaries respected the Constitution they had framed because of its lofty sentiments and high ideals, because it embodied the best practices of all other governments with original features, or even because it seemed to them to represent on the behavioristic level the best features of Newtonian machines. Franklin disagreed with many aspects of the Constitution, but the feature that made it acceptable to him was the provision for amendment on trial, the possibility that in the light of actual experience alterations could be made, just as scientific theories are modified by the experiments that they suggest. I am, therefore, convinced that from Franklin's point of view the greatest experiment to which he had ever been party was not the analysis of the Leyden jar, the examination of electrification in clouds, or any of the other laboratory experiments which won him international fame, but the test as to whether a new republic, governed wisely and justly according to principles that could be adapted to changing conditions, could survive in this world.

The Science of Benjamin Franklin

I. BERNARD COHEN

Many Americans tend to think of Benjamin Franklin as a tinkerer or gadgeteer, an inventor or practical man who "allegedly" made one experiment: the lightning kite. American historians generally have not understood that Franklin was, in fact, a true scientist or a "serious" scientist. They would be at a loss to explain how Joseph Priestley and other contemporaries could have referred to Franklin as a "Newton," in fact as the "Newton" of electricity. But the evidence as to the importance of Franklin in basic or fundamental science is not hard to find. His book on electricity, *Experiments and Observations on Electricity, Made at Philadelphia in America* (first published in London in 1751) was one of the most often reprinted books of the age. In the eighteenth century it appeared in five editions in English, three in French (in two separate translations), one in German and one in Italian—all prior to his rise to international political fame during the Revolution. Containing Franklin's unitary theory of electrical action and the many experiments that illustrated the theory, this book established the basic language that we still use in discussing electrical phenomena: such terms as negative or minus, positive or plus, battery—introduced into electrical discourse for the first time by Benjamin Franklin.

Franklin, furthermore, was honored by the scientific community to a degree that was unmatched in his day. He was awarded the Copley Medal of the Royal Society of London and was then elected a Fellow of that society and a member of its Council. He was elected in 1773 (two years before the Declaration of Independence) a "foreign associate" of the French Academy of Sciences in Paris, a very great honor indeed, since by the statutes of the Academy there could be only eight such foreign scientists as associates at any one time. No other American would be distinguished enough in his research to be so honored for another hundred years, when Louis Agassiz became a "foreign associate." Yet, despite such visible signs of eminence in the domain of pure or basic or fundamental science, Franklin's place in the history of science remains obscure and most Americans (even historians) do not recognize his stature and eminence in science as such and have even tended to confuse his scientific research and thought with his inventions.

For many years I have pondered as to why most Americans have not appreciated Franklin's stature as a scientist. A probable reason is to be found in the fact that, well into the twentieth century, the United States was a "developing nation," or an "underdeveloped nation," with regard to the sciences. Before that time the country produced very few first-rate scientists on a world scale. The physicist J. Williard Gibbs stands out as a great nineteenth-century exception, and he was recognized abroad long before his own countrymen knew of him. Until the present century, there was no adequate provision in America for advanced scientific education and very little opportunity for a lifetime of research. Americans specialized in applied science and invention, rather than pure science. Science, for all to many, was equated with practical needs rather than advances in knowledge. Accordingly, being a scientist was not traditionally included among the careers that led to greatness. The nation's rise to true scientific eminence came during the 1930's, following the immigration of so many scientific refugees from Europe, and national support of science on the present large scale dates only from the 1950's. Now that the United States has at last assumed a leading role among the scientific nations of the world, it is time that our history books set Benjamin Franklin in the proper perspective of the greatness of his scientific achievement, as a leading theoretical and experimental physical scientist of the Age of Reason.[1]

---

[1] These initial paragraphs repeat the argument in the introduction to my *Benjamin Franklin: Scientist and Stateman* (New York: Charles Scribner's Sons, 1975), pp. 11-14; the remainder of this essay is based largely on an article, "In Defense of Benjamin Franklin," *Scientific American,* August 1948, vol. 179, pp. 36-43.

Franklin first became acquainted with the subject of electrical science sometime aroung 1744.[2] Between 1747 and 1751 he made his major discoveries and began to win scientific acclaim. Contrary to the supposed general rule that the great discoveries in physics are made by men in their twenties and thirties, Franklin began his scientific work at about the age of 40; he had previously been too busy earning a living to devote much time to scientific pursuits. Having been successful in the world of affairs and now finding the pursuit of truth congenial to his tastes and gifts, he decided, as he tells us in his autobiography, to give up his business and to spend his time conducting experiments. No sooner had he retired from business, however, than a great national crisis arose and he put aside his scientific research in order to participate in the defense of Philadelphia. From then on until he died, he pursued his research only in his spare time. His city, colony and nation never ceased to require his services. At 81 years of age, when American independence had been won, and when his work in Paris was finished and he was ready to come home to America, Franklin wrote to his most intimate scientific correspondent, the Dutch physician and physicist Jan Ingenhousz, that he was once more a free man "after fifty years in public affairs." He hoped that his friend would come with him to America, where "in the little remainder of my life...we will make plenty of experiments together."[3] Alas, even this was to be denied him, for ahead there lay not days of joyful interrogation of nature but the trying and tedious work of the Constitutional Convention. Long before, Franklin had been forced to choose between the role of a quiet philosopher and a

---

[2] On Franklin's introduction to electricity, see my "Benjamin Franklin and the Mysterious 'Dr. Spence': the Date and Source of Franklin's Interest in Electricity," *Journal of the Franklin Institute,* 1943, vol. 235, pp. 1–25 (reprinted, with revisions, in I.B. Cohen, *The Science of Benjamin Franklin* [New York: Neal Watson Associates, 1981], and my *Franklin and Newton* (Philadelphia: American Philosophical Society, 1956; Cambridge, MA: Harvard University Press, 1966 [revised reprint, 1981]. More recently, this topic has been discussed in Bernard S. Finn, "An Appraisal of the Origins of Franklin's Electrical Theory," *Isis,* 1969, vol. 60, pp. 362–369, and in John L. Heilbron, "Franklin, Haller, and Franklinist History," *Isis,* 1977, vol. 68, pp. 539–549. In particular, Heilbron has identified a source of Franklin's early knowledge of electricity in an article in *The Gentleman's Magazine* (1745, vol. 15, pp. 193–197), entitled "An Historical Account of the New German Experiments in Electricity," a translation from a French text by Albrecht von Haller.

[3] Benjamin Franklin to Ingenhousz, 29 Apr., 1785.

"public man." He had decided the issue without hesitation, saying: "Had Newton been pilot of but a single common ship, the finest of his discoveries would scarce have excused, or atoned for his abandoning the helm one hour in time of danger; how much less if she carried the fate of the Commonwealth."[4]

As we read these lines today, we cannot help thinking of our own scientists who, during World War II, gave up their own individual research to serve their nation. But there is a fundamental difference between their problem and Franklin's. In Franklin's day, the one outstanding American scientist, the only one with a world-wide reputation, found that he could serve his country best by going abroad to plead its cause, rather than by applying his scientific skills to devising new instruments of destruction. Yet such was Franklin's stature in science—and he *was* the Newton of his age — that some suspected the man who dared to tame the lightning bolts of Jove had turned his talents to the perfection of a new and terrible weapon. "The natural philosophers in power," wrote Horace Walpole in 1777, "believe that Dr. Franklin has invented a machine of the size of a toothpick case, and materials that would reduce St. Paul's to a handful of ashes."

Benjamin Franklin made scientific contributions in many fields, including pioneer studies of heat conduction, the origins of storms, and so on, but his most significant work was done in electricity. He worked in electrostatics — the science of electricity at rest or in sudden swift surges. Before Franklin, the known facts of this subject were meager and their explanation was inadequate. When he left the field, a whole new set of observed data had been entered in the record and the Franklinian theory of electrical action had unified all the known facts, preparing the way for the progress of the future.[5]

Franklin's theory of electrical action is simple and straightforward. It is based on the fundamental idea that there is a "com-

---

[4] Benjamin Franklin to Cadwallader Colden, 11 October, 1750.

[5] See the essay (in the present volume) by R.A. Millikan, in which the discoverer of the electron pays a founder's tribute to the author of the first unitary theory of electrical action. Millikan even went so far as to hail Franklin as the discoverer of the electron. For a balanced view of Franklin's achievement, see John L. Heilbron, *Electricity in the 17th and 18th Centuries* (Berkeley, Los Angeles, London: University of California Press, 1979).

mon matter,'' of which the bulk of bodies is composed, and an "electrical matter,'' or, to use other 18th-century terms, "electrical fluid'' or "electrical fire.''[7] In its normal state, every body contains a fixed amount of the electrical fluid. But a body may, under certain conditions, gain an excess of the electrical fluid or lose some of its normal complement of it. In such a state a body is "electrified'' or "charged''; in the first case, when there is an excess of the fluid, said Franklin, the charge is to be denoted as "positive''or "plus,''indicating that something has been added to it; in the second case, "minus'' or "negative,'' indicating that something has been lost. When a piece of glass has been rubbed with a silk rag, the glass acquires an excess of the electrical fluid and becomes charged plus. Franklin insisted that electric charges are not "created'' by friction, as some of his contemporaries believed, but rather are the redistribution of the electrical fluid that results from the act of rubbing. If the glass gains an excess of fluid, Franklin held, the silk must have lost the very same amount, thereby gaining a negative charge of the same magnitude. Today we call this principle the law of conservation of charge. This principle declares that whenever charges appear or disappear, they do so in exactly equal quantities of positive and negative charge. Although this principle had been implicit in the thought of other scientists, it was Franklin who made it central to his theory and illustrated it by a number of different experimental examples.[8]

Franklin applied his theory to a number of experiments, including the following. He placed two experimenters on insulated glass stools, one charged plus and the other minus. When the two experimenters touched hands,both lost their charges because the excess of one supplied the deficiency of the other. If a third uncharged experimenter touched either of the charged ones, he drew

---

[7] Franklin's concept of a particulate electrical fluid arose from the Newtonian natural philosophy and was one of the "imponderables" used by eighteenth-century physicists; cf. my *Franklin and Newton* (cited in n.2 *supra*).

[8] On the origins and background of the concept of conservation of charge, see Heilbron's book (cited in n.6 *supra*), p. 330.

a spark or got a shock, because he had relatively more electric fluid than the man charged minus, and less than the man charged plus.[9]

This was a simple, dramatic demonstration of Franklin's contention that electrical phenomena are caused by the action of a single "fluid."[10] The chief rival theory held that electrical phenomena derive from two "currents" of an electric matter "which differ only in direction, not in kind," and which "nearly or exactly balance, so that a body can never be emptied of its electrical matter." These jets of matter ("effluences" and "affluences") produce electrical attraction and replusions from "the direct inpact of the electrical matter in motion."[11] A French contemporary pointed out that the beauty of Franklin's theory over its rival was that "Franklin says: do that and this is what must happen; change that circumstance and this will be the result. In this way you can take advantage of a certain thing; in that way you will suffer an inconvenience."[12] The late J.J. Thomson, discoverer of the fundamental properties of moving electrons, wrote only a few years ago: "The service which Franklin's one-fluid theory has rendered to the science of electricity by suggesting and coordinating researches can hardly be overestimated."[13]

---

[9]This experiment is described in Franklin's first letter on electricity to Peter Collinson (11 July 1747), printed in the later editions of Franklin's book under the date of 11 July 1974. See *Benjamin Franklin's Experiments: a New Edition of Franklin's "Experiments and Observations on Electricity"*, edited, with a critical and historical introduction, by I. Bernard Cohen (Cambridge, Mass.: Harvard University Press, 1941). A new facsimile of the first edition of Franklin's book (London, 1751-1753-1754), with introduction and appendixes by I.B. Cohen, is scheduled for publication in 1981 by the Dibner Library of the History of Science and Technology, Washington, D.C. On the dates of Franklin's letters, see I.B. Cohen, "Some Problems in Relation to the Dates of Benjamin Franklin's First Letters on Electricity," *Proceedings of the American Philosophical Society*, 1956, vol. 100, pp. 537-542.

[10] See my *Franklin and Newton*, ch. 8 & 10, and R.A. Millikan's essay in the present volume.

[11] These quotations concerning Nollet's theory come from John L. Heilbron's essay in the *Dictionary of Scientific Biography*, vol. 10 (New York: Charles Scribner's Sons, 1974), pp. 145-148. See, further, ch. 11 of Heilbron's book (cited in n.6 *supra*).

[12] This quotation comes from the introductory comment in Jacques Barbeu-Duboung's two-volume translation of Franklin's book on electricity, *Oeuvres de M. Franklin* (Paris, 1773).

[13] J.J. Thomson, *Recollections and Reflections* (London: G. Bell and Sons, 1936), pp. 252-253.

To understand the application of Franklin's theory, let us follow him through two series of significant experiments.[14] The first begins with one of the many facts first discovered by Franklin and now part of the basic data of the science—what he called the "wonderful effect of pointed bodies, both *drawing off* and *throwing off* the electrical fire." Franklin found that if a pointed conductor such as a needle is brought into the neighborhood of a charged insulated body, the needle will draw off the charge, but it will do so only if it is grounded, that is, in contact with the experimenter's hand or a grounded wire. If the needle is inserted in wax, a non-conductor or insulator, it will not draw off the charge.[15] He also found that if you try to charge a metal object with a jagged edge or point, the object will "throw off the charge" as fast as you put it on. He discovered further that a charged object could be discharged by sifting fine sand on it, by breathing on it, by bringing a burning candle near it, or by surrounding it with smoke.

For at least 50 years before Franklin's research, there had been speculation that lightning is probably electrical in nature. But what distinguished Franklin from his predecessors was the fact that he was able to design an experiment to test this hypothesis.[16] He made a small model showing how a discharge might take place between two electrified clouds or between a cloud and the earth. He then predicted that since a small pointed conductor would draw off the charge from an insulated charged body in his laboratory, a large pointed conductor erected in the ground ought to draw the electricity from passing clouds. This suggested to his active mind that "the knowledge of this power of points might be of use to

---

[14] See my *Franklin and Newton* (cited in n.2 *supra*), ch. 10; the experiments are described in Franklin's book (see n.9 *supra*).

[15] As Franklin stated explicitly in the later editions of his book, this "power" of pointed bodies to "draw off" the electrical fluid was discovered by his Philadelphia co-experimentor, Thomas Hopkinson.

[16] In a letter to John Lining, 18 March 1755, published in Franklin's book on electricity, an extract is given from Franklin's record book of experiments to show — as Franklin says—that the thought that the lightning discharge is an electrical phenomenon "was not so much 'an out-of-the-way one,'" but that it might have occurred to any electrician." But the important difference between Franklin's thoughts on this matter and those of others is expressed in the final sentence of the extract, "Let the experiment be made."

mankind, in preserving houses, churches, ships, &c., from the stroke of lightning, by directing us to fix on the highest parts of those edifices, upright rods of iron made sharp as a needle, and gilt to prevent rusting, and from the foot of those rods a wire down the outside of the building into the ground, or down round one of the shrouds of a ship, and down her side till it reaches the water."[17]

The experiment which Franklin proposed to test his hypothesis was described by him in these words: "On the top of some high tower or steeple, place a kind of sentry-box...big enough to contain a man and an electrical stand. From the middle of the stand let an iron rod rise and pass bending out of the door, and then upright 20 or 30 feet, pointed very sharp at the end. If the electrical stand be kept clean and dry, a man standing on it when such clouds are passing low, might be electrified and afford sparks, the rod drawing [electrical] fire to him from the cloud. If any danger to the man should be apprehended (though I think there should be none) let him stand on the floor of his box, and now and then bring to the rod the loop of a wire that has one end fastened to the leads, he holding it by a wax handle; so the sparks, it the rod is electrified, will strike from the rod to the wire and not affect him."[18]

This famous "sentry-box experiment" was first performed in France on 10 May 1752, under the directions of a French scientist named Jean Dalibard (or d'Alibard), who had translated Franklin's book into French at the request of the great naturalist Georges de Buffon.[19] (King Louis XV had been so fascinated by Franklin's book that he ordered some of the experiments it described to be performed in his presence.)[20] The Franklin sentry-box experiment was soon repeated in England. Glowing testimonials to the Philadelphia scientist speedily increased in

---

[17] Quoted from Franklin's "Opinions and Conjectures Concerning the Properties and Effects of the Electrical Matter...1749," printed in Franklin's book on electricity. See, further, I.B. Cohen, "The Two-Hundredth Anniversary of Benjamin Franklin's Two Lightning Experiments and the Introduction of the Lightning Rod," *Proceedings of the American Philosophical Society,* 1952, vol. 96, pp. 331-366.

[18] "Opinions and Conjectures..." (see n.17 *supra*), §21.

[19] Buffon's interest in having Franklin's book translated into French was related to his active controversy with Reaumur, since the Abbe Nollet was a protege of Reaumur's and Franklin's book offered an alternative to Nollet's theory of electricity. See Heilbron's article (cited in n.2 *supra*) and his biography of Nollet (cited in n.11 *supra*).

[20] Franklin described his reactions to the commendations of Louis XV of France in a letter to Jared Eliot, 12 April 1753.

number. An enterprising British manufacturer advertised for sale a ready-made machine "for making the Experiment by which *Franklin's* new theory of Thunder is demonstrated." Franklin did not perform this experiment himself, apparently because he thought that a very high building would be necessary; he was waiting for the completion of the high spire of Christ Church in Philadelphia. After the book was published, but before he had heard from Europe of Dalibard's successful execution of the experiment, the kite project occurred to him as a good substitute and he carried it through instead.[21]

Franklin devised other experiments and instruments to test the charge of clouds, of which one of the most interesting was a pair of bells located in his study. One of the bells was grounded by a rod going into the earth and the other was connected to a rod ending in a point on the roof. A little ball hung between the bells. Whenever an electrified cloud passed overhead, the ball was set in motion and rang the bells. Franklin's careful studies soon showed him that clouds may be charged either plus or minus, and he concluded, therefore, that lightning probably goes from the earth to a cloud at least as often as from a cloud to the earth—an idea which has been confirmed only in our own time by such research as that of B.J.F. Schonland and his associates in South Africa.[22]

Franklin's studies of lightning and his invention of the lightning rod brought him universal fame, but the scientists even more impressed by his analysis set the seal to his scientific reputation. In the form in which the 18th century knew it, the condenser was a glass jar coated on the outside with metal foil and filled with either metal shot or water. It was fitted with a wooden cover into which a rod ending in a knob was inserted. From the lower end of the rod a metal chain depended, going down into the water or shot. This device, invented in the late 1740's, was known as a "Leyden jar," because one of its several independent discoverers, Pieter van Musschenbroek, was a professor in Leyden. The essential feature of a condenser is the placement of an insulator or dielectric (*e.g.,* air, glass, wax or paper) between two conducting surfaces in close

---

[21] See the article cited in n.17 *supra,* reprinted in *The Science of Benjamin Franklin* (see n.2 *supra*).

[22] See Schonland's article in the issue of the *Journal of the Franklin Institute* devoted to the two hundredth anniversary of Franklin's lightning experiments (vol. 253, n. 5, May 1952); see also B.J.F. Schonland, *The Flight of Thunderbolts* (Oxford: Clarendon Press, 1950).

contact with it. In the first Leyden jar the inner conductor was water, the dielectric was the glass, and the outer conductor was a man's hand. Musschenbroek developed his version of it while carrying out some experiments with an electrical machine which charged a whirling glass globe by rubbing it against an experimenter's hands. The charge was transferred to a gun barrel, from the end of which hung a wire that was partly immersed in a round glass vessel filled with water. When Musschenbroek held the vessel in his right hand and attempted to draw a spark from the gun barrel with his left hand, he "was struck with such violence that my whole body was shaken as by a thunderbolt...in a word, I thought it was all up with me."[23]

The condenser was a wonderful instrument. By making it bigger and bigger, the shocks it could give were made stronger and stronger. Apparently, somehow or other electricity accumulated in it, and through some little-understood aspect of its construction, it could hold more electricity than anything else of its size. The electric fluids must, it was thought, be "condensed" in it. Musschenbroek wrote a letter describing this experiment which was published in the *Memoires* of the French Academy of Sciences. It ended with the famous statement that he would never again receive such a shock, even if he were to be offered the Kingdom of France! For such ignoble sentiments he was publicly rebuked by Priestley, who called him a "cowardly professor" and contrasted him with the "magnanimous Mr. Boze, who with a truly philosophic heroism worthy of the renowned Empedocles, said he might die by the electric shock, that the account of his death might furnish an article for the memoirs of the French Academy of Sciences." Then, referring to a German physicist named Richmann, who had just been killed while performing a variation of Franklin's sentry-box experiment, Priestley concluded, "But it is not given to every electrician to die the death of the justly envied Richman."[24]

All the electricians of Europe wondered what made the Leyden jar work. "Everybody," wrote Priestley, "was eager to see, and,

---

[23] On the Leyden jar, see Heilbron's book (cited in n.6 *supra*) and his article, "A propos de l'invention de la bouteille de Leyde," *Revue d'Histoire des Sciences,* 1966, vol. 19, pp. 133-142.

[24] Joseph Priestley, *The History and Present State of Electricity* (third ed., 2 vols., London, 1755), reprinted with an introduction by Robert E. Schofield (New York, London: Johnson Reprint corporation, 1966), vol. 1, pp. 107-108.

notwithstanding the terrible account that was reported, to *feel* the experiment.'' In France the new device provided a means of satisfying simultaneously the court's love of spectacles and the great interest in science. One hundred and eighty soldiers of the guard were made to jump into the air with a greater precision than soldiers of the guard displayed in any other maneuvers. Seven hundred monks from the Couvent de Paris, joined hand to hand, had a Leyden jar discharged through them all. They flew up into the air with finer timing than could be achieved by the most gifted corps of ballet dancers. From one end of the world to the other, traveling demonstrators sought their fortunes by showing the public experiments of electrical phenomena.

Franklin's step-by-step analysis of the vexing problem of the condenser showed him to be a great master of the technique of scientific experimentation. He found that the charge on the inner conductor was always the opposite of the charge on the outer conductor and that the amount of charge given to both was the same in magnitude. In other words, by the "charging" of the jar, one of the two conductors gained the exact quantity of "electrical fluid" that the other lost. "There is really no more electrical fire in the [Leyden] phial after what is called its *charging,* than before, nor less a *discharging,*" Franklin wrote the lead coating of a Leyden jar and placed it so that it was near the knob leading to the water inside the jar, but not near enough to produce a spark when the jar was charged. He then placed the jar on an insulating stand (a block of wax) and suspended a small cork on a string between the wire and the knob. The cork, he noted, "will play incessantly from one to the other, 'till the bottle is no longer electrized.'' In other words, the cork carried the charge from the plus conductor to the minus until equilibrium was restored.

Most important of all, Franklin showed that "the whole force of the bottle, and power of giving a shock, is in the GLASS ITSELF.'' How would *you,* reader, go about finding "wherein its strength lay''? Every student knows today that the only way to proceed is to test the instrument one element at a time, and to find the role played by each. But this apparently simple rule was not taken for granted in the time of Franklin, as can readily be seen in the fact that none of his contemporaries made the kind of analysis that Franklin now proceeded to carry out.

He charged a Leyden jar that stood on glass and carefully drew out the cork with its wire that hung down into the water. Then he took the bottle in one hand, and brought the other hand near its mouth. "A strong spark came from the water, and the shock was as violent as if the wire had remained in it, which shewed that the force did not lie in the wire." If it was not in the wire, then perhaps it was in the water itself. Franklin recharged the Leyden jar, drew out the cork and wire as before, and carefully poured the water into an empty Leyden jar which likewise stood on a glass insulator. The second jar did not become charged in this process. "We judged then," Franklin wrote, "that [the charge, or force] must either be lost in decanting, or remain in the first bottle. The latter we found to be true; for that bottle on trial gave the shock, though filled up as it stood with fresh unelectrified water from a tea-pot." Apparently the essential element was glass, the insulator between the two conductors. But it still remained to be demonstrated whether "glass had this property merely as glass, or whether the form [of the jar] contributed anything to it."[25]

The next part of the experiment involved the invention of the parallel plate condenser.[26] Franklin sandwiched a large piece of glass between two square plates of lead, equal to each other in size but slightly smaller than the glass. When this condenser was charged, he removed the lead plates, which had but little charge, and noted that a small spark could be taken from the glass at almost any point that it was touched. When the two completely uncharged plates were put back in place, one on each side of the glass, and a circuit made between them, then "a violent shock ensued." When we demonstrate this phenomenon to our students in physics classes today, we call it the experiment of the dissectible condenser. We explain it by stating that the dielectric, or glass, has been polarized during charging, *i.e.,* it has become an electret. There are certain types of wax that can be polarized in this way simply by being heated and then cooled. Such an electret will give off little or no charge by itself, but if we put a conductor on two sides of it, we

---

[25] The analysis of the Leyden jar occurs in a letter to Peter Collinson, 29 April 1749, containing "Farther Experiments and Observations in Electricity, 1748," printed in Franklin's book on electricity.

[26] Franklin observed in a note, "I have since heard that Mr. [John] Smeaton was the first who used panes of glass for that purpose."

have a charged condenser which can be then discharged like any other. Another fact about such condensers that we teach students today was also discovered by Franklin: the amount of charge is greater when the dielectric separating the two conductors is very thin than when it is thick.

Franklin's experiment of the cork that traveled back and forth between the two conductors contained, by the way, the germ of an important idea, although he did not realize it. We know today that a condenser never discharges in one complete stroke, but rather in a series of oscillations — a fact of great importance in radio and modern electronics.

Franklin's extraordinary experiments and his splendid theory marked the beginning of a new era in the subject of electricity. His theory showed its usefulness in many ways. Franklin discovered what is known today as the Faraday effect, namely that the charge on a hollow cylindrical condenser (or a hollow sphere) is on the outside surface only. At first he could not explain this. Later the answer came to him: the "electrical fluid" is self-repellent and the symmetry of the conductor couses it to distribute itself on the outside. From this explanation, Franklin's friend Joseph Priestley deduced that the law of electrical action must be an inverse square law similar to the law of gravitation. This deduction, although published, was overlooked and had to await rediscovery decades later by Charles Coulomb, when it became know as Coulomb's law.[27]

Yet another advantage of Franklin's theory was the ease with which it lent itself to the making of measurements, by concentrating attention on the amount of "electrical fluid" or charge which a body gained or lost. When working with two bodies, it did not matter which one was used because Franklin's law of conservation of charge meant that the quantity gained by one was exactly the quantity that the other lost. The first electricians to make quantitative measurements — such men as Volta, Bennet, Canton, Cavendish and Henley — built upon the convenient one-fluid theory of Benjamin Franklin and the law of conservation of charge which followed from it.

Of course, Franklin's experiments with lightning gave his general research program and his theory a spectacular fame. But

---

[27] On the discovery of the law, see Heilbron's book (cited in n.6 *supra*).

this subject is not very well understood. The invention of the lightning rod did not just show that Franklin was practical minded; rather, this invention proved what every scientist since Francis Bacon and Rene Descartes fully believed, that the road to practical inventions lies in pure or disinterested or basic or fundamental research. Franklin did not "direct" his research so that it would lead to something useful, as a historian woefully ignorant of science once declared, but rather used the results of his research to produce something of practical use *after* the research had been completed and when he *then* saw that it might have some practical application. The lightning experiments caused Franklin's name to become known throughout Europe to the public at large and not merely to men of science. Joseph Priestley, in his *History...of Electricity,* characterized the experimental discovery that the lightning discharge is an electrical phenomenon as "the greatest, perhaps, since the time of Sir Isaac Newton." Of course, one reason for satisfaction in this discovery was that it subjected one of the most mysterious and frightening natural phenomena to rational explanation. It also proved that Bacon had been right in asserting that a knowledge of how nature really works might lead to a better control of nature itself: that valuable practical innovations might be the fruit of pure disinterested scientific research.

No doubt the most important effect of the lightning experiments was to show that the laboratory phenomena in which rods or globes of glass were rubbed, to the accompaniment of sparks, and induced charges and electrical shocks, belong to a class of phenomena occurring naturally. Franklin's lightning experiments proved that electrical effects do not result exclusively from man's artifice, from his intervention in phenomena, but are in fact part of the routine operations of nature. And every "electrician" learned from Franklin's investigations of the nature of the lightning discharge that experiments performed with little toys in the laboratory could reveal new aspects of one of the most dramatic of nature's catastrophic forces. "The discoveries made in the summer of the year 1752 will make it memorable in the history of electricity," William Watson wrote in 1753. "These have opened a new field to [natural] philosophers, and have given them room to hope, that what they have learned before in their museums, they may apply, with more propriety than they hitherto could have done, in illustrating the nature and effects of thunder; a phaenomenon hitherto almost inaccessable to their inquiries."[28] Franklin's achievement of a highly successful career wholly in the field of electricity marked the coming of age of electrical science and the full acceptance of the new field of specialization. On 30 November 1753, awarding Franklin the Royal Society's Sir Godfrey Copley gold medal for his discoveries in electricity, the Earl of Macclesfield emphasized this very point: "Electricity is a neglected subject," he said, "which not many years since was thought to be of little importance, and was at that time only applied to illustrate the nature of attraction and repulsion; nor was anything worth much notice expected to ensue from it." But now, thanks to the labors of Franklin, it "appears to have a most surprising share of power in nature."[29]

It is often said that Franklin was typically American in his approach to science—a utilitarian interested in science chiefly, if not solely, because of its practical applications. It is true that when he had discovered the action of pointed grounded conductors and proved that clouds are electrified, he applied these discoveries to the invention of the lightning rod. But he did not make these discoveries in order to invent a lightning rod![30] Franklin's inventions were of two kinds. One type was pure gadgetry; in this class were his inventions of bifocal glasses, which required no recondite knowledge of optical principles, and of a device for taking books down from the shelf without getting up from one's chair. The lightning rod, on the other hand, developed from pure scientific research. If Franklin's approach to science had been strictly utilitarian, it is doubtful that he would ever have studied the subject of electricity at all. In the 18th century there was only one practical application of electricity, and that was the giving of electric shocks for therapeutic purposes, chiefly to cure paralysis. (Although Franklin on occasion participated in such therapy, he did not believe that the shock itself ever cured a case of paralysis. With shrewd psychological insight, he guessed that the reported cures arose from the desire of the patient to be cured rather than from the passage of electric fluid.)

---

[28] See my *Franklin and Newton* (cited in n.2 *supra*), p. 490.
[29] *Ibid.*
[30] How could he have done so, since he could have had no prevision as to what his future discoveries would be?

Franklin studied nature because he wanted to discover its in-
nermost secrets, and he chose electrostatics because chance
brought him the instruments with which to study this subject, and
because he quickly found out that this was a subject well fitted to
his particular talents. In a spirit which might well be emulated by
all men engaged in research, he wrote humbly at the end of one of
his communications: "These thoughts, my dear friend, are many
of them crude and hasty; and if I were merely ambitious of acquiring some reputation in philosophy [*i.e.,* natural philosophy, or
science], I ought to keep them by me, 'till corrected and improved
by time, and farther experience. But since even short hints and imperfect experiments in any new branch of science, being communicated, have oftentimes a good effect, in exciting the attention
of the ingenious to the subject...you are at liberty to communicate this paper to whom you please, it being of more importance that knowledge should increase, than that your friend
should be thought an accurate philosopher."[31]

In fact, Franklin's theory of electricity — though widely accepted and used — proved to have defects.[32] A major one arose in
two ways. First of all, Franklin had assumed that neutral or non-
electrified bodies are composed of "common" matter and a "normal" quantity of electrical fluid. The electrical fluid was
postulated to be composed of particles that repel one another and
that mutually attract and are attracted by the particles of common
matter.[33] In the case of two positively charged bodies, the excess
electrical fluid in one will — according to the theory — repel the excess electrical fluid in the other, and hence the theory explains or
predicts the mutual repulsion of two bodies, each of which has a
positive charge or more electrical fluid than in the normal or uncharged state. Similarly, a body that has lost some of its electrical

[31] Benjamin Franklin to Peter Collinson, 14 August 1747.

[32] For example, Franklin used extensively the concept of "electrical atmospheres,"
clouds of electrical fluid or electrical matter surrounding positively charged bodies. The
production of a condenser made of two parallel plates separated by air showed that this
concept was untenable and had to be abandoned. See Roderick W. Home, *The Effluvial
Theory of Electricity* (New York: Arno Press, 1981), and his article, "Franklin's Electrical Atmospheres," *British Journal for the History of Science,* 1972, vol. 6, pp.
131-151. See also Heilbron's book (cited in n.6 *supra*), pp. 241-242, 262-263, 388-389,
414-418, 426-430.

[33] See R.A. Millikan's essay, elsewhere in this volume.

fluid (charged negatively) and a body with an excess of electrical fluid (charged positively) will attract one another. But what of two bodies that are both negatively charged? In fact, as Franklin reluctantly had to admit, they are observed to repel one another.[34] This defect in the theory was a serious one. An attempt to remedy the situation was made by Franz Ulrich Theodosius Aepinus in his *Tentamen theoriae electricitatis et magnetismi* (Essay on the theory of electricity and magnetism), published in St. Petersburg in 1759. Aepinus here added a postulate to the Franklinian theory, according to which the particles of common matter not only attract particles of the electrical fluid but also repel one another. At once, it follows that negatively charged bodies should repel one another just as positively charged bodies do.[35]

Aepinus did not, however, introduce his radical postulate primarily to take care of a fundamental deficiency in the Franklinian theory of electrical action, as has usually been alleged. Rather, that result was merely a major by-product of a logical and mathematical analysis of the Franklinian scheme amended. As Aepinus makes clear, and as R.W. Home sums up the situation, Aepinus's new electrical postulate (about particles of common matter repelling one another) was a product of logical analysis and clear thinking rather than having been simply "an ad hoc modification of Franklin's theory to enable it to account for the observed mutual repulsion between two negatively charged bodies." Rather, as Home puts the matter:

With his skilled mathematician's eye, Aepinus perceived that if the principles Franklin had laid down were taken literally and their consequences rigorously traced out, they led to absurd conclusions. In particular, they led to the ludicrous proposition that two unelectrified bodies exerted electrical forces on each other. Hence Aepinus's additional postulate, or something formally equivalent to it, far from being a merely incidental modification of Franklin's theory, was absolutely essential if the foundations of the theory were to be rendered coherent. Only if this were done could the theory be refor-

---

[34] On Franklin's reluctance to admit that two negatively charged bodies mutually repel one another, see my *Franklin and Newton* (cited in n.2 *supra*), pp. 491–494, and also Heilbron's book (cited in n.6 *supra*). This phenomenon of repulsion was brought forcibly to Franklin's attention by his Philadelphia co-experimentor, Ebenezer Kinnersley.

[35] See *Aepinus's Essay on the Theory of Electricity and Magnetism*, with an introductory monograph and notes by R.W. Home and a translation by P.J. Connor (Princeton: Princeton University Press, 1979).

mulated in mathematical terms. In other words, Aepinus's innovation was an important step in the subjection of this particular branch of physical theory to mathematical analysis.[36]

Aepinus's theory was not widely accepted, although it won Franklin's support. Home has traced the stages of reception of Aepinus's ideas and suggests some possible causes for the lack of general acceptance. Many electricians of that day objected to the austere mathematical mode of thinking of Aepinus and others rejected a mathematical theory that was not based on a definite, certain, and established law of force. Furthermore, Aepinus's book was expensive and often difficult to obtain; the edition was small, limited to 650 copies. Franklin accepted Aepinus's conclusion that the impermeability of glass in condensers or Leyden jars was not related to unique aspects of glass (as Franklin had at first believed), but was a property of all non-conductors (or "electrics *per se*"); this became a feature of the Franklinian theory thereafter. Franklin strongly commended Aepinus's theory of magnetism. Aepinus had also shown that the Franklinian supposition of "electrical atmospheres" (supposedly, the excess electrical fluid on positively charged bodies formed a kind of ethereal cloud or atmosphere surrounding such bodies) was untenable.[37] But Franklin was silent on the subject of the new postulate; we have no information as to whether he did not fully grasp its import or whether he did so but refused to believe that particles of common matter can repel one another.

Franklin's contributions to science were not limited to electricity; he concerned himself with such other branches of science as oceanography, meteorology, general physics, and even medicine. Especially well known were his experiments to see whether oil spread on the surface of water would in fact still the waves. He made a spetacular demonstration of this phenomenon in Portsmouth harbor for the benefit of a group of Fellows of the Royal Society. He printed the first chart of the Gulf Steam and conceived of using a marine thermometer as an aid to navigation in relation to the Gulf Stream. He measured surface temperatures in the ocean during Atlantic crossings and devised a special instrument to

---

[36] *Ibid.,* pp. 119–120.
[37] See n.32 *supra.*

measure ocean temperatures to a depth of 100 feet. He also was concerned to produce more efficient shapes for ships.[38]

Franklin was interested in meteorology and especially cloud formation and the electrification of clouds. He is generally acknowledged to have been the first scientist to report that northeast storms move toward the southwest, and he was a pioneer in observing convection phenomena in the atmosphere. He argued in favor of a wave theory of light, rejecting the strict Newtonian corpuscular theory. He was considered among the primary supporters of the wave theory.

Franklin tried to apply his doctrine of conservation, which had worked so well for electricity, to explain thermal phenomena. He assumed that there is a constant amount of heat, which is simply distributed, redistributed, conducted, or nonconducted, according to the kind of material in question. Interested in problems of heat conductivity, he designed a famous experiment, still performed in most introductory physics courses, in which a number of rods of different metals are joined together at one end and fanned out at the other, with little wax rings placed on them at regular intervals. The ends that are joined together are placed in a flame, and the "conductivity" is indicated by the relative speeds with which the wax rings melt and fall off. Franklin (in France) never had the occasion to perform the experiment, although he did obtain the necessary materials for doing so, and he suggested that Ingenhousz and he might do the experiment together. Ingenhousz, however, did it on his own. Franklin's experiments on heat were not fully understood until Joseph Black introduced the concepts of specific heat and latent heat.[39]

Franklin's only major contribution to the theory of heat is in the specific area of differential thermal conduction. The success of his fluid theory of electricity, and his writings on heat as a fluid, did, however, influence the later development of the concept of "caloric." Lavoisier wrote in 1777 that if he were to be asked what he understood by "matter of fire," he would reply, "with Franklin, Boerhaave, and some of the older [natural]

---

[38] See my *Benjamin Franklin: Scientist and Statesman* (cited in n.1 *supra*), ch. 6.
[39] See, further, my *Franklin and Newton* (cited in n.2 *supra*), ch.8.

philosophers, that the matter of fire or of light is a very subtle and very elastic fluid. . ."[40]

Franklin was an advocate of fresh air and exercise. He invented (or perhaps reinvented independently) bifocal glasses and designed a flexible catheter. He wrote on a variety of medical subjects: lead poisoning, gout, the heat of the blood, the physiology of sleep, deafness, nyctalopia, infection from dead bodies, infant mortality, and medical education. He accumulated an impressive set of statistics in favor of the practice of inoculation and published them in a pamphlet (London, 1759), accompanying William Heberden's instructions on inoculation. Although Franklin gave electric shocks to patients suffering from "palsies," he believed that any temporary help was not due so much to the electricity as to "the exercise in the patients' journey, and coming daily to my house" or even — we may note with special interest today — the "spirits given by the hope of success, enabling them to exert more strength in moving their limbs." Franklin was a member of the Paris commission in 1787 to investigate the claims of Mesmerism to cure diseases by the manipulation of "animal magnetism." It is curious that neither Franklin nor the other members of the commission recognized the deep psychological significance of their conclusion that "the imagination does everything, the magnetism nothing."

None of these other scientific activities is in a class with the electrical research. Indeed, Franklin is sometimes described as the first scientist to have gained international fame for work wholly in this new branch of science. But Franklin's contributions to science in general include his aid in getting the work of other scientists published and his activities in founding the American Philosophical Society, our oldest scientific or learned society or academy.

With the discovery of electrons, protons and neutrons, many modern writers have argued about whether Franklin's one-fluid theory was or was not closer to the modern conception than the two-fluid theory of his rivals. To my mind, such debates are wholly without value. The value of Franklin's contribution to electricity does not lie in the degree to which it resembles our modern theory,

---

[40] Antoine-Laurent Lavoisier, *Oeuvres* (Paris: Imprimerie Nationale, 1862), vol. 2, p. 228.

but rather in the effect his researches had in getting us along on the road to our modern theory.

At the time that Franklin undertook his studies, the world of science lay under the spell of Isaac Newton, whose great *Principia* had shown that the motions of the universe could be explained by simple mathematical laws. Newton thus convinced almost everyone that mathematics and mathematical laws were the only key to the understanding of nature. What many people forgot, however, was that Newton's success in applying mathematics to celestial and terrestrial mechanics was possible only because the facts had been accumulated and classified, and were in a state where his great genius could produce the general system of physics which became a paradigm for all other branches of science thereafter. But when it came to optics, Newton did not create a mathematical system of nature in the style that in the *Principia* had served so well for celestial and terrestrial mechanics, nor was he able to reduce his quantitative and qualitative discoveries to the form of general mathematical law.[41] In the field of optics, Newton was but one of the giants[42] upon whose shoulders some later mathematical physicist would stand so as to produce a mathematical system. In contrast with the austere *Principia,* whose motto was *Hypotheses non fingo* ("I frame [or feign] no hypotheses"), his *Opticks* contains a long set of "queries" in which Newton discussed the possible explanations that might be given to his observed facts. These resemble Franklin's speculations concerning electrical phenomena.[43] In Franklin's time, as with optics in Newton's time, the state of electrical science did not yet permit a full mathematical synthesis. What was required were "giants" to uncover the facts of charge, of induction, of grounding and insulation, of the effect of shapes of conductors and so on, giants to build a workable manipulative theory to unify these facts and to draw attention to essential elements that might be

---

[41] See my *The Newtonian Revolution* (New York: Cambridge University Press, 1980).

[42] See Robert K. Merton, *On the Shoulders of Giants: a Shandean Postscript* (New York: The Free Press; London: Collier-Macmillan Limited, 1965).

[43] On the relation of Franklin's electrical theory to the tradition of experimental science associated with Newton's *Opticks,* see my *Franklin and Newton* (cited in n.2 *supra*).

measured. Franklin's success paved the way for the mathematical theorists of the 19th century.[44]

But, even more, his mastery of the technique of experimentation, his successful and consistent explanations in terms of a simple physical conceptual scheme, and the many new and curious facts of nature he revealed, gave experimental science a new dignity in the eyes of his 18th-century contemporaries. The French philosopher Diderot wrote, in his essay on the interpretation of nature, that Franklin's book on electricity, like the works of the chemists, was the best teacher of the nature of the experimental art and the way to use the principles of experimental research to draw back the veil of nature without multiplying its mysteries. This was the sense, then, in which Franklin's contemporaries believed him to be the new Newton, and this was the first great contribution made by America to the mind of science. In this light, there can be no doubt of Franklin's stature in science, nor that he deserves to stand as the first American scientist.

---

[44] On this topic, see the concluding section of Heilbron's book (cited in n.6 *supra*).

Index of Historical Figures

Penn, William, 161
Peters, Richard, 247, 248, 251
Pope, Alexander, 91, 103
Price, Richard, 96, 97, 104
Priestley, Joseph, 96, 97, 104, 115
    119, 262, 265, 274, 277, 278
Quincy, Edmund, 231
Quincy, Josiah Jr., 96, 140
Reed, Charles, 219, 220, 221
Reed, George, 224
Reed, Joseph, 55
Rittenhouse, David, 16
Robertson, William, 98, 148
Rousseau, Jean-Jacques, 111, 148, 238
    240, 242
Rush, Dr. Benjamin, 16, 75
Scarouaday, 249
Shikellamy, 244
Smith, Adam, 98, 148
Smyth, Albert Henry, 126, 133
Stevenson, Polly, 83, 155

Stiles, Dr. Ezra, 90, 91, 105, 119
    121, 157, 166
Strahan, William, •130, 132, 138, 183
    197, 202, 204, 213
Teedyuscung, 239, 244, 251, 252
Thomas, Gov. George, 244, 248
Thoreau, Henry David, 160, 161
Tocqueville, Alexis de, 109, 159
Todd, Anthony, 63
Vaughn, Benjamin, 10, 11, 14, 22, 69
    125, 126, 127, 128, 135, 147
Washington, George, 20, 68, 166, 256
    263
Watson, James, 190, 193
Watts, John, 190, 191, 193, 194
Weiser, Conrad, 239, 244, 250
West, Benjamin, 75
Whatley, George, 120, 121
Whitman, Walt, 161, 174
Wollaston, William, 102, 191, 192
Woodfall, Henry S., 129, 135, 139